Advanced Computational
Engineering and Experimenting

Edited by
Andreas Öchsner
Lucas F.M. da Silva
Holm Altenbach

Advanced Computational Engineering and Experimenting

Selected, peer reviewed papers from the
Fourth International Conference on
Advanced Computational Engineering and Experimenting
(ACE-X 2010)
July 8th-9th, 2010,
Held at Hotel Concorde La Fayette Paris, France

Edited by

Andreas Öchsner, Lucas F.M. da Silva
and Holm Altenbach

TTP

Trans Tech Publications Ltd
Kreuzstrasse 10
CH-8635 Durnten-Zurich
Switzerland
http://www.ttp.net

Volume 478 of
Key Engineering Materials
ISSN 1013-9826
Full text available online at *http://www.scientific.net*

Distributed *worldwide by*

Trans Tech Publications Ltd.
Kreuzstrasse 10
CH-8635 Durnten-Zurich
Switzerland

Fax: +41 (44) 922 10 33
e-mail: sales@ttp.net

and in the Americas by

Trans Tech Publications Inc.
PO Box 699, May Street
Enfield, NH 03748
USA

Phone: +1 (603) 632-7377
Fax: +1 (603) 632-5611
e-mail: sales-usa@ttp.net

printed in Germany

Preface

This special issue of Key Engineering Materials contains selected refereed papers presented at the Fourth International Conference on Advanced Computational Engineering and Experimenting (ACE-X 2010) held at the Hotel Concorde La Fayette Paris, France during the period 8th-9th July, 2010.

The goal of the conference was to provide a unique opportunity to exchange information, to present the latest results as well as to review the relevant issues on contemporary research in mechanical engineering. Young scientists were especially encouraged to attend the conference and to establish international networks with well-known scientists.

During the conference, special sessions related to *SCIENTIFIC VISUALIZATION AND IMAGING SYSTEMS* (organised by Prof. Fabiana R. Leta), *ADHESIVE BONDING* (organised by Dr. Lucas F.M. da Silva and Prof. Jean-Yves Cognard), *BIOMECHANICS* (organised by Prof. Saied Darwish), *DAMAGE AND FRACTURE OF COMPOSITE MATERIALS AND STRUCTURES* (organised by Prof. M.N. Tamin), *NUMERICAL MODELING OF MATERIALS UNDER EXTREME CONDITIONS* (organised by Prof. Nicola Bonora and Dr. Eric N Brown) were held. In addition, two short courses related to *ELASTO-PLASTIC MATERIAL BEHAVIOUR: CONTINUUM MECHANICAL MODELLING AND FINITE ELEMENT IMPLEMENTATION* (organised by Prof. Holm Altenbach and Prof. Andreas Öchsner), and *PREDICTING THE DURABILITY OF ADHESIVE BONDED JOINTS* (organised by Dr. Ian A. Ashcroft) were organised.

More than 283 scientists and researchers coming from more than 54 countries attended the conference. The large number of presented papers emphasises the considerable academic and industrial interest in the conference theme. The editors wish to thank the authors and delegates for their participation and cooperation, which made this sixth conference especially successful.

Finally, we wish to express our warm thanks and appreciation to our colleagues and associates for their sustained assistance, help and enthusiasm during the preparation of the conference.

The fifth conference, ACE-X-2011, will be held in Algarve, Portugal, from 3-6 July, 2011 (http://www.ace-x2011.com/).

March 2011

Andreas Öchsner
Lucas F.M. da Silva
Holm Altenbach

Table of Contents

Key Engineering Materials Vol. 478 (2011) pp 1-6
© (2011) Trans Tech Publications, Switzerland
doi:10.4028/www.scientific.net/KEM.478.1

Production of Magnesium Titanate-Based Nanocomposites via Mechanochemical Method

Abbas Fahami[a], Reza Ebrahimi-Kahrizsangi[b], Bahman Nasiri-Tabrizi[c]

Materials Engineering Department, Islamic Azad University, Najafabad Branch, Isfahan, Iran

[a]a.fahami@hotmail.com, [b]rezaebrahimi@iaun.ac.ir, [c]bahman_nasiri@hotmail.com

Key words: Magnesium titanate, Hydroxyapatite, Whitlockite, Mechanical alloying, Nanocrystalline, Structural features.

Abstract. The mechanical activation was employed to study the phase evolution of the $Mg-TiO_2-CaHPO_4-CaO$ nanocrystalline system. The powders mixture with certain weight percent was grinded. Thermal annealing process at 650°C, 900°C and 1100°C temperatures resulted in generation of different compounds like $MgTiO_3/MgO/$Hydroxyapatite (HAp) and $MgTiO_3/MgO/\beta$-TCP and $MgTiO_3/Mg_2TiO_4/MgO/\beta$-TCP, respectively. The compounds were characterized by X-ray diffraction (XRD), scanning electron microscopy (SEM), transmission electron microscopy (TEM), and energy dispersive X-ray spectroscopy (EDX). The consequences of XRD analysis revealed that by increasing temperature, some composites with different morphological and structural features were detected. Beside, due to decomposing of HAp around 800°C, HAp converted to whitlockite (β-TCP) with growth of temperature. According to SEM and TEM observations, it was found that the synthesized powder contained large agglomerates which significant content of finer particles and agglomerates with spherical morphology. Because magnesium titanates based dielectric materials are useful for electrical applications, the electrical property of HAp has been proved, and the incorporation of these materials could result in new nanocrystalline dielectric materials.

Introduction

The preparation and characterization of nano-dielectric materials have attracted increasing attention in the last two decades [1]. Nanostructured materials exhibit unusual physical and chemical properties, significantly different from those of conventional materials, due to their extremely small size or large specific surface area [2].

Magnesium titanates are important as dielectric ceramic industrial materials. There are three intermediate phases between MgO and TiO_2 such as qandilite (Mg_2TiO_4), geigielite ($MgTiO_3$), and karrooite ($MgTi_2O_5$). The formation of these phases depends on the relative stoichiometry of materials in the precursor [3]. The geigielite and qandilite, due to their dielectric properties like low dielectric loss (high quality factor), high dielectric constant, and near zero temperature coefficient of resonant frequency [4,5], have widespread applications in resonators, pigments, filters, antennas for communication, radar, direct broadcasting satellite and global positioning system operating at microwave frequencies and in the electrical and electronic industries as a dielectric material for manufacturing on-chip capacitors, high frequency capacitors and temperature compensating capacitors [6]. Various methods for the preparation of magnesium titanates microcrystalline powders were reported including solid state reactions [7], co-precipitation [8], and thermal decomposition of peroxide precursors [9], mechanochemical complexation [10], and sol–gel route [11]. On the other hand, the most important calcium phosphate based nanocomposites comprised of HAp and β-TCP. In addition of the good biocompatibility of HAp, the dielectric properties of these bioceramics have been evaluated in numerous studies [12-14]. Also, it has been found that such properties of HAp are greatly affected by various parameters such as Ca/P ratio and sintering temperature [15]. However, precise investigation is demanded for these compounds in the future.

Nowadays, the various methods like chemical precipitation [16], hydrothermal [17] and microwave irradiation [18] have been used to synthesize of calcium phosphate-based ceramics. Among different dry processes, mechanical alloying (MA) [19] is one of the most current methods for manufacturing of dielectric ceramics.

In this paper, the phase transformation of the $Mg–TiO_2–CaHPO_4–CaO$ nanocrystalline system is investigated. Also the preparation of $MgTiO_3/MgO/HAp$, $MgTiO_3/MgO/\beta$-TCP and $MgTiO_3/Mg_2TiO_4/MgO/\beta$-TCP nanocomposites through mechanical activation and subsequent thermal treatment are studied. In fact, the aim of this work is to discuss the synthesis and structural evaluation of the nanocomposites. The dielectric properties of $MgTiO_3$, Mg_2TiO_4 and MgO and their effective applications in electric equipments have been proven [20]. In addition, HAp has such as these characteristics as well [15]. For all these reasons, compound of these materials could be derived to create new nanocrystalline dielectric materials.

Experimental Procedures

Preparation Method. Fig. 1 depicts the flow chart for the synthesis of various nanocomposites by mechanical activation and subsequent thermal annealing. Calcium hydrogen phosphate ($CaHPO_4$, Merck $\geq$ 98%), calcium oxide (CaO, Merck), titanium oxide (TiO_2, Merck), and magnesium (Mg, Merck) were the starting reactant materials for the MA processing. In order to prepare the composites, a distinct amount of calcium hydrogen phosphate and calcium oxide (Ca/P = 1.67) blend (20 wt.%) was milled with a mixture of titanium oxide and magnesium for 60 h and subsequent thermal treatments were performed in an electrical furnace at 650°C, 900°C and 1100°C for 2 h in air. The powder mixture with the desired stoichiometric proportionality was milled by a high energy planetary ball mill under ambient air atmosphere. The grinding process was performed in polymeric vial using Zirconia balls (diameter 20 mm). The charge to ball ratio and rotational speed were 1:20 and 600 rpm, respectively.

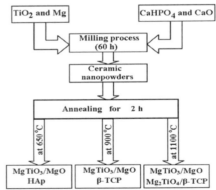

Fig. 1 Flow chart for the synthesis of magnesium titanate- based nanocomposites by mechanochemical method and subsequent heat treatment.

Characterization Techniques. Phase identification was carried out by XRD analysis with Xpert-Philips diffractometer using *Cu Kα* radiation. The diffractometer was operated at 40 kV and 30 mA. All measurements were performed at room temperature with the diffraction range of $2\theta = 10° – 80°$ at 1°/sec speed. The diffraction patterns of products were compared to proposed standards by the Joint Committee on Powder Diffraction and Standards (JCPDS), which involved card # 003-0747 for HAp, # 003-0713 for $Ca_3(PO_4)_2$, # 006-0494 for $MgTiO_3$, # 025-1157 for Mg_2TiO_4, # 021-1272 for TiO_2, # 004-0829 for MgO, and # 037-1497 for CaO. Energy dispersive X-ray spectroscopy (EDX) which is coupled to SEM was used to the semi-quantitative examination of the synthesized powders. Scanning electron microscope (SEM, SERON AIS-2100)was applied to characterize the morphological characteristics of the samples which were sputter-coated with a thin layer of gold. The size and morphology of the fine powders were observed in a transmission electron microscope (Philips CM10).

Results and Discussions

XRD Analyses. Fig. 2 (a-b) shows spectra of XRD patterns which belong to milled mixtures and subsequent thermal annealing powders, respectively. Fig. 2a, illustrates the peaks that is significant for TiO_2 and MgO and $MgTiO_3$.

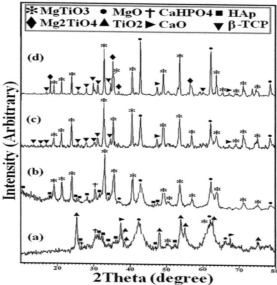

Fig. 2 XRD patterns of nanocomposites milled powders (a) and heat treated at different temperatures, (b) 650°C (c) 900°C and (d) 1100°C.

It should be noted that the presence of $MgTiO_3$ in milled powder indicate that milling during 60 h can lead to the formation of magnesium titanates phases such as $MgTiO_3$ (geigielite), Mg_2TiO_4 (qandilite), and $MgTi_2O_5$ (karrooite). On the other hand, a few certain peaks exist which are representative for HAp. It indicates that CaO was reacted with $CaHPO_4$ according to reaction (1).

$$6CaHPO_4 + 4CaO \rightarrow Ca_{10}(PO_4)_6(OH)_2 + 2H_2O \qquad (1)$$

The XRD patterns of milled powder after annealing at 650 °C, 900 °C and 1100 °C are displayed in Fig.2 (b-d). According to Fig. 2b, the heat treated sample at 650 °C produced a $MgTiO_3$/ MgO/ HAp nanocomposite. It shows that TiO_2 has reacted with MgO which formed MgTiO3. Hence, HAp and some of the magnesia has remained intact. By increasing temperature till 900 °C, MgTiO3 and MgO have remained sharply but according to reaction (2) HAp was decomposed and converted to β-TCP and CaO. The XRD analysis of this sample is shown in Fig. 2c.

$$Ca_{10}(PO_4)_6(OH)_2 \rightarrow CaO + 3Ca_3(PO_4)_2 + H_2O \qquad (2)$$

It is reported in [21] that the decomposition temperature (600–800 °C) strongly depends on the preparation method of the HAp powder. As shown in Fig. 2d, thermal treatment at 1100 °C leads to formation of a $MgTiO_3/Mg_2TiO_4/MgO/\beta$-TCP nanocomposite. Since, qandilite and karrooite are stable at high temperature, some magnesia and geigielite have reacted together and formed qandilite (reaction 3).

$$MgTiO_3 + MgO \rightarrow Mg_2TiO_4 \qquad (3)$$

Based on XRD patterns of the heat treated samples, the width of the peaks become narrower as compared to the results for the milled powder which shows an increase in the degree of crystallinity.

SEM-EDX Analyses. The SEM micrographs of the samples after the milling and annealing processes are shown in Fig. 3. The SEM micrographs show that particles of products can be attached at crystallographically specific surfaces and form elongated agglomerates composed of many primary crystallites. In fact, the chemical interactions at the contacting surface of particles result in very compact particles forming large agglomerates with spheroidal morphology. Based on Fig. 3a the mean size of the powder particles decreases after 60 h of milling. On the other hand, the mean size of the milled powder particles increases after annealing at 650°C, 900°C, and 1100°C. However, only a slight change in particle size is observed in these samples (Fig. 3 b-d). As temperature increases, the SEM micrographs show a continuous evolution of the morphological features. In fact, the mean size of the powder particles increases after the annealing process. Moreover, with an increase of the annealing temperature from 650°C to 1100°C the spheroidal particles become considerably large in size. Fig.4 (a-d) displays the concentrations of elements by the EDX spectra. The results of EDX analyses indicate a higher Mg/Ti ratio in small area of EDX analysis compared to Ca/P ratio which agrees with the chemical composition of the powder mixture. Furthermore, chemically stable contaminants are not detected due to the excessive adhesion of powders to the vial and balls.

Fig. 3 SEM micrographs of nanocomposites (a) mixed powder and heat treated at different temperatures, (b) 650°C (c) 900°C and (d) 1100°C.

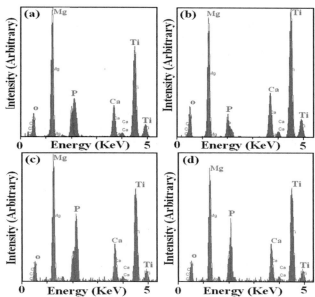

Fig. 4 EDX analysis of nanocomposites mixed powder (a) and heat treated at different temperatures,
(b) 650°C (c) 900°C and (d) 1100°C.

TEM Analyses. Fig. 5 (a) and (b) shows the transmission electron images of milled powder after 60 h and a heat treated sample at 1100°C for 2 h. In Fig. 5a, it can be seen that the agglomerates (100 nm in size) are formed after milling. The agglomerates consist of radially attached fibers. Also, Fig. 5b shows a growth of the powder particle after annealing at 1100°C which agrees with the data obtained from the SEM micrographs. It is revealed that particles with spheroidal shapes are formed after the thermal annealing process.

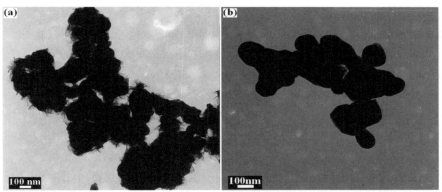

Fig. 5 TEM images of (a) milled sample and (b) heat treated sample at 1100°C.

This is the first report of the preparation of MgTiO$_3$/MgO/HAp, MgTiO$_3$/MgO/β-TCP, and MgTiO$_3$/Mg$_2$TiO$_4$/MgO/β-TCP nanocomposites and, therefore, there is no directly comparable data in the literature. However, further work is needed to investigate the electrical properties and identify optimal HAp and β-TCP levels that satisfy electrical performance criteria. Other properties and electrical performance of these nanostructured materials will be carried out in our research center.

Conclusions

In this work, we have investigated the phase transformation in a $Mg–TiO_2–CaHPO_4–CaO$ system. Based on XRD analysis, the presence of $MgTiO_3$ in milled powder indicates that the mechanical activation during 60 h can lead to the formation of magnesium titanates phases and thermal annealing of the milled powders at various temperatures resulted in the formation of three different nanocomposites. According to evaluations of the structural and morphological features, the best annealing temperature for the $MgTiO_3$ based nanocomposites is 650°C. SEM and TEM micrographs show that the crystal growth behavior of compounds depends on thermal annealing temperatures. The results confirmed that the solid state combination in polymeric vial and appropriate thermal annealing process is a suitable route to produce commercial amount of magnesium titanate nanocomposites.

References

[1] N. Stubicar, A. Tonejc and M. Stubicar: J. Alloys Compd. Vol. 370 (2004), p. 296.

[2] C.L. De Castro, B.S. Mitchell, in: Synthesis, functionalization and surface treatment of nanoparticles, Baraton MI, editors, chapter, American Scientific Publishers (2002).

[3] K. Hamada, Sh.I. Yamamoto and M. Senna: Adv. Powder Technol. Vol. 11 (2000), p.361.

[4] D. Li, L. Wang and D. Xue: J. Alloys Compd. Vol. 492 (2010), p. 564.

[5] M. Valant, M. Macek-Krzmanc and D. Suvorov: J. Eur. Ceram. Soc. Vol. 27 (2007), p. 2963.

[6] N. Dharmaraj, H.C. Park, B.M. Lee, P. Viswanathamurthi, H.Y. Kim and D.R. Lee: Inorg. Chem. Commun. Vol. 7 (2004), p. 431.

[7] B. Wechsler, A. Navrotsky: J. Solid State Chem. Vol. 55 (1984), p. 165.

[8] M.J. Martinez-Lope, M.P. Baura-Pena and M.E. Garcia-Clavel: Thermochim. Acta Vol. 194 (1992), p. 247.

[9] G. Pfaff: Ceram. Int. Vol. 20 (1994), p. 111.

[10] J. Liao, M. Senna, Mater. Res. Bull. Vol. 30 (1995), p. 385.

[11] I.R. Abothu, A.V. Prasada Rao and S. Komarneni: Mater. Lett. Vol. 38 (1999), p. 186.

[12] M.A. Fanovich, M.S. Castro and J.M. Porto Lopez: Ceram. Int. Vol. 25 (1999), p. 517.

[13] T. Ikoma, A. Yamazaki, S. Nakamura and M. Akao: J. Mater. Sci. Lett. Vol. 18 (1999), p. 1225.

[14] M.S. Khalil, H.H. Beheri and W.I. Abdel Fattah: Ceram. Int. Vol. 28 (2002), p. 451.

[15] M. Quilitz, K. Steingrover and M. Veith: J. Mater. Sci. - Mater. Med. Vol. 21 (2009), p.399.

[16] Y. Liu, W. Wang, Y. Zhan, C. Zheng and G. Wang: Mater. Lett. Vol. 56 (2002), p. 496.

[17] K. Lin, J. Chang, R. Cheng and M. Ruan: Mater. Lett. Vol. 61 (2007), p. 1683.

[18] A.L. Macipe, J.G. Morales and R.R. Clemente: Adv. Mater. Vol. 10 (1998), p. 49.

[19] S.H. Rhee: Biomaterials Vol. 23 (2002), p. 1147.

[20] I.R. Abothu, A.V. Prasada Rao and S. Komarneni: Mater. Lett. Vol. 38 (1999), p. 186.

[21] M.H. Fathi, A. Hanifi: Mater. Lett. Vol. 61 (2007), p. 3978.

Key Engineering Materials Vol. 478 (2011) pp 7-12
© *(2011) Trans Tech Publications, Switzerland*
doi:10.4028/www.scientific.net/KEM.478.7

Simultaneously Synthesis and Encapsulation of Metallic Nanoparticles using Linear–Dendritic Block Copolymers of Poly (ethylene glycol)-Poly (citric acid)

Ashkan Tavakoli Naeini[1,4,a], Manouchehr Vossoughi[1,2,b], Mohsen Adeli[2,3,c]

[1]Department of Chemical and Petroleum Engineering, Sharif University of Technology, Tehran, Iran

[2]Institute for Nanoscience and Nanotechnology, Sharif University of Technology, Tehran, Iran

[3]Department of Chemistry, Sharif University of Technology, Tehran, Iran

[4]Biochemical and Bioenvironmental Engineering Research Center, Sharif University of Technology, Tehran, Iran

[a]ashkan.tavakolin@gmail.com, [b]vosoughi@sharif.edu, [c]mohadeli@yahoo.com

Key words: Encapsulation, Block copolymer, Gold nanoparticles, Silver nanoparticles, Loading capacity

Abstract. Linear-dendritic triblock copolymers of linear poly(ethylene glycol) and hyperbranched poly(citric acid) (PCA-PEG-PCA) were used as the reducing and capping agents to encapsulate gold and silver nanoparticles (AuNPs and AgNPs). PCA-PEG-PCA copolymers in four different molecular weights were synthesized using 2, 5, 10 and 20 citric acid/PEG molar ratios and were called A_1, A_2, A_3 and A_4, respectively. Nanoparticles were encapsulated simultaneously during the preparation process. AuNPs were simply synthesized and encapsulated by addition a boiling aqueous solution of $HAuCl_4$ to aqueous solutions of A_1, A_2, A_3 and A_4. In the case of silver, an aqueous solution of $AgNO_3$ was reduced using $NaBH_4$ and AgNPs were encapsulated simultaneously by adding aqueous solutions of different PCA-PEG-PCA to protect the fabricated silver nanoparticles from aggregation. Encapsulated AuNPs and AgNPs were stable in water for several months and agglomeration did not occur. The synthesized silver and gold nanoparticles have been encapsulated within PCA-PEG-PCA macromolecules and have been studied using Transmission Electron Microscopy (TEM) and UV/Vis absorption spectroscopy. Studies reveal that there was a reverse relation between the size of synthesized AuNPs/AgNPs and the size of citric acid parts of PCA-PEG-PCA copolymers. For example, the prepared gold and silver nanoparticles by A_3 copolymer are of an average size of 8 nm and 16 nm respectively. Finally, the loading capacity of A_1, A_2, A_3 and A_4 and the size of synthesized AuNPs and AgNPs were investigated using UV/Vis data and the corresponding calibration curve. It was found that the loading capacity of copolymers depends directly on the concentration of copolymers and their molecular weight.

Introduction

Synthesis of metallic nanoparticles and the study of their size and properties is of fundamental importance in the advancement of recent research [1,2,3]. It is found that the optical, electronic, magnetic, and catalytic properties of metallic nanoparticles depend on their size, shape and chemical surroundings [2,3]. In nanoparticle synthesis it is very important to control not only the particle size but also the particle shape and morphology. Properties of metallic nanoparticles are different from those of bulk materials made from the same atoms. For example, the striking effect of nanoparticles on color has been known since antiquity when tiny metal particles were used to color glass in church windows. Silver particles stained the glass yellow, while gold particles were used to make ruby-colored glass. Nanogold or gold nanoparticles (AuNPs) have been widely studied in the past 10 years because of their unique properties, such as catalysis, quantum size effect, and optical properties [4]. Due to the requirements to control the nanoparticle size and surface functionalization for this broad range of applications, different synthetic methods have been developed to generate monodisperse gold and silver nanoparticles. In the case of AuNPs, one of the most widely used methods is the reduction of tetrachloroaurate ions (AuCl$_4$-) in aqueous medium using sodium citrate to generate particles with diameters typically ranging from 10 to 100 nm [5]. Although this method allows good control to produce a particular particle size, it is limited to the synthesis of larger particles. The Brust method and various modifications are useful for the generation of AuNPs having core sizes ranging from 1 to 4 nm [6-8]. A multitude of chemical reduction methods have been used to synthesize silver nanoparticles from silver salts. The reactions considered in the present study were limited to those using silver nitrate as the starting material. They vary in the choice of reducing agent, the relative quantities and concentrations of reagents, temperature, duration of reaction, as well as the diameters of the nanoparticles produced. Alternative synthetic strategies based on using polymers as both the reducing and stabilizing agent for the generation of stable metal nanoparticles without the use of an additional stabilizing agent have been developed. The resulting nanoparticle-polymer composites have been shown to be useful in catalytic transformations [9] and they could be useful for nanostructured solar cells, photonic band gap materials, storage devices, and drug delivery. Some polymers can fulfill the required dual role as a reducer and stabilizer [10]. However, even in the syntheses using those polymers, either the reduction reaction was carried out in organic solvents or polydisperse nanoparticles were produced. In both situations, the use of the nanoparticles is restricted, or at least complicated for aqueous-based (e.g. biological) applications or for applications that require monodisperse particles (e.g. electronics). The major advantage of using a polymer as a stabilizing agent is that it can be used to tailor the nanocomposite properties and also to provide long-term stability of the nanoparticles (specially metallic nanoparticles) by preventing particle agglomeration [11,12]. Recently, the functionalized AuNPs were synthesized through different stabilizing and capping agents and showed the potential in several applications [13]. Although many block copolymers and dendrimers have been used as stabilizing agents to synthesize Au/AgNPs in the literature [14], reports of the preparation and characterization of polymer–Au/AgNPs nanocomposites are occasional. Linear–dendritic macromolecules are hybrid large molecules containing dendrimers and linear polymers. Interesting properties and applications of this type of dendritic macromolecules for the use in encapsulation and entrap nanoparticles such as metallic nanoparticles have stimulated investigation in this area [15-19]. In the present study, we used poly (citric acid)-poly (ethylene glycol)-poly (citric acid) triblock copolymers as the Au and Ag nanoparticle supporter and simultaneously synthesis and encapsulation of gold and silver nanoparticles is discussed, which is an easy, simple and convenient route for preparing metallic particles in the nanometer range. The synthesized silver and gold nanoparticles have been encapsulated within PCA-PEG-PCA macromolecules and have been studied and investigated using Transmission Electron Microscopy (TEM) and UV/Vis absorption spectroscopy. These studies reveal that the prepared gold and silver nanoprticles are uniform and similar in shape and morphology which indicates the importance of the present work. Perhaps the most important factor in this process is that the gold and silver nanoparticles prepared by this process are stable for months.

Materials and Methods

Materials
Citric acid (extra pure anhydrous powder), HAuCl4, 3H2O (99.5%, for analysis), poly (ethylene glycol) (Mn =1500) and NaBH4 were purchased from Merck (Germany). The silver nitrate (> 99% AgNO3), sodium borohydride (99% NaBH4) and dialyze bag (a semipermeable membrane cut off 2000) were purchased from Sigma, Aldrich (St Louis, Missouri).

Experimental
Absorption spectra (300-800 nm) were collected using a Perkin-Elmer Lambda 900 UV-Vis/NIR spectrophotometer. Samples of encapsulated nanoparticles were prepared and left at room temperature overnight. Then, they were transferred to the spectrophotometer cell and spectra were recorded at 25°C. TEM images were recorded using a Philips CH 200 microscope with a LaB6-Cathode of 160 kV.

Synthesis of PCA-PEG-PCA linear-dendritic copolymers
PCA-PEG-PCA linear-dendritic triblock copolymers were synthesized through a reported procedure in the literature [20].

Preparation of encapsulated nanoparticles
In the case of synthesis gold nanoparticles, a 20 ml aqueous solution of $HAuCl_4$ with a constant concentration (200 µM) was added to aqueous solutions of PCA-PEG-PCA copolymers in different concentrations (500, 400, 300, 200, 100, 50, 25, 12.5 µM) at the boiling point [19]. After 20 minutes the color of $HAuCl_4$ solution changed from clear pale yellow to red concerning the reduction of the gold nanoparticles and trapping by PCA-PEG-PCA copolymers. In the case of synthesis and encapsulation of silver nanoparticles, a 10 mL of silver nitrate (1.0 mM) was added dropwise (1 drop/second) to a 30 mL of 2.0 mM sodium borohydride solution [21]. Meanwhile, aqueous solutions of PCA-PEG-PCA copolymers in different concentrations (500, 400, 300, 200, 100, 50, 25, 12.5 µM) were added dropwise (multiple drops/second). The reaction mixture was stirred vigorously on a magnetic stir plate. Finally, the obtained solutions were cooled to reach room temperature (25°C) for further UV-visible in a regular time schedule and TEM analyses.

Results and Discussion

PCA-PEG-PCA copolymers were synthesized through condensation of citric acid on hydroxyl functional groups of PEG. The degree of polymerization of poly (citric acid) parts was dominated through the citric acid/PEG molar ratio. In this work, ratios of citric acid/PEG = 2, 5, 10 and 20 were used to synthesize PCA-PEG-PCA copolymers which were called A_1, A_2, A_3 and A_4 respectively. The citric acid parts of the PCA-PEG-PCA copolymers were used to reduce gold and encapsulate gold and silver nanoparticles. The size of metallic nanoparticles encapsulated within PCA-PEG-PCA linear-dendritic copolymers depended on the concentration and the molecular weight of the linear-dendritic copolymers.

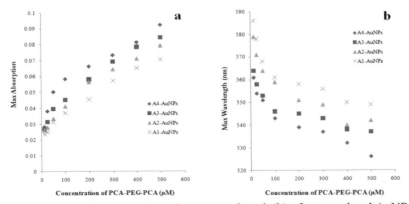

Figure 1. Maximum absorption (a) and maximum wavelength (b) of encapsulated AuNPs in A_1, A_2, A_3 and A_4 in 8 different concentrations (concentration of $HAuCl_4$ was 200 µM).

The dependence of loading capacities of copolymers on the molecular weight of PCA-PEG-PCA was investigated using UV experiments and results are shown in Figure 1.a and 2.a. Due to a direct relationship between the intensity of the maximum absorption of encapsulated nanoparticles and the molecular weight of PCA-PEG-PCA block copolymers, it could be found that the loading capacity of these PCA-PEG-PCA copolymers is directly related to the molecular weight. Figure 1.a shows the intensity of maximum wavelengths (λ_{max}) of AuNPs versus the concentration of PCA-PEG-PCA copolymers for A_1, A_2, A_3 and A_4 (concentration of $HAuCl_4$ was constant in all experiments and equal to 200 µM). As can be seen the intensity of λ_{max} of synthesized AuNPs increases by increasing the concentration of PCA-PEG-PCA copolymers which proves a direct relationship between the loading capacities of PCA-PEG-PCA copolymers and their concentration. Figure 1.b shows the λ_{max} of AuNPs versus concentration of PCA-PEG-PCA copolymers for A_1, A_2, A_3 and A_4. Clearly λ_{max} of the nanoparticles has a blue shift when the molecular weight and also the concentration of PCA-PEG-PCA copolymers increase. This diagram shows that the size of AuNPs inversely depends on the molecular weight and the concentration of PCA-PEG-PCA copolymers. Maximum absorption of A_{1-4}-AuNPs and loading capacities of A_1, A_2, A_3 and A_4 in a 500–12.5 µM concentration range are shown in Table 1.

Table 1. Maximum absorption of AuNPs loaded by different PCA–PEG–PCA copolymers and loading capacities of A_1, A_2, A_3 and A_4 (concentration of $HAuCl_4$ was 200 µM).

Concentration of PCA-PEG-PCA [µM]	Maximum absorption				Loading capacity [µM]			
	A_4-AuNPs	A_3-AuNPs	A_2-AuNPs	A_1-AuNPs	A_4	A_3	A_2	A_1
500	0.0923	0.0842	0.0793	0.0705	71.6287	63.2785	58.2268	49.1546
400	0.0814	0.0783	0.0711	0.0652	60.3975	57.1958	49.7732	43.6907
300	0.0733	0.0691	0.0645	0.0572	52.0424	47.7114	42.9690	35.4433
200	0.0663	0.0582	0.0566	0.0454	44.8274	36.4743	34.8247	23.2783
100	0.0585	0.0454	0.0413	0.0371	36.7851	23.2785	19.0515	14.7216
50	0.0504	0.0397	0.0336	0.0312	28.499	17.4026	11.1134	8.6391
25	0.0383	0.0315	0.0281	0.0251	15.976	8.9484	5.4432	2.3505
12.5	0.0284	0.0271	0.0263	0.0238	5.7527	4.4171	3.5876	1.0103

Table 2. Maximum absorption of AgNPs loaded by different PCA–PEG–PCA copolymers and loading capacities of A_1, A_2, A_3 and A_4 (concentration of $AgNO_3$ was 1 mM).

Concentration of PCA-PEG-PCA [µM]	Maximum absorption				Loading capacity [µM]			
	A_4-AgNPs	A_3-AgNPs	A_2-AgNPs	A_1-AgNPs	A_4	A_3	A_2	A_1
500	0.7431	0.7746	0.7191	0.6522	320.3144	270.2754	230.0116	170.8618
400	0.6878	0.7265	0.6844	0.6225	260.7858	230.5789	200.3361	150.5772
300	0.6451	0.6665	0.6329	0.5861	220.5106	180.9635	160.3778	120.7773
200	0.6191	0.5956	0.5998	0.5163	190.9123	130.5115	130.8368	70.4153
100	0.5799	0.5412	0.5367	0.4735	150.9917	90.3277	80.9789	40.0886
50	0.5373	0.4931	0.4788	0.4415	110.7364	50.6295	40.5275	10.6556
25	0.4737	0.4513	0.4442	0.4258	50.3753	20.4142	10.8623	10.4457
12.5	0.4437	0.4449	0.4311	0.4211	20.3762	10.919	10.8554	10.0900

Figure 2.a shows the intensity of maximum wavelengths (λ_{max}) of AgNPs versus the concentration of PCA-PEG-PCA copolymers for A_1, A_2, A_3 and A_4 (concentration of $AgNO_3$ was constant in all experiments and equal to 1 mM). As can be seen, generally, the intensity of λ_{max} of synthesized AgNPs increases by increasing the concentration of PCA-PEG-PCA copolymers which proves a direct relationship between the loading capacities of PCA-PEG-PCA copolymers and their concentration. As a point in figure 2.a, we can see that although A3 has lower molecular weight than A_4, but for higher concentrations than 300 µM the maximum absorption of encapsulated AgNPs within A_3 is higher than the maximum absorption of encapsulated AgNPs within A_4 in the

same concentrations. It seems that it would be better to use an aqueous solution of A_3 with concentration of 300 µM or higher in order to obtain maximum support and encapsulation of AgNPs. In other words, higher concentrations of A_3 would be the optimum solution for encapsulating silver nanoparticles.

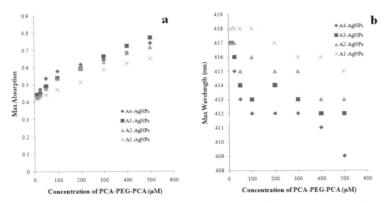

Figure 2. Maximum absorption (a) and maximum wavelength (b) of encapsulated AgNPs in A_1, A_2, A_3 and A_4 in 8 different concentrations (concentration of AgNO3 was 1 mM).

Figure 2.b shows the λ_{max} of AgNPs versus concentration of PCA-PEG-PCA copolymers for A_1, A_2, A_3 and A_4. Clearly λ_{max} of the nanoparticles has a blue shift when the molecular weight of PCA-PEG-PCA copolymers increases, but here the λ_{max} is not as dependent on concentration as in the case of AuNPs. This diagram shows that the size of AgNPs inversely depends on the molecular weight and the concentration of PCA-PEG-PCA copolymers but is a weak function of these two parameters in comparison with the same in the case of AuNPs. The maximum absorption of A_{1-4}-AgNPs and loading capacities of A_1, A_2, A_3 and A_4 in a 500–12.5 µM concentration range are shown in Table 2. The size and morphology of AgNPs were investigated using TEM experiments are shown in Fig. 3b.

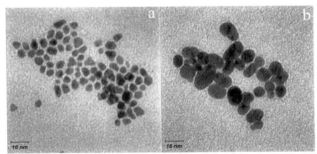

Figure 3. TEM images of AuNPs (a) and AgNPs (b) synthesized by A_3 PCA-PEG-PCA copolymers

Fig. 3.a shows a TEM image of the supported gold nanoparticles by A_3. The diameter of the nanoparticles is found to be approximately 8 nm. Fig. 3.b shows a TEM image of the supported silver nanoparticles by A_3. The Ag nanoparticles are spherical in shape with a smooth surface morphology. The diameter of the nanoparticles is found to be approximately 16 nm. The both TEM images also show that the produced nanoparticles are more or less uniform in size and shape. Generally, it could be investigated that in the case of PCA-PEG-PCA copolymers with higher molecular weight such as A_3, the synthesized gold and silver nanoparticles array in a hyperbranched order. In this case, the two ending citric acid parts are big enough to interact with two or more nanoparticles and make dendritic structures of nanoparticles. As figure 3 shows, with the same protector (A$_3$), the encapsulated AgNPs are bigger in diameter and have smoother surface in comparison with AuNPs. Moreover, for several months and in a regular time schedule, solutions of nanoparticles were stored in a dark place at room temperature and their UV-visible spectra were recorded in interval times to compare with previous results and investigate whether the nanoparticles were agglomerated or not. Based on these experiments it was found that under the mentioned storing conditions, protected and encapsulated gold and silver nanoparticles by PCA-PEG-PCA copolymers were stable for several months and agglomeration did not occur.

Conclusion

PCA-PEG-PCA copolymers containing dendritic poly(citric acid) parts were used to synthesize and support gold and silver nanoparticles successfully. The results showed that generally, the loading capacity of PCA-PEG-PCA copolymers was directly related to the concentration and molecular weight of copolymers whereas the size of nanoparticles was inversely depended on these parameters. But according to the UV/visible data, the size of encapsulated silver nanoparticles is a week function of these two parameters. The supported silver nanoparticles seem to be much more spherical in shape with a smooth surface morphology in comparison with gold nanoparticles. Moreover, it could be investigated that aqueous solutions of A$_3$ with a concentration of 300 or higher would be the optimum solution for encapsulating AgNPs whereas in the case of AuNPs the higher concentrations of A4 solutions have the most loading capacity. Supported gold and silver nanoparticles were stable in water for several months and agglomeration did not occur.

References

[1] S.S. Nath, D. Chakdar, G. Gope and D.K. Avasthi: J. Nanotech. Vol. 83-87 (2008) (1992), p. 119.

[2] G. Cao; *Nanostructures and Nanomaterials*, Imperial College Press (2004).

[3] K. Chang: *Tiny is Beautiful, Translating "Nano" into Practical*, The New York Times (2005).

[4] M.C. Daniel, D. Astruc: Chem. Rev. 104 (2004), p. 293.

[5] J. Turkevich, P.C. Stevenson, J. A. Hillier: Faraday Soc. Vol. 11 (1951), p. 55

[6] M. Brust, M. Walker, D. Bethell, D.J. Schiffrin, R. Whyman: J. Chem. Soc. Chem. Commun. (1994) p. 801.

[7] C.P. Collier, R.J. Saykally, J.J. Shiang, S.E. Henrichs, J.R. Heath: Science Vol. 277 (1997), p. 1978.

[8] D.E. Cliffel, F.P. Zamborini, S.M. Gross, R.W. Murray: Langmuir. Vol. 16 (2000), p. 9699.

[9] S. Rajesh, J.W. Park and Jennifer S. Shumaker-Parry: Langmuir. Vol. 23 (2007), p. 11883.

[10] B.P.S. Chauhan, R. Sardar: Macromolecules. Vol. 37 (2004), p. 5136.

[11] B.J. Kim, J. Bang, C.J. Hawker, E.J. Kramer: Macromolecules. Vol. 39 (2006), p. 4108.

[12] A.C. Balaza, T. Emrick, T.P. Russell: Science. Vol. 314 (2006), p. 1107.

[13] C.C. Chang, P.H. Chen, C.M Chang: J. Sol-Gel Sci. Technol. Vol. 47 (2008), p. 268.

[14] V. Pardo-Yissar, R. Gabai, A.N. Shipway, T. Bourenko, I. Willner: Adv. Mater. Vol. 13 (2001), p. 1320.

[15] I. Gitsov, C. Zhu: J Am Chem Soc. Vol. 125 (2003), p. 11228.

[16] H. Namazi, M. Adeli, Z. Zarnegar, S. Jafari, A. Dadkhah, A. Shukla: Colloid. Polym. Sci. Vol. 285 (2007), p. 1527.

[17] H. Namazi, M. Adeli: Eur. Polym. J. Vol. 39 (2003), p. 1491.

[18] H. Namazi, M. Adeli: Biomaterials. Vol. 26 (2005), p. 1175.

[19] A. Tavakoli Naeini, M. Adeli, M. Vossoughi: Eur. Polym. J. Vol. 46 (2010), p. 165.

[20] A. Tavakoli Naeini, M. Adeli, M. Vossoughi: Nanomedicine, NBM. Vol. 6 (2010), p. 556.

[21] S.D. Solomon, M. Bahadory, A.V. Jeyarajasingam, S.A. Rutkowsky, C. Boritz, L. Mulfinger: J. Chem. Edu. Vol. 84 (2007), p. 322.

Key Engineering Materials Vol. 478 (2011) pp 13-18
© (2011) Trans Tech Publications, Switzerland
doi:10.4028/www.scientific.net/KEM.478.13

Study of the Properties of Al$_2$O$_3$-Ag Nanopowders Produced by an Innovative Thermal Decomposition–Reduction and Silver Nitrate Reduction Methods

Agnieszka Maria Jastrzębska[1,a], Antoni Ryszard Kunicki[2,b],
Andrzej Roman Olszyna[1,c]

[1]Warsaw University of Technology, Faculty of Materials Science and Engineering, Woloska 141, 02-507 Warsaw, Poland

[2]Warsaw University of Technology, Faculty of Chemistry, Noakowskiego 3, 00-664 Warsaw, Poland

[a]agnieszka.jastrzebska@inmat.pw.edu.pl, [b]kunicki@ch.pw.edu.pl, [c]aolszyna@meil.pw.edu.pl

Key words: nanosilver, biocidal, alumina, thermal decomposition-reduction, silver nitrate, reduction

Abstract. The present study is concerned with the morphology, physical properties and biocidal activity of Al$_2$O$_3$-Ag nanopowders produced by two methods: thermal decomposition-reduction and the silver nitrate reduction. The innovative method of thermal decomposition-reduction has been described in our earlier publication and is protected by our patent application, whereas the silver nitrate reduction method is commonly used in industry at the present. The nano-powders produced by these two methods differ considerably from one another in terms of their morphology and physical properties. The proposed method of thermal decomposition-reduction gives Al$_2$O$_3$-Ag nano-powders which are not only much less agglomerated with the average agglomerate sizes below 1 µm, but also the average size of their particles is considerably smaller (below 60 nm). Moreover, their specific surface is larger (above 200 m^{2}g^{-1}) and they have good bactericidal and fungicidal properties.

Introduction

At the present, there is great demand from the industry for materials that show biocidal properties. This is why, since several years, many research centers all over the world have focused their interest on silver nano-particles. Because of their small size, the silver nano-particles show high chemical activity dependent on both their sizes and shapes [1]. They have also good anti-rheumatic and anti-inflammatory properties.

Like silver cations, the nano-particles of this element have the ability of destroying a vide variety of Gram-positive and Gram-negative strains of bacteria and fungi [2]. Moreover, recent researches have shown that, micro-organisms cannot create immunity against silver nano-particles as they do against antibiotics [3]. Therefore, the potential application range of silver nano-particles seems to be unlimited.

In view of their bactericide properties, silver nano-particles are considered to be an advantageous addition to matrices of various types. Their more important recent applications include dressing materials [4], coatings on implants [5], filtration membranes, and anti-fouling coatings [6]. However, unbound silver particles can easily be removed from the carrier material during exploitation. An additional problem is the natural liability of silver nano-particles to agglomeration, which results in loss of their biological activity. It is therefore necessary that the nano-particles should be built into the surface of the carrier material. This can be achieved by using a specially designed carrier.

Among many known inert carriers, the most promising material is aluminum nano-oxide. It is most often used in the form of shaped porous pieces [7], micro-spheres [8] or nano-needles [4]. The particles of aluminum oxide have very large specific surface. They are also considered to be the most inert material with respect to the human organism and show good biocompatibility [5]. In view of these properties they can be successfully used as the carrier for silver nano-particles.

Technology of the Al_2O_3-Ag nano-particles

Silver nanoparticles (20 nm) were deposited on an aluminum oxide nanopowder carrier using the method described in our earlier paper [9] (protected by a patent application). The method uses a mild reaction that takes place between a metal-organic and aluminum-organic compound and oxygen from the air. The reaction is conducted in an organic solvent with an addition, introduced later, of a silver compound [10,11]. After the completion of the reaction, the solvent is evaporated and the organic precursor powder obtained is subjected to thermal decomposition at a temperature of 700°C for 24 h (as established in our earlier study [11], these are the optimum conditions for this process), which results in Al_2O_3-Ag_2O nanoparticles being formed. Then, the nano-powders are subjected to reduction in a hydrogen atmosphere to obtain a series of Al_2O_3-Ag nanopowders with silver contents of 0.30, 1.40, 2.85, and 12.70 wt%.

There are many alternative methods of producing silver nanoparticles deposited on an inert carrier, such as the impregnation with nano-silver from a colloidal system [12], or the popular method consisting of the chemical reduction of silver nitrate ($AgNO_3$). The latter method is widely used in industry, but the carriers are chiefly porous forms of aluminum oxide. In the present study we compare the properties of the nanopowders produced by our method and by the chemical reduction of silver nitrate. The carrier was an aluminum oxide nanopowder prepared by the thermal decomposition. The procedure was as follows. First an aqueous solution (distilled water) was prepared of $AgNO_3$ (0.1 M, POCH) with an appropriate concentration of silver nitrate. The $AgNO_3$ solution was stirred, added with an Al_2O_3 nanopowder to obtain a homogeneous suspension, and then added with $5cm^3$ of an aqueous solution of formalin (30%, POCH). Finally, an aqueous solution of ammonia was dropped into the solution and the reaction run according to formulae (Eq. 1) and (Eg. 2):

$$2AgNO_3 + 4NH_3 + H_2O \rightarrow 2[Ag(NH_3)_2]^+ + 2OH^- + 2NO_3^-, \tag{1}$$

$$2[Ag(NH_3)_2]^+ + HCHO + 3OH^- \rightarrow 2Ag + HCOO^- + 2H_2O + 4NH_3. \tag{2}$$

The sediments were rinsed 3 times and dried. The contents of silver in the Al_2O_3-Ag samples thus obtained were 0.30, 1.40, 2.85 and 12.7wt%.

Measurements

The morphology of the nanopowders was examined in a scanning electron microscope (SEM, Zeiss LEO 1530) at an accelerating voltage of 2.0 kV. The microscopic samples were prepared by depositing drops of a dispersion of the nanopowder in 2-propanol on silicon plates which were then dried and covered with a thin carbon film using a BAL-TEC SCD duster equipped with a CEA 035 unit.

A quantitative analysis of the nanopowders was performed by the stereological method [13]. The stereological parameters were estimated using the MicroMeter v.086b computer program. The estimation of the average sizes of the particles and agglomerates was based on their size distributions. The standard deviation of the measured values was also determined.

The physical properties of the nano-powders were examined by the physical sorption of nitrogen. The nitrogen adsorption and desorption from the nanopowder surface was measured with a Quantachrome Quadrasorb-SI device. Before the measurements, the samples were dried at 350°C for 24 h. The adsorption was examined in a bath at -195°C, whereas the desorption was examined at room temperature. The specific surface area of the nanopowders was determined by the Brunauer-Emmet-Teller (BET) method, and the open pores present in the agglomerates were analyzed by the Barret-Joyer-Halends method (BJH).

The biocidal activity of the nanopowders was analyzed qualitatively using the classical inoculation technique [14]. Bacteria species (E.Coli, Sarcina, Bacillus sp.) and fungi species (A.niger) were placed on the Petri plates with an Agar culture and covered by the nanopowder. Then the plates were put in an incubator for 72 h to multiply the microorganisms. After the incubation, the plates were photographed.

Results and Discussion

The morphology of the Al$_2$O$_3$-Ag nanopowders produced by the thermal decomposition-reduction method was examined in a scanning electron microscope. Examples of SEM images of the powders are shown in Fig. 1. In the photographs we can see both single nano-particles and agglomerates. The stereological analysis shows that the average size of the powder particles does not change much at lower silver contents where it oscillates around the value of 46 nm, whereas in the sample with 12.55 wt% of silver, it increases to above 60 nm. Moreover, in all the powders, the average size of the agglomerates increases with increasing silver share (wt.%).

Fig. 1. SEM images of the Al$_2$O$_3$-Ag nanopowders, produced by the thermal decomposition-reduction method, with the Ag content (wt,%): (a) 0.30, (b) 2.84, and (c) 12.55.

Figure 2 shows SEM images of the Al$_2$O$_3$ nanopowder without nano-silver addition prepared by thermal decomposition (the same carrier was used in the method of AgNO$_3$ chemical reduction described later in the text) had a much greater average particle size (65 nm) than the powders containing nano-silver (Table 1). This can be attributed to the fact that the presence of much smaller silver nanoparticles contributes to the decrease of the average particle size of the powder.

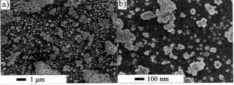

Fig. 2. SEM images of the Al$_2$O$_3$ nanopowder (without an addition of nano-silver), produced by thermal decomposition.

The Al$_2$O$_3$-Ag nanopowders, produced by the proposed thermal decomposition-reduction method were also examined for their physical properties such as the specific surface area and the open porosity of the agglomerates. The results are given in Table 1. The specific surface area of all the nanopowders appeared to be above 150 m^{2}g^{-1}, and the share of open pores in the agglomerates was high (above 0.5 cm^{-3}g^{-1}). The best physical parameters were achieved in the nanopowder with 1.35 wt%Ag. Its specific surface area was greatly developed (208 m^{2}g^{-1}) and the open porosity was 1.320 cm^{3}g^{-1}.

Table 1. Stereological parameters and physical properties of the Al$_2$O$_3$-Ag nanopowders produced by the thermal decomposition-reduction method.

Ag [wt%]	E(d$_2$) particle [nm]	E(d$_2$) agglomerate [nm]	S$_{BET}$ [m^{2}g^{-1}]	V$_{BJH}$ [m^{2}g^{-1}]
0	65 ± 12	312 ± 167	169.60 ± 0.01	0.758 ± 0.001
0.30	48 ± 12	380 ± 200	148.50 ± 0.01	0.613 ± 0.001
1.35	47 ± 15	330 ± 100	208.00 ± 0.01	1.320 ± 0.001
2.84	43 ± 13	520 ± 200	157.60 ± 0.01	0.605 ± 0.001
12.55	60 ± 16	870 ± 400	172.90 ± 0.01	0.525 ± 0.001

The properties of the Al_2O_3-Ag nanopowders produced by the proposed thermal decomposition-reduction method were compared with the properties of Al_3O_3-Ag nanopowders produced by the chemical reduction of $AgNO_3$. The morphology of these powders was also examined by SEM (Fig. 3). We can see that these nanopowders also contain single nanoparticles and larger agglomerates, but here the nano-particles, except those with the highest silver content (12.55 wt.% - Fig. 3d) have elongated shapes and their number increases with increasing nanosilver addition (Fig. 3c). The stereological analysis confirmed this relationship (Table 2) and showed that with increasing nanosilver content the average particle size increases from 66 to 115 nm. Moreover, the average size of the agglomerates appeared to be much greater than that in the nanopowders produced by the thermal decomposition-reduction method, and considerably increases (from 1.74 to 7.90 µm) as the nanosilver addition increases, except for the sample with 12.55 wt%Ag.

Fig. 3. SEM images of the Al_2O_3-Ag nanopowders produced by chemical reduction added with: (a) 0.30 wt%, (b) 1.35 wt%, (c) 2.84 wt%, (d) 12.55 wt% of silver.

The specific surface area of the nanopowders produced by the chemical reduction appeared to be markedly greater (exceeding 370 m^2g^{-1}) than that of the nanopowders powders produced by our method, whereas the open porosity of the agglomerates was low (below 0.8 cm^3g^{-1}).

The best physical properties were achieved in the nanopowder with 1.35 wt.% of nanosilver, just as was the case with the nanopowder produced by our method, but its specific surface area is considerably greater (440.40 m^2g^{-1}). The open porosity of this powder was, however, relatively low (0.577 cm^3g^{-1}).

Table 2. Stereological parameters and physical properties of the Al_2O_3-Ag nanopowders produced by the chemical reduction of silver nitrate.

Ag [%wag]	E(d_2) particle [nm]	E(d_2) agglomerate [µm]	S_{BET} [m^2g^{-1}]	V_{BJH} [m^2g^{-1}]
0	65 ± 12	0.31 ± 0.16	169.60 ± 0.01	0.758 ± 0.001
0.30	66 ± 22	1.74 ± 1.36	371.50 ± 0.01	0.417 ± 0.001
1.35	81 ± 24	1.84 ± 1.29	440.40 ± 0.01	0.577 ± 0.001
2.84	89 ± 21	7.90 ± 4.85	410.10 ± 0.01	0.801 ± 0.001
12.55	115 ± 36	4.83 ± 2.61	218.40 ± 0.01	0.743 ± 0.001

The nanopowders produced by these two methods were also examined in terms of their bactericidal and fungicidal properties using the classical inoculation technique. Fig. 4 shows the Petrie plates after 72 hours of incubation. The 'dark rings' visible around the nanopowder dispersed on the plates represent the regions where the bacteria (E.Coli, Sarcina, Bacillus sp.) and fungi (A.niger) were not able to multiply. The nanopowders of both types show a similar inhibitory action against the growth of bacteria and fungi. An exception was the nanopowder with 12.55 wt% of nanosilver, produced by the thermal decomposition-reduction, which was evidently more effective against A.niger fungi than the nanopowder produced by the chemical reduction with the same nanosilver content. Moreover, the nanopowders produced by the latter method were more effective against bacteria, which may however be attributed to the $AgNO_3$ remnants left on the nanopowder surface.

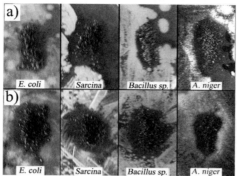

Fig. 4. Photographs of the surfaces of the Petri plates covered with the Al_2O_3-Ag powder with 12.55 wt% of nanosilver, produced by: (a) thermal decomposition-reduction, (b) chemical reduction of silver nitrate.

Conclusions

Silver nanoparticles deposited on an aluminum oxide nanopowder carrier were produced by the thermal decomposition-reduction method, developed earlier at our laboratory, and the method of chemical reduction of silver nitrate which is commonly used in industry. Both methods gave nanopowders with good bactericide and fungicide properties, although the nanopowders of these two types differ in their morphology and physical properties. The nanopowders produced by our method not only are much less agglomerated with the average size of the agglomerates below 1μm (against 5 μm in the nanopowders produced by the other method), but also the average size of their particles is considerably smaller (below 60 nm). The nanopowders produced by the chemical reduction of silver nitrate have, however, a much greater specific surface (above 400 m^2g^{-1}) and relatively better bactericide properties.

It is, however, worth noting that the thermal decomposition-reduction method, proposed by us, is much more 'clean' from the chemical point of view, since during this process, apart from carbon dioxide, no other undesired side products appear which could be harmful to the environment. Furthermore, the final product (Al_2O_3-Ag nanopowder) is not contaminated with the reaction reagents as is the case in the nanopowder produced by the $AgNO_3$ chemical reduction, which in addition is much more complicated in technological terms.

These are the reasons why we believe that the Al_2O_3-Ag powders produced by our method have much greater applicative possibilities than the Al_2O_3-Ag powders produced by the other method.

Acknowledgements

The study was accomplished thanks to the funds allotted by the European Union within the framework of the project entitled 'Program for the Development of the Warsaw University of Technology' financed by the European Social Funds and the National Budget and also thanks to the funds allotted by the Ministry of Science and Higher Education within the framework of the research project no. N N507 469538.

References

[1] S. Pal, Y.K. Tak, J.M. Song: Appl. Environ. Microbiol. Vol. 73 (2007), p. 1712

[2] M.J. Pike-Biegunski: Lek w Polsce (Drug in Poland) Vol. 11 (2005), p. 98

[3] M.J. Pike-Biegunski: Lek w Polsce (Drug in Poland) Vol. 9 (2005), p. 30

[4] J.J. Buckeley, P.L. Gai, A.F. Lee, L. Olivid, K. Wilson: Chem. Commun. (2008), p. 4013

[5] V.A. Dubok: Powder Metallurgy and Metal Ceramics Vol. 39 (2000), p. 381

[6] E. Weir, A. Lawlor, A. Whelan, F. Regan: Analyst Vol. 133 (2008), p. 835

[7] G. Wang, C. Shi, N. Zhao, X. Du: Mat. Letters Vol. 61 (2007), p. 3795

[8] A. Esteban-Cubillo, C. Diaz, A. Fernàndez, L.A. Diaz, C. Percharromàn, R. Torrecillas, J.S. Moya: J. Europ. Ceram. Soc. Vol. 26 (2006), p. 1

[9] A. Kunicki, A. Olszyna, A. Sołgała, PL Patent Application P-386489 (2008).

[10] A. Sołgała, A. Kunicki. A. Olszyna: Materiały Ceramiczne (Ceramic Materials) Vol. 60 (2008), p. 262

[11] A. Jastrzębska, A. Kunicki, A. Olszyna, Kompozyty (Composites) Vol. 10 (2010), p. 270

[12] A. Jastrzębska, A. Olszyna, A. Kunicki: Mat. Sci. and Engineering Vol. 3 (2010), p. 514

[13] K.J. Kurzydłowski, B. Ralph, in: *The quantitative description of the microstructure of the materials*, CRC Press LLC (1995).

[14] T. Thiel in: *Streaking microbial cultures on agar plates*. Science in the Real World: Microbes in Action (1999).

Key Engineering Materials Vol. 478 (2011) pp 19-24
© (2011) Trans Tech Publications, Switzerland
doi:10.4028/www.scientific.net/KEM.478.19

Mechanical and Microstructural Properties of Cement Paste Incorporating Nano Silica Particles with Various Specific Surface Areas

Ali Reza Khaloo[1, a], Asghar Gholizadeh Vayghan[2, b], Mohammad Bolhasani[3, c]

[1]Department of Civil Engineering, Sharif University of Technology, Tehran, Azadi St., Iran.

[2]MS in Structural Engineering, Sharif University of Technology, Tehran, Azadi St, Iran.

[3]MS in Geotechnical Engineering, KNT University of Technology, Tehran, Mirdamad St, Iran.

[a]khaloo@sharif.edu, [b]a.v.gholizadeh@gmail.com, [c]bolhassani_kntu_ac@yahoo.com,

Key words: Nanosilica, Specific surface area, Agglomeration.

Abstract. In this study, the effect of agglomeration and non-uniform dispersion of silica particles on the mechanical and microstructural properties of cement paste incorporating silica fume and nanosilica (NS) with various specific surface areas (SSA) is experimentally investigated. The SSA and replacement percent of silica particles were considered as test variables and four series of mixes were made including one set of mixes for silica fume with a SSA of 20 m^2/g and three sets of mixes for three different types of NS with SSA equal to 90, 200 and 380 m^2/g. In each series of mix designs three different cement replacement percents of 1.5%, 3% and 5% were applied. The results indicate that as the SSA and replacement percent of silica particles increase, the domain of variation of compressive strength results rises dramatically. It is observed that an increase in SSA of silica particles results in further agglomeration and difficulty in dispersion of NS particles within the paste. Also, there is significant variation on distribution of NS particles between similar specimens.

Introduction

It has been long found that fine amorphous silica particles can improve the mechanical properties and durability of concrete through the pozzolanic effect [1]. A new amorphous silica source recently introduced to the world of science is nanosilica. Nowadays, this material is produced with specific surface areas between 60-650 m^2/g in powder and colloidal forms by different companies [2]. Because of the amorphous structure and the filler effect and also appropriate physical and chemical characteristics, NS is a suitable supplementary material to enhance the microstructure of cement mixtures [3, 4]. In a research conducted by Y. Qing et al. the effect of nanosilica on the physical characteristics of cement paste has been studied in which by utilization of 5% of nanosilica with a SSA of 160 m^2/g and an average particle size of 15 nm, a maximum increase of 41% in compressive strength of 3-day samples was observed [5]. Also, Jo et al. has investigated the effect of NS particles with a SSA of 60 m^2/g and an average particle size of 40 nm on the characteristics of cement mortars in which by utilization of 12% of the considered NS a unique value of 177% increase in the compressive strength of 7-day samples was achieved [6].

Because of their high specific surface area, microstructural and electrical aspects, NS particles have high tendency to agglomerate and, therefore, the distribution is rather difficult. What is more, this problem is intensified as SSA increases. However, because of inadequate attention of the previous researches to the agglomeration and non-uniform dispersion of NS particles a general conclusion cannot be drawn on the precise effect of NS on the mechanical properties of cement mixtures (i.e. only one kind of NS has been utilized in each research). Therefore, the effect of agglomeration of NS particles on the compressive strength of cement pastes is investigated in this paper.

Experimental Program

Materials. The Materials used in this study include: Type I ordinary Portland cement (OPC), silica fume (SF), and three different types of nanosilica. The chemical composition and physical properties of the materials are shown in Table 1.

Table 1. Physical and chemical characteristics of cementitious materials.

Items	Chemical composition (%)				
	OPC	SF	NS-1	NS-2	NS-3
SiO_2	21.34	93	99.8	99.8	99.8
CaO	64.83	0.3	-	-	-
Al_2O_3	5.79	1.2	-	-	-
Fe_2O_3	2.75	0.9	-	-	-
MgO	2.85	0.5	-	-	-
SO_3	1.66	0.6	-	-	-
L.O.I	0.59	3.1	0.2	0.2	0.2
Physical properties					
SSA (m^2/g)	0.35	20	90	200	380
Avg. particle size	15 µm	140 nm	20 nm	12 nm	7 nm

Three different types of powder formed NS have been provided from Aerosil Evonik Degussa Company of Germany with SSA of 90, 200 and 380 m^2/g and treated as NS-1, NS-2 and NS-3, respectively. The utilized superplasticizer (SP) is Premia-180, provided from Dirgodaz Arshia Company of Iran, based on polyacrylate with a maximum allowable replacement percent of 2%, pH= 8.5 and a water content of 60%.

Mix design. Tests were performed on 5 cm × 5 cm × 5 cm cubic specimens and four specimens were cast for each mix design. In all of the mixes, the water/binder ratio was held constant and adopted equal to 0.23. The mix designs consist of four series of pastes including SF and the three different types of nanosilica. In each series, three cement replacement percents of 1.5%, 3% and 5% were applied. Also, a control paste was produced as reference. The pastes incorporating 1.5%, 3% and 5% of silica fume are treated as A-1, A-2 and A-3, respectively. Also, pastes incorporating NS-1, NS-2 and NS-3 are treated as B, C and D respectively and the labels 1, 2 and 3 show the replacement percent of cement (i.e. 1.5%, 3% and 5%). For the test mixtures the superplasticizer was added so that the flow of all pastes is the same as the flow of the control paste, which is equal to 100 mm. The details of the aforesaid mix designs are shown in Table 2.

Results and discussion

Table 2 exhibits the compressive test results of mix designs. Fig. 1 indicates that an increase in SSA from 20 m^2/g up to 200 m^2/g results in an increase of the average compressive strength. However, utilization of NS-3, in which the SSA equals 380 m^2/g, results in loss of strength. Moreover, it seems that an increase in NS content up to a definite percent leads to an increase in the average compressive strength of specimens and for higher percents of NS the mentioned parameter decreases.

The variations of the standard deviation of strength results versus the cement replacement percent are shown in Fig. 2. It is observed that an increase in silica percent and SSA leads to dramatic increase of the results standard deviation.

Table 2. Mix designs, strength results and statistical data.

Sample Label	Mix proportions by percent					28-day strength (MPa)				Statistical data	
	C	NS/C	SF/C	W/B	SP/B	1	2	3	4	Average	Std. deviation
Co	100	0	0	23	0	55	54	55	56	55	0.71
A-1	98.5	0	1.5	23	0.039	66	70	68	60	66	3.74
A-2	97	0	3	23	0.09	77	75	70	65	71.75	4.66
A-3	95	0	5	23	0.14	81.5	78	70	68	74.38	5.56
B-1	98.5	1.5	0	23	0.087	64	75	80	82	75.25	6.98
B-2	97	3	0	23	0.2	84.25	77.5	64	87	78.19	8.89
B-3	95	5	0	23	0.54	56.25	52.5	83.5	74	66.56	12.71
C-1	98.5	1.5	0	23	0.72	90.5	88	102.3	108.5	97.31	8.41
C-2	97	3	0	23	1.14	111.5	106.5	91.25	83.5	98.19	11.29
C-3	95	5	0	23	2.2	75.5	92.5	115.5	85	92.13	14.78
D-1	98.5	1.5	0	23	0.93	109.5	80	75	88.75	88.31	13.19
D-2	97	3	0	23	1.68	100.5	71.25	93.75	62.5	82	15.62
D-3	95	5	0	23	3.93	91.75	68.75	102	55.5	79.5	18.36

Increase in replacement percent and SSA of silica particles makes the distribution of these particles more difficult and, also, results in an increased tendency to agglomerate. Therefore, this problem will cause to considerable differences between compressive strength results of specimens produced from the same mix design and an increase in replacement percent and SSA of silica particles intensify this problem. As the results show, adding superplasticizer and use of mechanical mixers are unable to solve this problem.

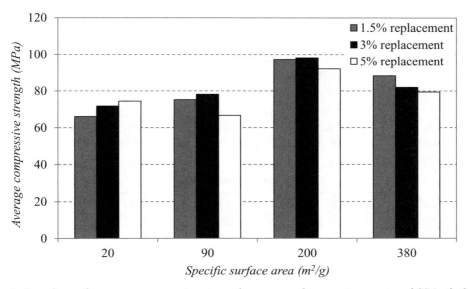

Fig. 1. Bar chart of average compressive strength versus replacement percent and SSA of silica.

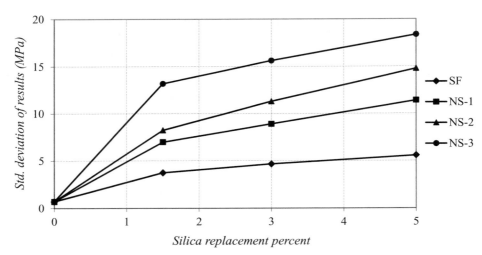

Fig. 2. Standard deviation of strength results versus silica percent and SSA.

According to Fig. 3a to Fig. 3c, SEM micrographs captured from D-3 samples indicate that in specimens containing nanosilica particles there are zones with very dense microstructure (shown with A) beside porous and weak zones (shown with B) and an abundance of agglomerated nanosilica particles are apparent (shown with C). On the other hand, the SEM micrographs taken from B-3 specimens indicate a moderately homogenous microstructure (see Fig. 3d). Table 3 shows the typical EDX analysis results for zone A and C of D-3 samples and also zone D of B-3 samples. The percentages of ingredients indicate presence of C-S-H gel in zone A and D and agglomerated silica in zone C.

Therefore, it can be concluded that increase in replacement percent and SSA of silica particles make the microstructure of the matrix heterogeneous. The decrease in compressive strength of samples and dramatic increase in results variance with increase of replacement percent and SSA of silica particles is due to this heterogeneity of microstructure and unequal content of silica particles in different specimens.

Regarding the obtained results and SEM micrographs it can be concluded that due to the large and meaningful differences found between compressive strengths of specimens, only relying on the arithmetic mean of the results without considering the dispersion problems and uncertainty issues is not convincing.

Table 3. EDX analysis results of different zones.

Ingredient	Zone A		Zone C		Zone D	
	Wt%	At%	Wt%	At%	Wt%	At%
Na	0.00	0.00	0.00	0.00	2.38	3.53
Mg	5.47	7.77	0.00	0.00	0.00	0.00
Al	8.06	10.32	6.63	6.68	6.64	8.38
Si	26.79	32.95	66.41	74.88	28.80	34.93
K	2.45	2.16	10.55	7.33	15.31	13.33
Ca	46.78	40.32	16.41	11.12	46.86	39.82
Fe	10.46	6.47	0.00	0.00	0.00	0.00
Total	100	100	100	100	100	100

Fig. 3. SEM micrographs captured from different matrices of destroyed samples: (a), (b) and (c) correspond to D-3 samples and (d) corresponds to B-3 samples.

Conclusions

The results obtained from the study indicate that:

Utilization of NS particles results in an increase of compressive strength by 78% and 30% at the optimum replacement percent of NS and SF, respectively.

The agglomeration and non-uniform dispersion of NS particles result in formation of different types of zones within the samples although the macroscopic appearances of samples seem homogenous and similar and all of them have the same workability. However, the SEM micrographs indicate that the NS particles have not been dispersed adequately and the microstructure of the hardened pastes incorporating nanosilica is heterogeneous.

The large dispersion of test results is due to agglomeration and non-uniform dispersion of NS particles. Increase in silica replacement percent and specific surface area lead to drastic increase in variation of results.

Acknowledgments:
Supports of research committee of Sharif University of Technology (SUT) and SEM laboratory personnel of Tarbiat Modares University are greatly appreciated.

References

[1] L. Hui, X. Hui-gang, Y. Jie, O. Jinping: Compos. PART B-Eng. Vol. 35 (2004), p. 185

[2] Y. Kazuaki, A. Yasuhiko, S. Hiroyo: Bulletin of Nippon Bunri University, Vol. 32 No. 1 (2004), p. 31

[3] W. Kuo, K. Lin, W. Chang, H. Luo: J. Ind. Eng. Chem. Vol. 12, No. 5 (2006), p. 702

[4] CP. Huang: NSF-REU University of Delaware (2006), August 11

[5] Y. Qing, Z. Zenan, K. Deyu, C. Rongshen: Constr. Build. Mater. Vol. 21 (2007), p. 539

[6] Byung-Wan Jo, Chang-Hyun Kim, Ghio-ho Tae, Jong-Bin Park: Constr. Build. Mater. Vol. 21 (2007), p. 1351

Key Engineering Materials Vol. 478 (2011) pp 25-33
© (2011) Trans Tech Publications, Switzerland
doi:10.4028/www.scientific.net/KEM.478.25

Improvement of the Corrosion Resistance for the Galvanic Coupling of Steel with Polypyrrole Coated Galvanized Steel

A. H. El-Shazly*, H. A. Al-Turaif

Chemical and Materials Engineering Dept., King Abdulaziz University, Jeddah, Saudi Arabia
*corresponding author: Elshazly_a@yahoo.com

Key words: Corrosion resistance, polypyrrole, galvanic corrosion, electropolymerization, conducting polymers

Abstract

The aim of the present work is to use intrinsically conducting polymers (ICPs) to improve the corrosion resistance ability of the galvanic coupling of galvanized steel coupled with steel by coating it with polypyrrole (PPy). The potentiostatic technique was used for forming the PPy layer using a potentiostat (EG&G A-273 Potentiostat/Galvanostat). Many variables were investigated for their effect on the characteristics of the formed coat layer such as: applied potential, electrolyte concentration (sodium tartrate concentration), solution pH, and type of electrode. The formed coat layer was investigated using X-Ray Photoelectron Spectroscopy (XPS) technique. Finally, the corrosion resistance ability of the galvanic coupling of PPy coated galvanized steel coupled with bare steel was investigated using electrochemical methods such as Tafel method. The results show that the galvanic coupling of PPy coated galvanized steel and bare steel has a corrosion current which is 31.8% less than the galvanic coupling of bare galvanized when coupled with steel.

Introduction

Steel galvanization is a sacrificial protection method for steel against corrosion where, a layer of zinc is applied on the surface of steel either electrochemically or by hot dipping of steel in molten zinc. This method of protection is widely used in most of industrial applications such as steel tanks and steel pipelines, as well as large buildings construction like metallic structures and bridges. The thickness of the formed galvanic layer is not only a controlling parameter in the lifetime determination of the galvanic layer, but also in the determination of the total cost of the galvanization process. Replacement of part of the galvanic layer by less expensive, durable, environmentally stable and easy to be synthesized polypyrrole coat might be used for reducing the cost of the galvanization process and increasing the lifetime of coated galvanized steel. Corrosion protection using intrinsically conducting polymers (ICPs) is now an important research field especially due to the restriction of using heavy metals due to the environmental problems. ICPs are considered an effective corrosion protection coating for many different metals such as mild steel [1-5], stainless steel [6-8], iron [9-13] , aluminium [14-18] copper [19,20] or zinc [21,22]. This can be demonstrated by the fact that the corrosion potential of these metals is shifted in the direction of noble metals and the corrosion current decreases. Brusic et al. [19] found that the chemical nature of the polymer backbone, oxidation state and the extent and nature of polymer doping significantly affect the corrosion protection properties of the coated metal. Polypyrrole (PPy) is one of the widely used ICPs for metals protection; in particular several studies have been devoted to thin polypyrrole film formation on common metals as Fe, Al, and Zn by anodic oxidation of pyrrole. Of all heterocyclic monomers, pyrrole alone can be easily electropolymerized in an aqueous solution over a wide pH range from 3 to 9 [20-25]. The use of appropriate electrolyte allows depositing PPy films on oxidizable metals by electrochemical oxidation of pyrrole. In their work, Martins dos Santos et al. [26] studied the effect of using different electrolyte such as oxalic acid, sodium oxalate, sodium/potassium tartrate and sodium salicylate as electrolytes and compared in terms of easiness for PPy deposition, and film characteristics. They found that electrochemical measurements in presence of these electrolytes with and without pyrrole demonstrate that copper can be efficiently passivated before polypyrrole electrodeposition. Aeiyach et al. [27] successfully electrodeposited PPy on zinc and these films showed considerable properties as a primer layer for protection applications. Iroh et al. [28] found that the presence of PPy coatings significantly increases the corrosion potential and drastically reduces the corrosion current and corrosion rate of steel. They concluded that the corrosion resistance of poly(N-methylpyrrole) coated steel was lower than that of PPy coated steel. Immersion tests on coated steel–copper galvanic couple showed that EB/ER coating offered 100 times more protection than ER coating against steel dissolution and coating delamination on copper. This was mainly attributed to the passive metal oxide films formed by EB blocking both the anodic and cathodic reactions. Salt spray tests showed that 100 μm EB/ER coating protected steel–copper couple for at least 2000 h. Martins et al. [29] investigated the electropolymerization of pyrrole on zinc-coated steel electrodes in aqueous medium under several techniques (potentiodynamic, galvanostatic and potentiostatic modes) by using carboxylate salts, such as citrate, succinate, oxalate, malate and tartrate. Adherent and homogeneous PPy coatings were obtained only with tartrate counter-ions.

The aim of the present work is to investigate the corrosion resistance ability improvement of PPy coated galvanized steel when it is in a galvanic coupling with steel in 3.5% sodium chloride solution as electrolyte. Potentiostatic technique was used for the electropolymerization of pyrrole using sodium tartrate as electrolyte. Replacement of part of the galvanic layer by less expensive, durable, environmentally stable and easy to be synthesized PPy coat is important for reducing the cost of the galvanization process and increasing the lifetime of the coated galvanized steel.

Experimental
Electropolymerization of pyrrole:
Aqueous electropolymerization of pyrrole was performed in one-compartment cell. The working electrode was made from galvanized steel sheet of 2x3x0.1 cm^3. The working electrode was polished and degreased with acetone for about half an hour prior to the electropolymerization. An Ag/AgCl reference electrode manufactured by Corning Company was used as the reference electrode. The potentiostatic technique (constant potential method) was used to electrochemically coat the galvanized steel with the PPy layer using an EG&G Princeton Applied Research Potentiostat/Galvanostat Model 273A. The working electrode was the galvanized steel while different counter electrodes were investigated such as galvanized steel, steel and stainless steel. The applied potential was varied from 1 to 2.5 V. The pH value of the solution containing 0.5 M pyrrole and sodium tartrate was varied between 7, 9, 11 and 13. The initial monomer (pyrrole) concentration was kept constant at 0.5 M while electrolyte concentration was varied between 0.1, 0.2, 0.3 and 0.4 M. The electropolymerization time was fixed at 800 s. After each experiment, the PPy coated galvanized steel sheet was rinsed with distilled water and methanol and left to dry.

Examination of the performance of the PPy coated galvanized steel against corrosion:
Tafel extrapolation was used for the examination of PPy coated galvanized steel when coupled with steel in 3.5% NaCl solution. PPy coated galvanized steel and steel were used as anode and cathode respectively, the corrosion current and potential were measured against Ag/AgCl reference electrode using the EG&G Princeton Applied Research Potentiostat/Galvanostat Model 273A provided with powerCorr software. Finally, the traditional gravimetric analysis was used by measuring the loss in weight of PPy coated galvanized steel coupled with steel for 30 days of immersion in 3.5% NaCl solution.

Results and discussions
A- Effect of applied potential
As shown in figure 1, four different applied potentials 1, 1.5, 2 and 2.5 volts vs saturated calomel electrode (SCE 3.5% KCl) were investigated. The results show that for potentials below 2 V the formation of the PPy layer on the galvanized steel is not succeeded. This may be attributed to the fact that below a certain potential level the nucleation rate of polymer on the electrode surface is lower than the rate of nucleus growth and each nucleus spreads on the overall surface before the next nucleus is formed [19,20]. At 2 V and 2.5 V the formation of PPy is succeeded. This is

because at higher over potentials the nucleation rate increases faster than the step propagation rate and the deposition of each layer proceeds with the formation of a large number of nuclei. When a 2 V potential is applied, the current decreases at 80 s, then, the insulating film continues to form till current reaches the PPy layer formation at 0.124 A, after 200 s. On the other hand, at 2.5 V applied potential, the current decreases at 25 s, then, the insulating film continues to form till it reaches the PPy layer formation at 0.24 A, after 150 s. The above results show that increasing the applied potential decrease the incubation period and increase the formation current.

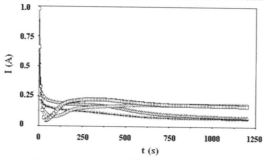

Legend: 1.0 V △, 1.5 V +, 2.0 V O, 2.5 V □.
Coating PPy layer at 0.5 M pyrrole + 0.2 M sodium tartrate, pH = 9.0
Figure 1: Current transient with time during polymerization at different oxidation potential

Examination of the performance of the galvanic coupling of PPy coated galvanized steel/steel against corrosion using Tafel extrapolation test:

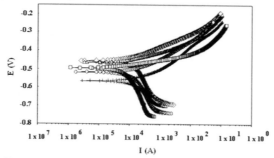

Legend: No Coating ◊, 1.0 V △, 1.5 V +, 2.0 V O, 2.5 V .
Figure 2: Tafel test for the galvanic coupling of steel and PPy coated galvanized steel at different applied potential using Ag/AgCl reference electrode in 3.5 % NaCl solution

As shown in figure 2 and table 1, the results show that the corrosion rate of the galvanic coupling have been decreased for layers formed at higher applied potential. The corrosion rate was changed by a factor ranging from 11 to 70% depending on the applied potential for layer formation. The rate was decreased from 0.1238 for bare galvanized steel to 0.03695 mm/yr for PPy coated galvanized steel at applied potential of 2.5 V.

Table 1: Corrosion rate for the galvanic coupling of steel and galvanized steel without coating and with PPy coating at different applied potentials.

Voltage(V)	I corr (A)	E corr (V)	Corrosion rate (mm/year)
No Coating	8.263E-6	-0.457	0.12380
1.0	4.975E-6	-0.465	0.11010
1.5	9.311E-6	-0.566	0.07455
2.0	4.184E-6	-0.518	0.06270
2.5	3.126E-6	-0.496	0.03695

B - Effect of electrolyte (sodium tartrate) concentration

The PPy layer was formed using different concentrations of sodium tartrate ranges from 0.1 to 0.4 M. As shown in figure 3, the formation of PPy layer was not succeeded at 0.1 M sodium tartrate concentration, while at higher concentrations (0.2, 0.3 and 0.4 M) the layer was formed successfully. These results may be attributed to the fact that at lower concentrations a continuous anodic dissolution take place for long time and the insulating film cannot be formed. The results show that the induction period has been decreased from 80 to 15 s by increasing the electrolyte concentration from 0.2 to 0.4 M, which may be attributed to the higher conductivity of the solution at higher electrolyte concentrations.

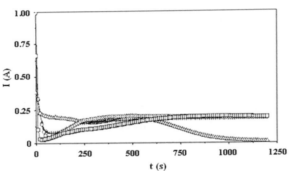

Legend: 0.1 M △, 0.2 M +, 0.3 M O, 0.4 M □

Figure 3: Transient current with time during polymerization in different sodium tartrate concentrations.

2.2. Tafel Extrapolation Test:

The Tafel extrapolation test for the galvanic coupling of the PPy coated galvanized steel coated at different electrolyte concentration and steel was carried out in 3.5% NaCl using Ag/AgCl reference electrode. Table 2 shows that the corrosion rate has been decreased by increasing the electrolyte (sodium tartrate) concentration up to 0.3 M sodium tartrate, which indicate that the corrosion resistance of the formed layer has been increased by increasing the electrolyte concentration. The rate was decreased from 0.1238 mm/year for the uncoated steel to 0.03147 mm/year for the PPy coated galvanized steel at 0.3 M sodium tartrate with improvement in the corrosion resistance of the galvanic coupling by a factor of 1.74 over the uncoated galvanized steel.

Table 2: Corrosion rate for the galvanic coupling of steel and galvanized steel without coating and with PPy coating at different electrolyte concentration:

Concentration	I corr (A)	E corr (V)	Corrosion rate (mm/year)
No Coating	8.263E-6	-0.457	0.1238
0.1	4.948E-6	-0.428	0.07415
0.2	4.184E-6	-0.518	0.06270
0.3	5.726E-6	-0.501	0.03147
0.4	2.221E-6	-0.394	0.08581

C- Effect of solution pH

The PPy layer was formed under different solution pH within the range of 5 to 11. The results show that the PPy layer was formed successfully for pH values in the range from 7 to 9. Higher and lower values of this pH values are not suitable for PPy layer formation. As shown in figure 4, the layer formation for pH values of 7 and 9 has the same induction period of 80 s and transition time for the PPy layer formation of 250 s with different current densities of 0.125 and 0.14 A respectively.

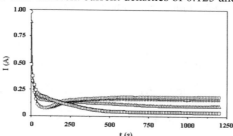

Legend: pH 5 Δ, pH 7 +, pH 9 O, pH 11 □

Figure 4: Transient current with time during electropolymerization in different solution pH

3.2. Tafel extrapolation test:

Table 3: Corrosion rate for the galvanic coupling of steel and galvanized steel without coating and with PPy coating at different solution pH.

pH	Icorr (A)	Ecorr (V)	Corrosion rate (mm/year)
No Coating	8.263E-6	-0.457	0.1238
5.0	4.723E-6	-0.469	0.07078
7.0	3.727E-6	-0.502	0.05585
9.0	4.184E-6	-0.518	0.06270
11.0	4.997E-6	-0.435	0.07487

The test was carried out for the galvanic coupling between the PPy coated galvanized steel and steel in 3.5%NaCl solution. As shown in table 3 the results show that samples coated with solutions of pH within the range of 7 to 9 have the lower corrosion rate, and that the corrosion rate decreased by a factor of 1.54 for PPy coated galvanized steel coated at pH 7 than the samples without coating

4. Effect of Different counter electrode:

4.1. Layer formation:

Three different counter electrodes such as steel, zinc and stainless steel were examined for their effect on the formed PPy layer on galvanized steel. As shown in figure 5, approximately the PPy layer formation conditions for using stainless steel is much close to steel while for zinc the induction period and the current required for layer formation are not clear.

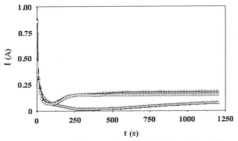

Legend: Zinc △, Steel +, Stainless Steel O

Figure 5: Transient current with time during polymerization using different counter electrode.

Tafel extrapolation test

Table 4 shows that the sample that has been coated using stainless steel as the counter electrode has the lowest corrosion rate of 0.04954 mm/year with an improvement of 60% over the sample without coating.

Table 4: Corrosion rate for the galvanic coupling of steel and galvanized steel with and without PPy coating at different counter electrodes.

Counter electrod	Icorr (A)	Ecorr (V)	Corrosion rate (mm/year)
No Coating	8.263E-6	-0.457	0.1238
Zinc	5.163E-6	-0.499	0.07737
Steel	4.184E-6	-0.518	0.06270
Stainless.S	3.306E-6	-0.452	0.04954

Surface elemental analysis and composition:

XPS investigation of the bare galvanized steel was conducted at the beginning of this study. Figure 6 is a typical XPS general survey spectrum of galvanized steel. Zn, O, and Cr elements were detected at the galvanized steel surface. The atomic weight percentages were calculated as 69, 20, and 11 % respectively. This result means that a uniform zinc oxide layer is covering the surface.

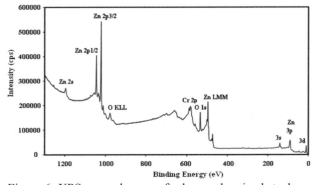

Figure 6: XPS general survey for bare galvanized steel

Examination of the elemental composition of PPy coated galvanized steel at different potentials of 1, 1.5, 2 and 2.5 V was carried out by XPS as shown in table 5.

Table 5: XPS atomic weight percentages of PPy coating compositions at different applied potentials.

Applied Potential	Atomic Weight Percent					
	C	O	N	Zn	Na	Fe
1.0 V	38.49	29.51	2.79	27.88	0.54	0.78
1.5 V	43.11	31.85	3.65	20.16	0.55	0.68
2.0 V	71.84	19.76	7.61	0.33	0.40	0
2.5 V	70.30	19.05	9.92	0.32	0.37	0

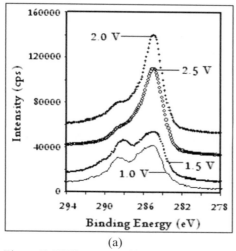
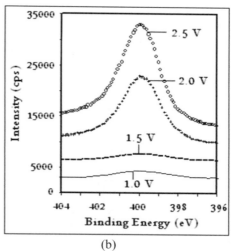

(a)   (b)

Figure 7: XPS spectra of (a) carbon {C1s} and (b) nitrogen {N1s} on galvanized steel coated with PPy film at different applied potentials

The results indicate the following:

- Zinc atomic weight percentages are high in samples coated at 1.0 and 1.5 V but are very low for samples coated at 2 and 2.5 V potentials. This means that the formed PPy layer is not uniform all over the surface at lower applied potentials and is covering the surface at applied potentials above 1.5 V.
- Samples coated at 2 and 2.5 V have the higher carbon and nitrogen atomic weight percentages which mean that the formed PPy layer is covering the entire surface.
- The double peaks in the carbon (C1s) spectra are originated from both the PPy coating and the sodium tartrate (Figure 7a). However, the single peak of the nitrogen (N1s) is originated from the PPy coating only (Figure 7b).

Gravimetric method

From the above results, the galvanized steel was coated with the PPy layer using a solution of 0.5 M pyrrole, 0.2 M sodium tartrate, and solution pH of 9 using the potentiostatic technique with stainless steel as the counter electrode and an applied potential of 2 V vs Ag/AgCl reference electrode. The PPy coated galvanized steel was coupled with bare steel in a solution of 3.5% NaCl, and the loss in weight of the galvanized steel was measured for a period of 30 days. As shown in figure 8 the results show that coating the galvanized steel with PPy layer improved the corrosion resistance ability of the galvanic coupling steel/galvanized steel by 31.8% in relation to the galvanic coupling of steel/bare galvanized steel.

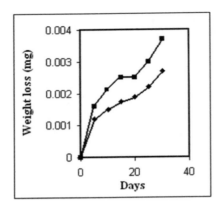

Figure 8: weight loss vs time for both PPy coated and uncoated galvanized steel

Conclusion

PPy coating was used to improve the corrosion resistance ability of the galvanic coupling of steel with PPy coated galvanized steel. The potentiostatic technique was used for forming the layer. The layer formed was investigated for its composition using the X-Ray Photoelectron Spectroscopy (XPS), while the corrosion current for the galvanic coupling of the PPy coated galvanized steel/steel was measured using the Tafel test. In addition, a gravimetric test was carried out to support the obtained results. Many factors were investigated for their effect on the performance of the formed layer. The results show that increasing the applied potential has increased the corrosion resistance ability of the layer formed applied potential of 2 V was proved to have the higher corrosion resistance. For electrolyte concentration the formed layer has shown good characteristics for a tartrate concentration of 2 M, solution pH of 9 and using steel or stainless steel as the counter electrodes gives good layer performance characteristics. Gravimetric tests of the galvanic coupling steel/PPy coated galvanized steel in 3.5% NaCl solution have shown that coating the galvanized steel with PPy layer improved the corrosion resistance ability of the coupling by a factor of 1.32 than bare galvanized steel when coupled with steel. The obtained results can find applications for the protection of steel constructions using the sacrificial protection methods in cathodic protection systems.

References

[1] G. Troch-Nagels, R. Winand, A. Weymeersch, L. Renard, J. Appl.Electrochem. Vol. 22 (1992), p.756.

[2] W. K. Lu, R.L. Elsenbaumer, B. Wessling, Synth. Met. Vol.71 (1995), p. 2163.

[3] J.L. Camalet, J.C. Lacroix, S. Aeiyach, K. Chane-Ching, P.C. Lacaze, J. Electroanal. Chem.Vol. 416 (1996), p. 179.

[4] N. Ahmad, A.G. MacDiarmid, Synth. Met. Vol.78 (1996), p. 103.

[5] P. Li, T.C. Tan, J.Y. Lee, Synth. Met. Vol.88 (1997), p. 237.

[6] S. Ren, D. Barkey, J. Electrochem. Soc. Vol. 139 (1992), p. 1021.

[7] J.R. Santos, L.H.C. Mattoso, A.J. Motheo, Electrochim. Acta Vol. 43(1998),p. 309.

[8] D.E. Tallman, Y. Pae, G.P. Bierwagen, Corrosion Vol.55 (1999), p. 779.

[91] D. Sazou, C. Georgolios, J. Electroanal. Chem. Vol. 429 (1997), p. 81.

[10] P.J. Kinlen, D.C. Silverman, C.R. Jeffreys, Synth. Met. Vol. 85 (1997), p. 1327.

[11] J.L. Camalet, J.C. Lacroix, S. Aeiyach, K. Chane-Ching, P.C. Lacaze, Synth. Met. Vol. 93 (1998), p. 133.

[12] M.C. Bernard, A. Hugot-Le Goff, S. Joiret, N.N. Dinh, N.N. Toan, J. Electrochem. Soc. Vol. 146 (1999), p. 995.

[13] A. Mirmohseni, A. Oladegaragoze, Synth. Met. Vol. 114 (2000), p. 105.

[14] S.C. Yang, R. Brown, R. Racicot, Y. Lin, F. McClarnon, ACS Sym.Ser. Vol. 843 (2003), p. 196.

[15] P. Montoya, F. Jaramillo, J. Calderón, S.I. Córdoba de Torresi, R.M. Torresi, Electrochim. Acta, Vol. 55- 21(2010), p.6116.

[16] G.G. Wallace, A. Dominis, G.M. Spinks, D.E. Tallman, ACS Sym.Ser. Vol. 843 (2003), p. 103.

[17] D. Huerta-Vilca, S.R. Moraes, A.J. Motheo, J. Brazil. Chem. Soc. Vol. 14 (2003), p. 52.

[18] D.E. Tallman, C. Vang, G.G. Wallace, G.P. Bierwagen, J. Electrochem. Soc. Vol. 149 (2002), p. C173.

[19] V. Brusic, M. Angelopoulos, T. Graham, J. Electrochem. Soc. Vol. 144(1997), p. 436

[20]C.A. Ferreira, S. Aeiyach, J.J. Aaron, P.C. Lacaze, Electrochim. Acta Vol. 41 (1996), p. 1801.

[21] P.C. Lacaze, C.A. Ferreira, S. Aeiyach, J.J. Aaron, French Pat. 92 14091 PSA-CitroeÈn, 1992.

[22] P.C. Lacaze, C.A. Ferreira, S. Aeiyach, French Pat. 9214092 PSA CitroeÈn, 1992.

[23] Z. Deng, W.H. Smyl, H.S. White, J. Electrochem. Soc. Vol. 136 (1989), p. 2152.

[24] J. Petitjean, S. Aeiyach, C.A. Ferreira, P.C. Lacaze, H.Takenouti, J. Electrochem. Soc. Vol. 142 (1995), p. 136.

[25] B. ZaõÈd, S. Aeiyach, H. Takenouti, P.C. Lacaze, Electrochim. Acta Vol. 43 (1998), p. 2331.

[26] L.M. Martins dos Santos, J.C. Lacroix, K.I. Chane-Ching, A. Adenier,L.M. Abrantes, P.C. Lacaze, J. Electroanal. Chem. Vol. 587 (2006), p. 67

[27] S. Aeiyach, B. Zaid, P.C. Lacaze, Electrochim. Acta Vol. 44 (1999), p. 2889.

[28] J. O. Iroh , W. Su, Electrochimica Acta Vol. 46 (2000), p. 15.

[29] J.I. Martins, T.C. Reis , M. Bazzaoui , E.A. Bazzaoui , L. Martins, Corrosion Science Vol. 46 (2004), p 2361.

Key Engineering Materials Vol. 478 (2011) pp 34-39
© (2011) Trans Tech Publications, Switzerland
doi:10.4028/www.scientific.net/KEM.478.34

Experimental Characterization of Hydrogen Embrittlement in API 5L X60 and API 5L X80 Steels

Araújo, Bruno Allison[a]; Travassos, Gabriel Dias[b], Silva, Antonio Almeida[c], Vilar, Eudésio Oliveira[d], Carrasco, Jorge Palma[e] and Araújo, Carlos José[f]

Federal University of Campina Grande, Campina Grande - PB, Brazil.

[a]bengmec@yahoo.com.br, [b]gabrieltravassos@yahoo.com.br, [c]almeida@dem.ufcg.edu.br, [d]vilar@deq.ufcg.edu.br, [e]jorge_palma_c@yahoo.com.br and [f]carlos@dem.ufcg.edu.br

Key words: hydrogen embrittlement, hydrogen trapping, fracture surface.

Abstract. The present work aims to study the hydrogen embrittlement process in API 5L X60 and API 5L X80 steels. The tests were performed using two kinds of hydrogen sources to work with two conditions of hydrogen damage: environmental hydrogen embrittlement and internal hydrogen embrittlement. The mechanical behavior of API 5L X60 and API 5L X80 steels in tensile tests, with and without hydrogen, were studied. Under environmental hydrogen embrittlement conditions, the API 5L X60 steel presented a softening process observed by the decrease in yield strength and increase in its deformation. The API 5L X80 steel was more susceptible to the phenomenon due the deformation decrease of hydrogenated samples. In notched samples, both steels were susceptible to embrittlement as shown by the decrease in elongation. Under internal hydrogen embrittlement conditions, in both steels the changes in deformation were significant and can be attributed to changes in the hydrogen trapping due to the hydrogenation process used, the chemical composition and microstructure. It was observed that the fracture surface morphology of hydrogenated samples of both steels was ductile by microvoids coalescence, and that the distribution of dimples per unit area was higher in the API 5L X60 steel. It can be concluded, as reported in the literature, that the reversible hydrogen trapping observable in environmental hydrogen embrittlement is more damaging than irreversible hydrogen trapping, observable in internal hydrogen embrittlement.

Introduction

There is great interest in understanding the role of hydrogen when interacting with metals and metallic alloys and of the damage produced by that interaction. In the industrial sectors affected for the hydrogen degradation, the petrochemical sector is one of the most prejudiced. The degradation of mechanical properties as a result of hydrogen interaction with metals and metallic alloys is manifested by diverse ways: blisters on the surface of the material or internal cracks due to Hydrogen-Induced Cracking, fisheyes due to Hydrogen Attack, failure in non-ferrous based materials structures for Cracking from Hydride Formation, failure due to residual hydrogen in Cracking from Precipitation of Internal Hydrogen and catastrophic cracking of high strength steels due to Hydrogen Embrittlement.

Depending on the source, Hydrogen Embrittlement has been classified into two forms: Environmental Hydrogen Embrittlement (EHE) and Internal Hydrogen Embrittlement (IHE) [1,2]. EHE takes place through adsorption of molecular hydrogen generated in a hydrogenated atmosphere or during a corrosion reaction, and its absorption within the lattice after dissociation into atomic form. IHE, in contrast, takes place in the absence of a hydrogenated atmosphere and is brought about by hydrogen which has entered the lattice during processing or fabrication of steel, i.e., prior testing or service. In the present work, an experimental investigation was carried out on the mechanical behavior of a API 5L X60 and API 5L X80 steels under tensile loading and environmental assisted conditions, with the purpose of studying the response of these steels to IHE and to EHE.

Experimental Procedures

This study was performed using the API 5L X60 and API 5L X80 steels with chemical composition shown in Table 1. The microstructure of API 5L X60 steel is composed of bands of ferrite and perlite, which is typical of rolled X60 steels. The microstructure of API 5L X80 steel consists of ferrite and bainite microstructure that is typical of steels produced by controlled rolling processes. The specimens were extracted from the wall of a pipe already conformed and were machined in the direction of lamination. The dimensions of the specimens are in accordance with ASTM E 8M-04.

Table 1. Chemical composition of API 5L X60 and API 5L X80 steels [%].

	C	**Mn**	**Si**	**P**	**S**	**Al**	**V**	**Mo**	**Cu**	**Nb**	**Ti**	**Cr**	**Ni**
X60	0.12	1.48	0.27	0.012	0.008	0.039	0.048	0.032	0.006	0.041	0.009	-	-
*	0.24	1.40	-	0.025	0.015	-	**	-	-	**	0.06	-	-
X80	0.084	1.61	0.23	0.01	0.011	0.035	0.015	0.17	0.029	-	-	0.135	0.011
*	0.24	1.40	-	0.025	0.015	-	**	-	-	**	0.06	-	-

* Maximum reference values;
** (Nb + V + Ti) < 0.15% [3].

To reproduce the EHE condition, the hydrogen was permeated through the Type I (Smooth specimen ASTM) and Type II (Specimens ASTM + notch) specimens. The hydrogen was produced on the specimen surface from galvanostatic condition utilizing a AC-DC power supply (Icel-PS7000) at room temperature in 0.1 M NaOH solution with 2 mg As_2O_3. A Pt-Ir Fisher electrode was utilized as anode. The constant charging current density was 2.5 mA.cm^{-2}. The charging of hydrogen was performed for 24 h in absence of mechanical stress. After hydrogenation, the Type I and Type II were immersed in a Cu_2SO_4 solution to reduce the hydrogen desorption.

To reproduce the IHE condition, the hydrogen was introduced cathodically at room temperature using a 0.1 M NaOH with 2 mg As_2O_3 solution with the same current density employed in EHE tests. The experimental setup was used according with the charging methodology proposed by Tiwari [1]: a) employ of a Type III specimen (specimen ASTM + notch + portion extended), that forms the cathode (portion extended) of the electrolytic cell used in the hydrogen charging; b) hydrogenation performed under tensile stress of 65% yield strength for 24 and 48 h to allow the hydrogen presence in the lattice above of solubility limit; c) After loading the hydrogen for a certain time, the electrolytic cell is removed and the load is maintained for 24 h for the initial stabilization of the concentration of hydrogen. Thus, only the irreversibly trapped hydrogen is present in the specimen. In this process, the hydrogen was generated in the extended portion of specimen and the hydrogenation was accomplished by diffusion due to a concentration gradient and due to a stress gradient created by a notch present in the middle of specimen. This hydrogenation under stress process was carried out in the fixture developed by Costa [4].

After hydrogenation, uniaxial tensile tests at room temperature under slow strain rate were performed using a universal testing machine INSTRON model 5582, according to the recommendations of ASTM E8M-04 standard. In the case of tests for EHE were utilized the Type I and Type II specimens. The strain rate applied was 2.5x10^{-5} s^{-1}. The fracture surfaces were studied by scanning electron microscopy (SEM).

Results and Discussions

EHE - Type I and Type II specimens. Figure 1(a) and Table 2 show that the hydrogenated API 5L X60 steel had a slight decrease in yield strength, suggesting that the steel in hydrogen condition suffered small softening, as can be observed by the decrease in yield strength. In addition, the elongation obtained in the tensile test was higher in hydrogenated condition. The susceptibility of

HSLA (High Strength Low Alloy) steels has been investigated by many researchers. Hardie *et al.* [5] studied X60, X80 and X100 steels. It was shown that there is a distinct susceptibility to loss of ductility after hydrogen charging and this tends to increase with the level of resistance of the steel. Analyzing the variation of elongation of the specimens with and without hydrogen from both steels, it can be observed that for the API 5L X60 steel there was an increase in elongation and to the API 5L X80 steel a decrease, and thus the API 5L X80 steel appears to be more susceptible to the phenomenon.

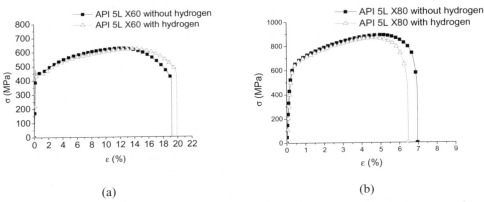

(a)   (b)

Figure 1. Stress-strain curves: (a) X60 steel, Type I specimens; (b) X80 steel, Type II specimens.

Table 2. Results from stress-strain curves for the X60 and X80 steels, Type I specimens.

	API 5L X60		API 5L X80	
	Without H	With H	Without H	With H
σ_{YS} [MPa]	462.13 ± 10.84	450.19 ± 8.47	487.93 ± 4.67	491.53 ± 5.39
σ_{UTS} [MPa]	629.20 ± 4.20	626.71 ± 4.75	719.84 ± 3.18	721.64 ± 9.47
Elongation [%]	19.08 ± 0.4	19.47 ± 0.12	16.69 ± 0.24	16.39 ± 0.09

From Figure 1(b) and Table 3, one can see that the API 5L X80 steel showed an embrittlement trend as can be seen in the values of elongation, showing that the effect of hydrogen is enhanced under a notch. This can be explained by the fact that the location of hydrogen in regions with high levels of stress triaxial state is a factor that increases the process of hydrogen embrittlement [6]. For notched specimens, however, hydrogen can decrease the stress fracture, and this decrease is proportional to the amount of hydrogen concentration. Moreover, it also influences the loss of ductility [7].

Table 3. Results from stress-strain curves for the X60 and X80 steels, Type II specimens.

	API 5L X60		API 5L X80	
	Without H	With H	Without H	With H
σ_{UTS} [MPa]	772.39 ± 6.66	765.63 ± 4.78	880.71 ± 20.82	868.16 ± 11.15
Elongation [%]	7.89 ± 0.38	6.85 ± 0.35	7.07 ± 0.35	6.18 ± 0.49

IHE –Type III specimens. As seen in Figure 2 and Table 4, both steels under these conditions showed good resistance to the phenomenon of internal hydrogen embrittlement.

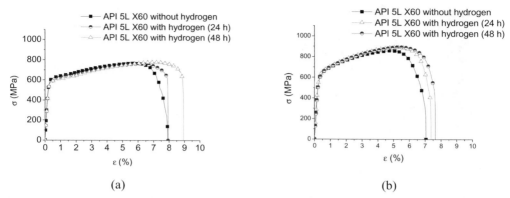

(a)   (b)

Figure 2. Stress-strain curves for Type III specimens: (a) API 5L X60 steel; (b) API 5L X80 steel.

Table 4. Results from stress-strain curves for the X60 and X80 steels, Type III specimens.

API 5L X60			
	Without hydrogen	Hydrogenation under stress (24 h)	Hydrogenation under stress (48 h)
σ_{UTS} [MPa]	772.39 ± 6.66	772.70 ± 18.73	785.38 ± 5.40
Elongation [%]	7.89 ± 0.38	7.70 ± 0.20	8.51 ± 0.31
API 5L X80			
	Without hydrogen	Hydrogenation under stress (24 h)	Hydrogenation under stress (48 h)
σ_{UTS} [MPa]	880.71 ± 20.82	901.16 ± 10.03	890.70 ± 0.77
Elongation [%]	7.07 ± 0.35	7.40 ± 0.18	7.19 ± 0.05

This behavior of API 5L X60 and API 5L X80 steels can be explained by their chemical composition and microstructure. It is known that alloys designed to resist to hydrogen embrittlement must have a large number of harmless trapping and that these should preferably be irreversible and well distributed through the microstructure [8]. Additions of elements that are carbides formers, which are used for grain refinement, precipitation hardening and improves the toughness, also provide irreversible trapping for hydrogen. For example, steels containing Nb have shown good resistance due to formation of particles of NbC in the ferrite matrix [9]. In addition, precipitates of Mo_2C, VC and TiC also increase resistance to hydrogen embrittlement [8]. Some researchers have shown that the hydrogen released by the microstructure is more significant in the process of hydrogen embrittlement [10], indicating that hydrogen reversibly trapped is more harmful than the hydrogen which is maintained irreversibly.

SEM analysis. The fracture surface morphology of API 5L X60 and API 5L X80 steels were predominantly by ductile coalescence of voids, as can be seen from Figures 3 and 4. The main features are the largest number of dimples in API 5L X60 steel and the presence of cracks on the fracture surfaces of API 5L X80 steel.

EHE - Type I specimens. It can be noted that the effect of hydrogen was to increase the number of dimples in the hydrogenated samples, and this effect was more pronounced in the API 5L X60 steel. Hydrogen accumulates in particle-matrix interfaces, which in turn contributes to the reduction of interfacial resistance of the particles, causing a larger number of dimples. In the API 5L X80 steel cracking at the fracture surface was observed in hydrogenated condition.

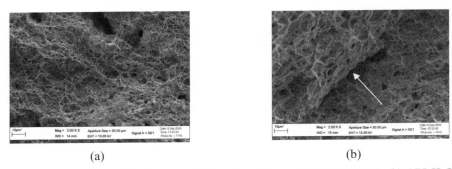

(a)   (b)

Figure 3. Fracture surface of hydrogenated Type I specimens: (a) API 5L X60; (b) API 5L X80.

EHE –Type II specimens. It can be noted that because the specimens were notched the results can be different from the any obtained in smooth specimens (Type I specimens). For API 5L X60 unnotched, cracking on the fracture surface did not appear, but occurred while under the action of a notch, as can be seen through Figure 4(a). According to [11] when hydrogenated specimens are subjected to deformation, it is postulated that the hydrogen concentration that occurs in the region of triaxial stress state ahead of a notch or a crack can further reduce the cohesive strength of the material, which explains the decrease in elongation in both steels.

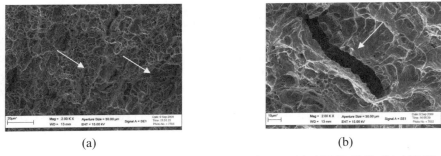

(a)   (b)

Figure 4. Fracture surface of hydrogenated Type II specimens: (a) API 5L X60; (b) API 5L X80.

IHE –Type III specimens. The results suggest that the reason for the effects of the action of hydrogen is due to high concentration of hydrogen within the matrix due to the type of hydrogenation used: it is known that a large amount of hydrogen (much larger than the equilibrium concentration) can be retained at room temperature in the matrix for some alloys due to the presence of numerous structural defects. According to [12], hydrogen induced softening may be expected in materials hardened by disperses particles of known composition and morphology distributed in the matrix, providing the extended paths of easy glide. As API 5L X60 steel has chemical elements such as Ti, Nb and V, and API 5L X80 steel has Ti, which are combined with other elements forming carbides and carbonitrides dispersed in the microstructure, they may be responsible for results in these test conditions.

Conclusions

After the tests in API 5L X60 and API 5L X80 steels, used in oil and gas pipelines, was established that the fracture morphology of both steels with and without hydrogen was predominately ductile by coalescence of voids.

For environmental hydrogen embrittlement tests, the variation of elongation in the samples without and with hydrogen for API 5L X60 and API 5L X80 steels is small. In the hydrogenated samples of API 5L X60 steel, the elongation increased while in the API 5L X80 steel it decreased. Therefore, the API 5L X80 steel was more susceptible to the phenomenon.

In the environmental hydrogen embrittlement process was observed that the presence of a notch enhances the action of hydrogen, because when hydrogen is accumulated in reversible traps, it diffuses to regions susceptible to cracking nucleation in sufficient quantities for the embrittlement process occur.

In the internal hydrogen embrittlement process, both steels were not susceptible to this phenomenon and this can be explained by the fact that these steels have micro-alloying elements that act beneficially in relation to internal hydrogen embrittlement.

Acknowledgements

The authors are very grateful to FINEP/CTPETRO/CNPq/PETROBRAS/RPCmod and to ANP/UFCG-PRH-25 for have financed the development of this investigation work, and the LEEQ/UFCG, LaMMEA/UFCG and NEPEM/UFPB laboratories by important contribution.

References

[1]   Tiwari,G. P.; Bose, A.; Chakravartty, J. K.; Wadekar, S. L.; Totlani, M. K.; Arya, R.N.; Fotedar, R. K. A Study of Internal Hydrogen Embrittlement of Steels. Materials Science and Engineering A, v. 286, pp.269-281, 2000.

[2]   Symons, D.M. A Comparation of Internal Hydrogen Embrittlement and Hydrogen Environment Embrittlement of X-750. Engineering Fracture Mechanics, v.68, pp. 751-771, 2001.

[3]   API SPEC 5L. Specification for Line Pipe. American Petroleum Institute, March, 2004.

[4]   Costa, E.B. Design and Construction of Equipment for Applying Loads of Tensile Test Specimen Subjected to Hydrogen Permeation. 2008. 69p. Monograph. Degree in Mechanical Engineering. UFCG.

[5]   Hardie, D.; Charles, E.A.; Lopez, A.H. Hydrogen Embrittlement of High Strength Pipeline Steels. Corrosion Science, v. 48, p. 4378-4385, 2006.

[6]   Trasatti, S.P.; Sivieri, E.; Mazza, F. Susceptibility of a X80 Steel to Hydrogen Embrittlement. Materials and Corrosion, v.56, n.2, p.111-117, 2005.

[7]   Wang, M.; Akiyama, E.; Tsuzaki, K. Effect of Hydrogen on the Fracture Behavior of High Strength Steel During Slow Strain Rate Test. Corrosion Science, v.49, p.4081–4097, 2007.

[8]   Offshore Tecnology Report - OTO. A Review of the Effects on the Hydrogen Embrittlement of High Strength Offshore Steels. Healt and Safety Executive, 1999.

[9]   Gojic, M.; Kosec, L.; Vehovar, L. The susceptibility to Sulphide Stress Cracking of Low Alloy Steels. Materials and Corrosion, v.49, p27-33, 1998.

[10] Luppo, M.; Garcia, O.J. The Influence of Microstructure on the Trapping and Diffusion of Hydrogen in a Low Carbon Steel. Corrosion science, v. 32, n.10, p.1125-1136, 1991.

[11] Hardie, D.; Liu, S. The Effect of Stress Concentration on Hydrogen Embrittlement of a Low Alloy Steel. Corrosion Science, v.38, n. 5, p.721-733, 1996.

[12] Lunarska, E.; Mikeladzey, A. Effect of Second Phase Particles on Hydrogen Embrittlement of Iron Alloys. International Journal of Hydrogen Energy, v.22, n.2/3, p.131-139, 1997.

Key Engineering Materials Vol. 478 (2011) pp 40-45
© (2011) Trans Tech Publications, Switzerland
doi:10.4028/www.scientific.net/KEM.478.40

Corrosion Monitoring in Marine Environment Using Wavelet Description

Ivica Kuzmanić[1, a], Igor Vujović[2,b] and Joško Šoda[3,c]

[1]University of Split, Faculty of Maritime Studies, vicedean office, Zrinsko-Frankopanska 38, 21000 Split, Croatia

[2] University of Split, Faculty of Maritime Studies, Department of Marine Electrical and Information Technology, Zrinsko-Frankopanska 38, 21000 Split, Croatia

[3] University of Split, Faculty of Electrical Engineering, Mechanical Engineering and Naval Architecture, Ruđera Boškovića bb, 21000 Split, Croatia

[a]ikuzman@pfst.hr, [b]ivujovic@pfst.hr, [c]jsoda@fesb.hr

Key words: dual-tree complex wavelet transform, image processing, marine environment, corrosion, monitoring, illumination variation.

Abstract. The paper proposes a method, the so-called wavelet description, for corrosion monitoring in marine environment which is based on taking the energy difference contained in energy from coefficients derived by applying complex wavelet transforms. Then the rms value of coefficients has been accounted that form an illumination-independent energy representation of corroded and corrosion-free parts. The robustness on illumination variations has been achieved because by applying the proposed algorithm the energy representation enables reduction of the noise, since getting the difference of two subsequent images leaves only greater values of differences.

Introduction

It is widely known that marine environment is highly aggressive and it is imperative to monitor as much parameters as possible. Among them a corrosion monitoring is an important parameter that has to be monitored since it is used as quality parameter in wide area of applications. For example in an extensively corrosive environment it is of vital importance to maintain operation capabilities of vessels.

The benefit of corrosion monitoring is in detection of corrosion even on dock in port during normal operation, which saves money and prevents environmental damage [1, 2], costs of accidents and loss of lives. Corrosion causes damage in the material structure [3], such as cracks. In case of chemical or oil tankers the corrosion that damages the material structure can be source of oil or chemical leaks that could cause for pollution of the environment.

In order to build a corrosion monitoring system, the cost of the system is very important factor. In order to implement a corrosion monitoring system, the system must be cheap and easy to use; it has to produce no additional costs and has to be maintainable.

Direct and indirect corrosion monitoring techniques are developed. Direct techniques include corrosion coupons, electrical resistance, inductive resistance probes, linear polarization resistance, electromechanical impedance spectroscopy, electrochemical frequency modulation, harmonic analysis, electrochemical noise, zero resistance ammetry, potentiodynamic polarization, thin layer activation and gamma radiography, electrical field signature method, and acoustic emission. On the other hand, indirect techniques include corrosion potential, hydrogen flux monitoring and chemical analyses.

Corrosion monitoring in real-time is proposed in [4] that is based on coupled multielectrode array sensors. The simulated environment was a marine environment. However, implementation of sensor networks requires adaptation of hardware into/nearby the ship's hull. The changes in the microtopography of a metal surface during a corrosion process are measured by applying decorrelation of the scattered speckle fields under coherent illumination [5]. However, real conditions are far from coherent illumination, which makes it hard to implement in real life. An image processing technique for corrosion monitoring is proposed in [6], holography in [7] and digital radiography in [8]. The last two references include image processing as well. Ultrasound images are considered in [9] that deal with corrosion in traffic (civil engineering, bridges), but not in marine traffic. Photoacoustic microscope is used in [10] to find corrosion at intersecting surfaces for testing industry products. Image comparison was used in [11]. Digital images of corrosion-free steel are compared with current images of steel in power lines. Therefore, degradation can be detected. Neural networks and morphology wavelets are combined in [12]. In [13], the parameters used for judging corrosion are the decrease in strand diameter and the strand's surface texture. Wavelets were already used for ultrasound detection of corrosion [9, 14]. Camera monitoring is an alternative for corrosion in marine environment which can be performed by image analysis as well.

In this paper, a system for corrosion monitoring is proposed where camera recording of the interested surface is performed periodically. Obtained images are compared using wavelet description (energy in complex wavelet transform) and conclusion about corrosion is reached. The proposed algorithm includes robustness to illumination variation by natural causes.

Although inspirited by maritime problems, the proposed algorithm can be used on land as well. Even more, in many land corrosion cases, this method is more appropriate for application.

The paper is organized as follows. The proposed method is explained in the following section. This section is followed by the results and conclusions section.

Proposed Corrosion Monitoring

The hardware for implementation of the proposed algorithm is cheep and available. It can be a self-standing digital camera or an analog/digital computer camera. The second piece of hardware is an ordinary PC or notebook. For the prototype we used the Matlab program package. The software can be further developed to become a self-standing application.

Contrary to other papers we propose monitoring in periodic intervals. The main reason for proposing monitoring in periodic intervals is based on the fact that slightly observable corrosion cannot be observable before it grows to observable size, i.e. there is no need for continuous monitoring. Basically, the proposed method of corrosion monitoring can be simply explained as follows: The condition of a metal surface is recorded by a camera into computer memory. In the next period of time, the metal surface is recorded again and compared with the previous data in the computer memory.

The proposed algorithm consists of several steps as follows.

The first step is to obtain a reference value of the wavelet descriptor. This is the process performed by acquisition of the training sequence. It is illustrated in Fig.1 on the right side. The training sequence consists of N frames obtained on-line or as input from the movie file (off-line mode of operation). The acquired frame block in Fig.1. can represent two things. In the on-line mode of operation, it represents a snapshot from the camera. In the off-line mode of operation, it represents an input frame from the movie file.

In order to obtain illumination-independent values of the image pixels, a summation is used. All wavelet coefficients are summated for all training frames (N). Then, the following average is obtained:

$$ referent\_coefficients^{wav.name} = \frac{1}{N}\sum_{i=1}^{N} frame\_coefficients_i^{wav.name} \qquad (1) $$

The wavelet descriptor is calculated for the average values of pixels. Two different wavelets are used for real and imaginary part of the dual-tree complex wavelet transform. The proposed wavelet descriptor is the energy description by complex wavelets and can be written as:

$$wavdescr = \left(referent\_coefficients^{wav.1}\right)^2 + \left(referent\_coefficients^{wav.2^2}\right)^2 \tag{2}$$

Which can be normalized in the following manner:

$$wavdescr = \frac{wavdescr}{\max(wavdescr)} \tag{3}$$

The second step of the proposed method is to save the wavelet descriptor into the data storage.

Then step 1 is repeated after some period of time which is usually measured in months. This gives another wavelet descriptor. The old and new wavelet descriptor is subtracted and the absolute value is taken. The output derived by subtraction will be a black image if the corrosion is not present. If corrosion is present, the derived image will show different colours at positions that indicate the presence of the corrosion. The obtained image can be analyzed from distance or on board.

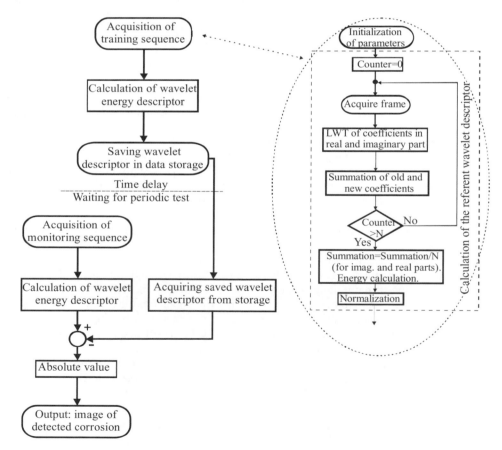

Fig. 1. Flow chart of the proposed algorithm

Results

Observation: Using the proposed method for monitoring corrosion does not compromise that accuracy of distinguishing of corrosion if the quality of obtained image is poor. The overall accuracy of distinguishing corrosion is increased by 4 times, because the energy of corrosion is 4 times weaker than the energy of a non-corroded surface of the same material under the same illumination conditions.

Additional advantage of the proposed algorithm is its adaptability. It is possible to use classic of wavelet technique for memory-based motion detection to eliminate variations of illumination. We want to emphasize that motion is not detected in image, but rather differences of two subsequent images, which means corrosion.

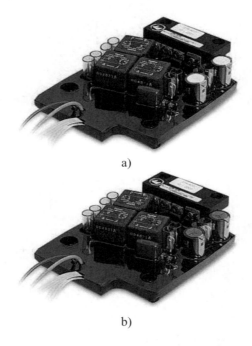

a)

b)

Fig. 2. Electronic part of equipment: a) before corrosion, b) after corrosion

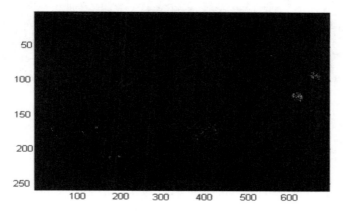

Fig. 3. An example of the detected corrosion by color recognition – noise produces false results

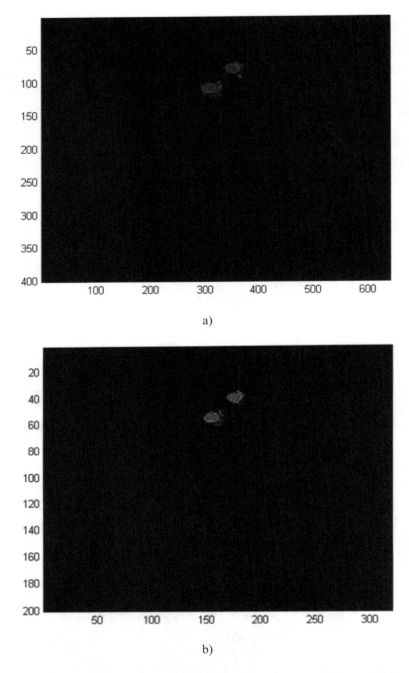

a)

b)

Fig. 4. Detected corrosion by proposed: a) in wavelet reconstructed image, b) in wavelet approximation

Fig.2 shows an example of corrosion. Fig. 3 shows detection of corrosion by color recognition algorithm, which is previously known. It can be seen that noise produces false results in scattered positions. Wavelet enhancement results are illustrated in Fig. 4.

Conclusions

This work presents a novel method for corrosion detection and monitoring. The proposed method is based on image processing and ordinary digital cameras, which means that the price is economically sustainable and attractive to private and multinational companies. It is a non-evasive method.

The overall accuracy of distinguishing corrosion is increased by 4 times, because the energy of corrosion is 4 times weaker than the energy of a non-corroded surface of the same material under the same illumination conditions. The approach is very robust to illumination variations. These variations can mislead non-robust algorithms and produce false results in corrosion detection. Therefore, false detection rate is reduced.

The advantage of the proposed algorithm is its adaptability. It is possible to use classic of wavelet technique for memory-based motion detection to eliminate variations of illumination.

The prototype of the proposed system has exhibited some promising results and the next step should be testing it in real world conditions.

References

[1] H. Sayyaadi and P. Hemati: MTTS/IEEE Techno-Ocean Vol. 1 (2004), p. 212

[2] Information on http://research.dnv.com/marmil/Pilotship/OPT_ENV_TECH_CRUISE.pdf

[3] J.A. Collins: *Failure of Materials in Mechanical Design* (John Wiley & Sons, USA, 1991).

[4] X. Sun and L. Yang: Corrosion, San Diego, March 12 - 16, 2006.

[5] T. Fricke-Begemann, G. Gülker, K. D. Hinsch and Karen Wolff: Applied Optics, Vol. 38 (1999), p. 5948

[6] Information on http://www.matmidia.mat.puc-rio.br/sibgrapi2009/media/posters/59880.pdf

[7] P. Carelli, D. Paoletti and G.S. Spagnolo: Industrial Metrology, Vol. 1 (1991), p. 277

[8] Information on http://www.ndt.net/article/wcndt00/papers/idn325/idn325.htm

[9] S.K. Sinha, A.J. Schokker and S.R. Iyer: Proceedings of IEEE, Vol.1 (2003), p. 487

[10] H. Endoh, R. Mukai, Y. Hiwatashi, T. Kumabayashi and T. Hoshimiya: IEEE Ultrasonics Symposium, Toronto, October 5-8, 1997.

[11] F. Tsutsumi, H. Murata, T. Onoda, O. Oguri and H. Tanaka: Transmission & Distribution Conference & Exposition: Asia and Pacific, Seoul, October 26-30, 2009.

[12] Y. Peixin and T. Jun, 2nd International Congress on Image and Signal Processing, Tianjin, October 17-19, 2009.

[13] H. Yoshida, K. Sobue and J. Masuda: 20th International Conference on Industrial Electronics, Control and Instrumentation, Bologna, Sptember 5-9, 1994.

[14] F. Truchetet and O. Laligant, in: Wavelet Applications in Industrial Processing II, edited by F. Truchetet and O. Laligant, Vol. 5607 of Proceedings of SPIE, cahpter, 1, SPIE (2004).

Key Engineering Materials Vol. 478 (2011) pp 46-53
© (2011) Trans Tech Publications, Switzerland
doi:10.4028/www.scientific.net/KEM.478.46

Experimental and FEM Analysis of the AA 6082 Processed by Equal Channel Angular Extrusion

J. León[a] , C.J. Luis Pérez[b] , D. Salcedo[c] , I. Pérez[d] , J.P. Fuertes[e] ,

I. Puertas[f] , R. Luri[g]

Mechanical, Energetics and Materials Engineering Department, Public University of Navarre, Campus Arrosadía s/n, 31006 Pamplona, Spain

[a]javier.leon@unavarra.es, [b]cluis.perez@unavarra.es, [c]daniel.salcedo@unavarra.es, [d]ivan.perez@unavarra.es, [e]juanpablo.fuertes@unavarra.es, [f]inaki.puerta@unavarra.es, [g]rodrigo.luri@unavarra.es

Key words: Equal Channel Angular Extrusion (ECAE), Severe Plastic Deformation (SPD), Finite Element Method (FEM).

Abstract. Recent studies have shown that severe plastic deformation processes (SPD) improve the mechanical properties of the processed parts. Some of the most outstanding SPD processes are as follows: High Pressure Torsion (HPT), Repetitive Corrugation and Straightening (RCS), Cyclic Extrusion Compression (CEC), Accumulative Roll Bonding (ARB), Conform and Continuous Combined Drawing and Rolling (CCDR), among others, but the most well-known is Equal Channel Angular Extrusion or Pressure (ECAE/ECAP). The aim of these processes is to introduce high values of deformation inside the parts in order to reduce the grain size and thus to improve the mechanical properties of the starting material. The study of the damage imparted to an AA-6082 alloy is made in the present work. This alloy is received as cast and it is quenched at a temperature of 530 °C during 4 hours in order to be processed by ECAE at room temperature using different geometries of the dies. The imparted damage is also studied by using FEM simulations.

Introduction

SPD processes have the aim of attaining materials with mechanical properties greatly improved with respect to the starting materials. This is achieved by means of the reduction in the grain size up to micrometric or even nanometric values [1]. The increase in the improvement on the mechanical properties of the materials processed by SPD processes depend on the starting material, the number of passages and the thermal treatments carried out [2]. Within the SPD processes, ECAE/ECAP is the process on which more research has been done [3-5]. This process consists in the extrusion of a material through two channels that intersect at a specific angle, where in most of bibliography this angle is 90°. The deformation in the material is mainly obtained by a shear effect. One of its most important advantages is that due to the fact that the dimensions of the processed billet remain practically constant, it is possible to carry out several passages with the same billet by introducing it again at the entrance channel and thus increasing the accumulated deformation. Most of the existing reference bibliography is related to the structure of the material after being processed a specific number of times and after diverse thermal treatments [1]. Nevertheless, there are only a few studies about the variation of the mechanical properties with respect to the die geometry, that is, the intersection angle between channels as well as the inner and the outer die radii, among others.

The present study deals with the analysis of how the extrusion force varies as a function of the geometry parameters of the ECAE dies, where this will be made through the technique of design of experiments and finite element simulations with the software MSC Marc Mentat™. Likewise, the homogeneity of the material deformation pattern will be studied after having been processed.

Finally, the level of the damage accumulated in the billet will be studied in order to be able to know in advance the number of passages the material can be processed before its fracture.

The present work will be focused on an AA-6082 aluminium alloy in water quenching state. Before starting the study here considered, the material law of this aluminium alloy was obtained in order to be able to introduce it in the FEM (Finite Element Modelling) simulations and thus to achieve a good correlation between the analytical and the experimental results. Furthermore, it is necessary to know the friction coefficient which exists in the ECAE process of the real machine and under the boundary conditions and the die material employed.

In order to make this study, the technique of Design of Experiments (DOE) is used and in this case, the selected model is a Central Composite Design (CCD) with two central points. The selected design factors are as follows: the inner and the outer radii of the intersection of the die channels, the intersection angle and the billet length. Table 1 shows the previously-mentioned factors with their corresponding low and high levels.

Table 1. Design of experiments selected

Factor	Low level	High level
(Ri) Internal radius [mm]	1.5	3.5
(Re) External radius [mm]	1.5	3.5
(α) Angle of intersection [°]	85	95
(L) Billet length [mm]	60	100

The starting material AA-6082 (initially in T39 state) is quenched at 530° C during 4 hours and with a heating slope of 1.5 hours. The time that passes between the quenching and the ECAE process should be as small as possible since if not, a natural aging of the material takes place, which would involve a change in the material law and therefore, in the processing force. In Fig. 1 the closure system of the dies (upper and lower) and their set-up in line with the extrusion punch can be observed. The extrusion velocity that was utilized is 50 mm/min.

Figure 1: ECAE machine from the Public University of Navarre employed in the experiments

Determination of the Flow Stress Curve and the Friction Coefficient

A very important aspect to consider in order to be able to achieve accurate results is to know as well as possible the boundary conditions of the process. The velocity of the process is given by the ECAE machine and the manufacturing of the dies has been made by CAD/CAM. The most complex process variables to know and to assess are the material law of AA-6082 and the friction coefficient. In order to obtain the material law, the methodology followed in [6-7] has been used because from a tension test of the starting material, it is only possible to get information up to a deformation value of 0.2 (depending on the ductility of the material). Since in ECAE, deformation values higher than $\varepsilon > 1$ are reached, this approach is not useful. The used methodology consists in predeforming the material up to different known deformation values and subsequently, performing tension tests on each of the billets. The same ECAE process is utilized to predeform the material up to a known value where this deformation value is known through finite element simulations. From each tension test, its plastic deformation part is selected and it is moved a deformation value equal to that accumulated in the predeforming process. Fig. 2(a) shows the points of each tension test at different initial values of accumulated deformation and the Voce curve fitted among them [8]. The so obtained curve corresponds with the plastic stress-strain curve, which is introduced in the software MSC Marc Mentat^{TM} in this way. The elastic component is introduced through the values of the elastic limit and the Young modulus. As can be observed in Fig 2(a), five zones with depicted points appear in the graph, where the first one corresponds with the starting material and the other four correspond with each of the four ECAE passages with route C. For each passage, three tension tests were performed so as to achieve a better approach in the results.

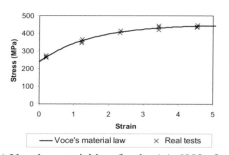

a) Voce's material law for the AA-6082 after water quenching

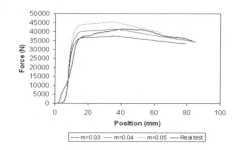

b) Determination of the friction coefficient

Figure 2: Determination of the flow stress curve and the friction coefficient

Once the material law of AA-6082 is obtained, the next step to take is to determine the friction coefficient which exists in the ECAE process for this material, taking into account that a lubrication by MoS_2 applied in spray was employed. The form of assessing it is to perform several simulations by FEM so that the extrusion force is calculated with the previously-evaluated material law and it is compared to that force given by a load cell attached to the ECAE machine [7,9]. This comparison is made with the central point from the previously-planned design of experiments, that is, external and internal radii (Re, Ri) equal to a value of 2.5 mm, an intersection angle (α) between channels of 90° and a billet length of 80 mm (L). Fig. 2(b) shows the real extrusion force (obtained from three tests) along with the force attained from the FEM simulations with different values of friction coefficient. The friction coefficient value whose corresponding force is closer to the real one is 0.04, where this will be taken as the value employed in the rest of the FEM simulations.

Force Results
In order to obtain the experimental values of the force in the ECAE machine, three billets were processed for each of the points from the design of experiments where the value finally taken for each point was the mean value of the maximum value obtained for the force. Fig. 3(a) shows the typical curve for an experimental test in which the value for the extrusion force is represented in function of the distance covered by the punch. Furthermore, Fig. 3(b) shows the same curve but obtained in the case of the FEM simulation. Both graphs are those corresponding to the central point of the design of experiments. As can be observed in Fig. 3, the similarity between both graphs is very high, not only for the values but also for the shape of the curve. At the beginning of the process, the force increases quickly up to a point where the billet is compressed at the entrance channel and it starts to pass through the intersection between both channels. Once the end of the billet begins to exit from the intersection, the force continues with a growing tendency but of low slope. This is because of the compression of the billet at the exit channel. Nevertheless, once the material starts to come out from the die channel (the length of the exit channel is 20 mm), the force tends to decrease slightly as the contact zone between billet and die diminishes.

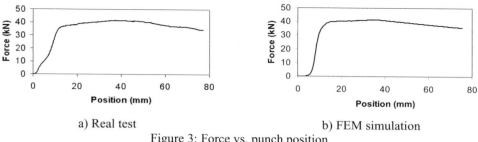

a) Real test   b) FEM simulation

Figure 3: Force vs. punch position

The small difference which can be appreciated between both graphs is in the value for the ascending slope at the beginning. This is due to two different effects. The first one is that the real billet is machined with a tolerance so that it can be fitted easily at the entrance die channel, where this involves that at the beginning the billet tends to fill the entire entrance channel before it starts to pass through the intersection. On the contrary, the FEM simulated billet has the same diameter as the entrance channel, with no difference between them. The second effect is the small value for the compression which undergoes the extrusion punch. Although the extrusion punch is more rigid than the aluminium billet, as very high values of pressure are reached, the punch is compressed as well, being part of its length reduced. In the case of the punch simulation, the contact is considered to be as rigid, that is to say, it does not undergo any deformation or its dimensions cannot be modified.

Once the values for the force in the FEM simulations were attained in each point of the design of experiments, the resulting ANOVA table can be observed in Table 2.

Table 2. ANOVA table for the extrusion force

Source	Sum of Squares	Df	Mean Square	F-Ratio	P-Value
A:Ri	16.3924	1	16.3924	88.17	0.0000
B:Re	56.0589	1	56.0589	301.53	0.0000
C:α	187.396	1	187.396	1007.96	0.0000
D:L	219.521	1	219.521	1180.75	0.0000
AB	0.878438	1	0.878438	4.72	0.0663
AC	0.0000225625	1	0.0000225625	0.00	0.9915
AD	0.0429526	1	0.0429526	0.23	0.6454
BC	2.2134	1	2.2134	11.91	0.0107
BD	0.0264876	1	0.0264876	0.14	0.7170
CD	0.254773	1	0.254773	1.37	0.2801
Total error	1.30141	7	0.185916		
Total (corr.)	484.086	17			

Table 2 shows the statistical significance of each effect by means of the comparison of the mean squares (MS), with an estimation of the experimental error. In the table, DF represents the number of degrees of freedom. The column corresponding to mean square, is obtained simply by dividing Sum of Squares (SS) by its corresponding degree of freedom. In contrast, column of F statistic is calculated as the quotient of each of the MS of the effects, divided by the value of the MS corresponding to the total error. Column of P values, gives the probability values associated with values that take the variable of a function of distribution F, for determined values of DF of the numerator and the denominator.

Eq. 1 shows the resulting model as a function of the selected factors.

$$F = 97,2444 + 1,36934 \cdot Ri - 7,81816 \cdot Re - 0,770075 \cdot \alpha + 0,297381 \cdot L - 0,234312 \cdot Ri \cdot Re +$$
$$+ 0,0002375 \cdot Ri \cdot \alpha + 0,00259063 \cdot Ri \cdot L + 0,0743875 \cdot Re \cdot \alpha - 0,00203437 \cdot Re \cdot L - \qquad (1)$$
$$- 0,00126187 \cdot \alpha \cdot L$$

The value obtained for the adjusted R^2 statistic was 99.35 %. Fig. 4 shows the estimated response surfaces for each case. The most significant factor is the length of the billet and as it is logical to expect, the higher the length, the higher is the required force. The second factor in importance is the intersection angle, where when this is increased, the necessary force decreases. In the third and in the fourth place, we have the external and the internal radius, respectively. Regarding the external radius, as its value increases, the force decreases, whereas with respect to the internal radius, the opposite effect is observed.

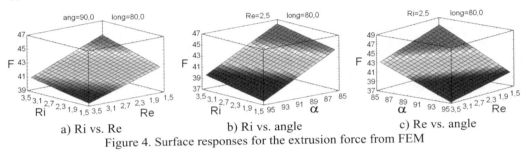

a) Ri vs. Re   b) Ri vs. angle   c) Re vs. angle

Figure 4. Surface responses for the extrusion force from FEM

The compression force is a factor very important to take into consideration when the optimum die geometry is wanted to be selected because of the problem associated with the buckling, as was previously-mentioned. Nevertheless, in order to obtain a material with homogeneous properties, it is interesting to study not only the deformation pattern but also the damage accumulated inside the material.

Equivalent Plastic Strain Distribution

A very important property to take into consideration in SPD processes is the homogeneity of the deformation in the cross-section of the material since this will have influence on the mechanical properties of the latter. In this way, in the present section, the results about the plastic deformation accumulated in each of the points from the planned DOE will be presented. In Fig 5(a), the deformation pattern obtained by FEM for the cross-section of the billet is shown in the case of the central point of the design of experiments. One way of measuring the homogeneity in the cross-section of the material processed by ECAE is through the study of microhardness. For this, in the present work, a total of 62 measurements of microhardness were taken in the material processed with the die corresponding with the central point of the design. The distribution of these was carried out along the radius of the cross-section and for different values of the angle, where in this case two measurements were made in each position of the present study. Five values for the angle study and six different points in each of them were taken. The two remaining measurements were made at the centre of the cross-section. Fig 5(b) shows the graphical representation of the experimental results obtained for the microhardness. Comparing both graphs in Fig 5(a) and Fig 5(b), it can be observed that a great similarity exists between them. Four different zones are appreciated. The upper zone of the cross-section coincides with the internal radius of the die and a higher value of deformation and microhardness is observed. In the lower zone (external radius of the intersection between channels), a small area appears showing the lowest values for the equivalent plastic deformation and for the microhardness. As we move from the lower zone towards the centre of the cross-section, the values of both properties increase although they decrease again when the cross-section centre is reached. Finally, in the zone which is on the right part of the billet, it can be observed that the values of deformation and microhardness have an intermediate value. The existing difference in size of each zone between both figures is given by the number of microhardness measurements that was carried out. In elements, the number of nodes in the cross-section is approximately 280 whereas the number of positions studied for the evaluation of microhardness is, as was mentioned, 32.

The equipment utilized to measure the microhardness was a Mitutoyo hardness testing machine with a resolution of 0.1 (HV) and an uncertainty of ±1.0 % (HV). The load employed to carry out the measurements was 200 g.

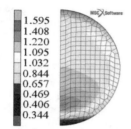
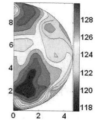

a) Total equivalent plastic strain from FEM　　　　b) Vickers micro-hardness measurements

Figure 5: Cross section homogeneity

Once the design of experiments was carried out, Table 3 shows the ANOVA table obtained in the case of the equivalent plastic strain.

Table 3. ANOVA table for the total equivalent plastic strain

Source	Sum of Squares	Df	Mean Square	F-Ratio	P-Value
A:Ri	0.038416	1	0.038416	579.83	0.0000
B:Re	0.0726303	1	0.0726303	1096.24	0.0000
C:α	0.190969	1	0.190969	2882.38	0.0000
D:L	0.000121	1	0.000121	1.83	0.2186
AB	0.000961	1	0.000961	14.50	0.0066
AC	0.00275625	1	0.00275625	41.60	0.0004
AD	0.00001225	1	0.00001225	0.18	0.6801
BC	0.0025	1	0.0025	37.73	0.0005
BD	0.0	1	0.0	0.00	1.0000
CD	0.00000625	1	0.00000625	0.09	0.7677
Total error	0.000463778	7	0.000066254		
Total (corr.)	0.308836	17			

The R^2_{adj} statistic obtained in the fitting of the model is 99.64 % and the equation of the complete model is depicted in Eq. 2. From the ANOVA table shown in Table 3, it can be observed that the most significant factors, arranged in decreasing order of importance, are as follows: the intersection angle between channels, the external radius and finally, the internal radius. On the contrary, as was logical to expect, the length of the billet does not have influence on the deformation value.

$$\bar{\varepsilon} = 3,08224 + 0,308125 \cdot Ri - 0,273 \cdot Re - 0,0220375 \cdot \alpha - 0,000315625 \cdot L - 0,00775 \cdot Ri \cdot Re -$$
$$- 0,002625 \cdot Ri \cdot \alpha - 0,00004375 \cdot Ri \cdot L + 0,0025 \cdot Re \cdot \alpha + 0,00000625 \cdot \alpha \cdot L \qquad (2)$$

Fig. 6 shows the estimated response surfaces of the deformation value as a function of the most significant factors, whereas the rest of the factors that are not represented in each graph are held at their central values. It can be observed that as the intersection angle between channels increases, the mean value of deformation in the cross-section decreases. The same tendency is observed in relation to the external radius between channels. Lastly, the contrary effect is just obtained in the case of the internal radius because the higher this factor is, the higher the deformation value is achieved.

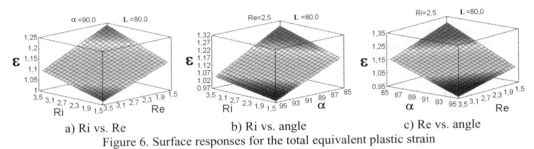

a) Ri vs. Re   b) Ri vs. angle   c) Re vs. angle

Figure 6. Surface responses for the total equivalent plastic strain

In this way, it is possible to determine the die geometry the highest value of deformation in the billet can be achieved with. At the same time that the accumulated deformation is controlled, it is also important to control the level of damage the material undergoes as in this way, a compromise solution could be taken when the most adequate geometry parameters must be selected.

Damage Study

One of the advantages in the ECAE process is the possibility to impart several passages to the material so that the accumulated plastic deformation is increased. Nevertheless, this can be only carried out a specific number of times until the fracture of the material occurs. In order to do this, it is very important to know the damage imparted to the material in each of the passages. In this section, the damage exerted on the material in the first passage will be studied considering the Cockcroft-Latham's damage model [10]. Fig. 7 shows the damage in the cross-section at a point in the middle of the billet along with the damage in the middle section throughout the length of it.

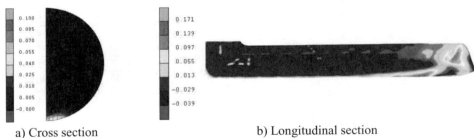

a) Cross section   b) Longitudinal section

Figure 7: Damage obtained from FEM

In Fig. 7(b), it can be observed that the highest value for the damage is reached at the initial part of the billet. It can be pointed out that the plastic deformation accumulated in this zone is very low and with a very low value of homogeneity as well, which means that the end is usually removed as well as the back part of the billet, which has undergone no deformation because it has not passed through the intersection between the channels. Therefore, the cracks that are generated during the successive passages will begin to appear at the end of the billet and at that zone in the material which passes by the outer radius of the channels.

Conclusions

In the present work, the variation of the extrusion force and the plastic deformation accumulated in the ECAE process were studied for different geometries of the channel, where the selected parameters were: the length of the billet, the intersection angle between channels and the external and the internal radii of them. All of this was carried out for billets with circular cross-section.

It is observed that the force increases with the length of the billet and it decreases with the intersection angle between the channels. Furthermore, it is shown that the accumulated plastic deformation increases when the angle between channels along with the internal and the external radii are decreased.

The damage introduced inside the material is accumulated at the front end of the billet and at the lower part of the cross-section, that is, just at the zone where the material has passed by the outer radius of the ECAE dies.

References

[1] F. J. Humphreys, P. B. Prangnell, J. R. Bowen, A. Gholinia, C. Harris: Trans. Royal Society London Vol. 357 (1999), p.1663.

[2] S. H. Chon, S. M. Liu, t. N. Kim, J. K. Park: Key Engineering Materials Vol. 345-346 (2007), p. 125.

[3] V. M. Segal: Materials Science and Engineering A Vol. 197 (1995), p. 157.

[4] R. Luri, C. J. Luis: Materials Science Forum Vol. 526 (2006), p. 193.

[5] R. Z. Valiev, R. K. Islamgaliev, I. V. Alexandrov: Progress in Materials Science Vol. 45 (2000), p. 103.

[6] B. Avitzur: Metal Forming: Processes and Analysis (McGraw Hill, 1979).

[7] R. Luri, J. León, C. J. Luis, I. Puertas: IMC 21 Conference (2004), p. 167.

[8] E. S. Puchi, M. H. Staia, Metallurgical and Materials Transactions A, Vol. 29 (1998), p. 2345.

[9] R. Luri, C. J. Luis: 1st CISIF-MESIC Conference (2005).

[10] M.G. Cockroft, D.J. Latham. Ductility and workability of metals. Journal Institute of Metals, Vol. 96 (1968), p. 33–39.

Key Engineering Materials Vol. 478 (2011) pp 54-63
© *(2011) Trans Tech Publications, Switzerland*
doi:10.4028/www.scientific.net/KEM.478.54

A probabilistic approach to the simulation of non-linear stress-strain relationships for oriented strandboard subject to in-plane tension

Anthony T McTigue [a], Annette M. Harte[b]

Department of Civil Engineering, National University of Ireland, University Road, Galway, Ireland

[a]a.mctigue1@nuigalway.ie, [b]annette.harte@nuigalway.ie

Key words: Oriented Strandboard, OSB, Non-Linear, Simulation, Probabilistic, Stress-Strain Relationship, Tension.

Abstract. This paper presents the results from an experimental test program conducted on commercially available oriented strandboard (OSB) panels and statistical analyses of the results. Standardised testing was used to determine the short-term behaviour of OSB/3 panels subjected to tension loading. A variety of thicknesses sourced from three different producers were used. Analysis of the results indicate that a quadratic expression in the form of $\sigma = a\varepsilon^2 + b\varepsilon$ provides the best description of the relationship between stress (σ) and strain (ε) up to the point of failure. It has also been shown that the coefficients a and b of the quadratic regression equations are negatively correlated to each other. Anderson-Darling goodness-of-fit tests were conducted on the results for tension strength and modulus of elasticity (MOE). The results indicate that the tension strength and MOE come from populations that follow either normal or lognormal probability distributions.

Introduction

Oriented strandboard (OSB) is a two-phase wood-based composite material made from elongated wood strands. The strands are sliced from small-diameter low-grade logs with the longest dimension aligned parallel to the grain of the log. They are coated in a thermosetting resin binder and are formed into a three-layered mat that is hot pressed to cure the binder, bonding the strands together to form large panels. OSB is typically used as a structural sheathing material in a similar fashion to plywood. Its main drawback is that its complex structure combined with the natural variability of the raw materials make its mechanical behaviour difficult to predict. Various attempts have been made to predict the mechanical behaviour of OSB by making major simplifying assumptions, limited geometric configurations and loading conditions. However, a generalised engineering approach to predict the mechanical response of OSB under all loading conditions while accounting for the natural variability is still not readily available.

The preliminary output of a study seeking to develop a method of predicting the mechanical response of OSB and its variability is presented in this paper. The focus is on results from a test program conducted to examine the short-term tension behaviour of commercially available OSB panels using standardised testing arrangements as per BS EN 789:2004 [1]. A variety of thicknesses of OSB/3 panels, produced in accordance with BS EN 300:2006 [2] by three different manufacturers, were tested. The results have been used to establish stress-strain relationships to describe the short-term mechanical behaviour up to the point of failure and to determine appropriate probability distribution models to describe the natural variability of the parameters.

Literature Review

A review of the use of probability based methods in the forest products industry conducted by Taylor *et al.* [3] described the effectiveness of these methods to accurately simulate the natural variability of structural wood systems. The Monte-Carlo method has proven to be a particularly useful tool to model the natural variability in both the physical characteristics and mechanical behaviour of wood-based composites. The effectiveness of the Monte-Carlo method is however dependent on knowledge of the probability distribution of each variable in the system.

The first attempt to predict the mechanical response of wood strand composites was conducted by Hunt and Suddarth [4]. A 2-D linear elastic finite element model was developed to predict the tension modulus and shear modulus of particleboard. Single layer random particleboard was modelled as a regular grid of beam elements (representing the binder) infilled with plate elements (representing the particles). The mechanical properties of individual particles were determined experimentally in the parallel and perpendicular to grain directions. The Monte-Carlo method was used to simulate the structure of the panel by randomly assigning a particle orientation to each plate element independently. Comparison with experimental results showed the average predicted tension MOE differed from the experimental value by 2% to 3% while the average predicted shear modulus differed from the experimental value by 10% to 12%.

Wang and Lam [5] made use of several probability based techniques in the development of a 3-D non-linear stochastic finite element model capable of predicting the probabilistic distribution of the tension strength and MOE of multi-layered parallel aligned wood strand composites. The model input was generated through testing of individual wood strands with standardised cross-sectional dimensions of 2.7x17 mm at a gauge length of 152 mm to evaluate the tension strength, MOE and to determine the underlying probability distributions of each material property. Assemblies of strands with 2, 3, 4 and 6 layers were also tested at a gauge length of 457 mm and the results were used for comparison with model predictions. The Monte-Carlo method was used to randomly assign material properties to individual strands based on the underlying probability distribution. Analysis of the results from testing wood strands also showed that a correlation existed between tension strength and tension MOE. This was one of the first attempts to preserve the relationship between two input variables during Monte-Carlo simulation using the standard bivariate normal distribution procedure developed by Lam *et al.* [6] and Wang *et al.* [7] to model the mechanical response of wood-based composites. A probability based technique was also used to simulate the size effect using the Weibull weakest link theory. Excellent agreement was achieved between the simulated and experimental probability distributions for tension strength and MOE of the multiply laminates.

Clouston and Lam [8] incorporated the probability based techniques developed by Wang and Lam into 2-D non-linear stochastic finite element model to predict the mechanical response of angle-ply wood strand laminates subjected to multiaxial stress conditions. This was one of the first attempts to model wood-strand composites with varying ply orientations and to model non-linear compression behaviour. Excellent agreement was observed between the predicted and experimental probability distributions of ultimate strength and MOE in tension, compression and bending. Further studies by Clouston and Lam [9, 10] developed the model into a 3-D non-linear stochastic finite element model for predicting the probabilistic distribution of strength, stiffness and failure load of angle-ply laminates subjected to tension, compression and bending. Clouston [11] and Arwade *et al.* [12] further developed this model to enable it to predict the strength and MOE of large section parallel strand lumber (PSL) members loaded in tension, compression and bending.

Past studies have largely concentrated on predicting the mechanical properties of wood-based composites based on the mechanical properties of the raw materials with model verification being achieved through experimental testing of small scale, laboratory produced panels. This study is focusing on predicting the mechanical properties of existing, large scale, commercially available panels based on the physical properties that can be controlled during panel production. It has been shown previously that both solid timber and timber-based composites behave elastically when loaded in tension [13-15] up to the point of failure. Therefore, it has been assumed in this study that OSB behaves elastically up to the point of failure when loaded in tension.

Testing

Materials. The materials tested were commercially available OSB/3 panels manufactured in accordance with BS EN 300:2006 [2].Three different panel thicknesses (11 mm, 15 mm and 18 mm) produced by Manufacturer A, one panel thickness (15 mm) produced by Manufacturer B and one panel thickness (15 mm) produced by Manufacturer C were tested. Panels were produced by Manufacturer A using Sitka spruce and Scots pine wood strands bound with Methylene di-Phenyl di-Isocyanate (MDI) resin stacked in a 0-90-0 lay-up pressed in a daylight press. Panels were produced by Manufacturer B using Scots pine and Lodgepole pine wood strands bound with Melamine Urea Phenol Formaldehyde (MUPF) resin in the surface layers and Polymeric di-Phenyl Methane di-Isocynate (PMDI) resin in the core stacked in a 0-90-0 lay-up pressed in a daylight press. Panels were produced by Manufacturer C using pine wood strands bound with Melamine Urea Phenol Formaldehyde (MUPF) resin in the surface layers and di-Phenylmethane di-Isocynate (pMDI) resin in the core layer stacked in a 0-90-0 lay-up pressed in a continuous press.

Specimen Preparation. A total of 32 cutting plans were prepared for each panel thickness in accordance with the guidelines in BS EN 789:2004 [1] of which 15 were selected at random for cutting. The remainder were retained for future study. Cutting plans (see Fig. 1) are designed to ensure that the panel can be cut to form one test piece per material property in both directions. Test pieces cut with their longer dimension aligned parallel to the longer dimension of the panel are designated longitudinal (LONG) while test pieces cut at 90° to the longer dimension of the panel are designated lateral (LAT). The surface strands were aligned parallel to the longer dimension for all panels tested. An additional set of eight 11mm thick panels from Manufacturer A were cut to produce 5 tension test pieces in each direction. Four pieces were tested in each direction from each of these additional panels with the remainder being retained for further study. All test pieces were conditioned at 20°C and 65% relative humidity prior to testing. Tension test pieces were cut to the basic shape as described in BS EN 789:2004 [1] using slightly modified dimensions shown in Fig. 1 as per two previous studies [16, 17]. Details of the number of test replications in each material property direction are given in Table 1.

Fig 1. Sample Cutting Plan and Tension Test Piece Details (Dimensions in mm)

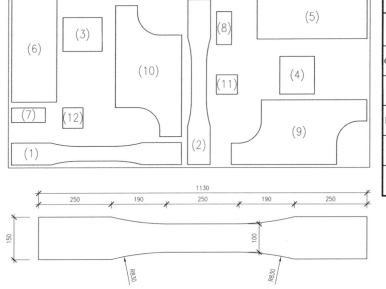

Material Property	Test Piece Number	Direction
Tension	(1)	Longitudinal
	(2)	Lateral
Compression	(3)	Longitudinal
	(4)	Lateral
Bending	(5)	Longitudinal
	(6)	Lateral
Planar Shear	(7)	Longitudinal
	(8)	Lateral
Panel Shear	(9)	Longitudinal
	(10)	Lateral
Bearing	(11)	Longitudinal
	(12)	Lateral

Table 1. Sample Sizes

Thickness	Manufacturer A		Manufacturer B		Manufacturer C	
	Longitudinal	Lateral	Longitudinal	Lateral	Longitudinal	Lateral
11mm	56**	39	-	-	-	-
15mm	15	15	15	15	15	15
18mm	15	15	-	-	-	-
** Includes results of previous study by O'Toole [16]						

Testing. Testing was performed using a Dartec universal hydraulic testing machine with hydraulic grips and a 250 kN load cell capable of reading load to an accuracy of 1% (see Fig. 2(a)). Two 5 mm, full bridge LVDT's with an accuracy of ± 1% were mounted to the test piece using custom made mounting blocks spaced 120 mm apart and bolted together through the test piece using M3 bolts (see Fig. 2(b)) as per the requirements of BS EN 789:2004 [1]. Load and displacement were continuously monitored using a National Instruments NI CDAQ-9172 data acquisition system and LabVIEW 8.2 software. Load was applied using a constant strain rate set such that the test pieces failed within 300 ± 120 s as specified in BS EN 789:2004 [1]. Moisture content was determined using the "oven dry method" as per in BS EN 322:1993 [18] to ensure consistency in the conditioning process.

Fig 2. Tension Test Setup

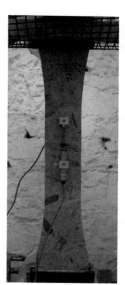

Fig. 2(a) – Tension test piece setup in Dartec 250 kN universal testing machine

Fig. 2(b) – Full-bridge LVDT's mounted to the test piece using custom made mounting blocks

Results

Strength and Elastic Stiffness. Tension strength and stiffness properties were calculated for each test piece as per BS EN 789:2004 [1]. A linear regression analysis on the section of the load-deflection curve from 0.1 to 0.4 times the failure load was performed and tension stiffness was calculated using Eq. 1. Tension strength is calculated using Eq. 2 and the cross sectional dimensions at the failure location.

$$E_t = [(F_2 - F_1)l_1]/[(u_2 - u_1)A].$$ (1)

$$f_t = F_{max}/A.$$ (2)

Where: F_2 = load at $0.4F_{max}$; F_1 = load at $0.1F_{max}$; u_2 = displacement corresponding to F_2; u_1 = displacement corresponding to F_1; F_{max} = failure load; l_1 = gauge length; A = cross-sectional area.

Summary statistics (including mean, 5th percentile and coefficient of variation (COV)) for tension strength and MOE are presented in Table 2 below for each panel manufacturer, thickness and material property direction.

Table 2. Tension Test Results Summary

| | Longitudinal | | | | | | Lateral | | | | | |
| | Strength | | | Stiffness | | | Strength | | | Stiffness | | |
Thickness	Mean (N/mm²)	5th Percentile (N/mm²)	CoV (%)	Mean (N/mm²)	5th Percentile (N/mm²)	CoV (%)	Mean (N/mm²)	5th Percentile (N/mm²)	CoV (%)	Mean (N/mm²)	5th Percentile (N/mm²)	CoV (%)
A-11mm	10.85	7.63	20.31	4089	3148	15.07	9.28	6.39	20.32	3531	2670	16.99
A-15mm	13.19	9.67	15.44	4458	3904	8.72	10.51	9.35	8.43	3267	2825	10.02
A-18mm	10.86	8.59	15.51	3775	3147	11.47	8.98	6.14	20.21	3294	2654	15.59
B-15mm	10.32	8.95	11.10	3684	3236	10.02	8.94	7.44	9.98	3423	2757	12.59
C-15mm	10.57	7.12	18.78	4376	3568	13.14	6.76	5.60	12.62	2736	2335	11.18

Regression Analysis. OSB is traditionally regarded by design codes as being a linear elastic material when loaded in tension under the serviceability limit state. Initial inspection of the results indicated that the relationship between stress and strain is linear at low strain but that non-linearity exists a strains above a certain level. Inspection of the plot of stress v's strain shown in Fig. 3 shows that the relationship is linear up to a point but deviates at strains higher than 0.002 . Linear and quadratic regression analyses showed that for all specimens, the R^2 values for the quadratic model were superior to those for the linear model. This confirmed that a quadratic model is better at describing material behaviour over the full strain range. A quadratic stress-strain equation in the form $\sigma = a\varepsilon^2 + b\varepsilon + c$ was fitted to the stress-strain data for each specimen tested. The constant term c approximates to 0 for all specimens, allowing the equations to be simplified to the form $\sigma = a\varepsilon^2 + b\varepsilon$.

Test specimens were grouped according to manufacturer, thickness and direction. An average stress-strain curve was generated for each group using the stress-strain data from each test specimen in the group by calculating the mean stress along lines of constant strain [8-10]. Fig. 3 shows a typical average stress-strain curve and the associated 95% confidence interval for 11 mm thick panels produced by Manufacturer A loaded in the longitudinal direction. Confidence intervals are used to estimate population parameters based on sample statistics [19, 20]. This allows us to state with 95% certainty that the average longitudinal tension stress-strain curve for all 11mm thick OSB panels produced by Manufacturer A will fall somewhere within the region shown in Fig 4. This can also be said for all the other manufacturers, panel thicknesses and material directions.

It was decided to investigate the strength of the relationship (if any) between the coefficients a and b of the quadratic stress-strain relationships. The quadratic regression equations for each test specimen were grouped according to manufacturer, panel thickness and direction and linear regression analyses were conducted between the coefficients for each group. Fig. 4 shows the results of a typical regression analysis for the 11mm thick panels produced by Manufacturer A loaded in the longitudinal direction. The results show that a negative linear correlation exists between coefficient b and coefficient a. The R^2 values indicate that the strength of the relationship in some cases is quite weak (R^2 = 0.165 for Manufacturer A, 11 mm longitudinal) and in some cases is quite strong (R^2 =0.830 for Manufacturer B, 15 mm lateral).

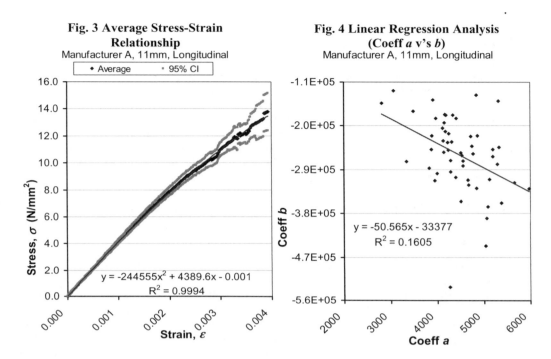

Fig. 3 Average Stress-Strain Relationship
Manufacturer A, 11mm, Longitudinal

Fig. 4 Linear Regression Analysis (Coeff *a* v's *b*)
Manufacturer A, 11mm, Longitudinal

Probability Model Distribution Fitting. The literature review suggested that strength and stiffness properties of wood-based composites tend to follow either the normal or lognormal probability distribution models [8-11]. A preliminary analysis using Minitab 15.0 statistical software confirmed this finding. It was decided focus on these two probability distributions and to develop a computer program to automatically determine the more suitable probability distribution to describe the results from the experimental test program.

The program was written using the Microsoft Visual Basic for Applications (VBA) for Microsoft Excel 2000. The computer program output included probability plots to facilitate visual inspection of the goodness of fit between the empirical distribution function (EDF) of the experimental data and cumulative distribution function (CDF) for each probability distribution being examined. The Anderson-Darling test was used to definitively determine the more suitable probability distribution model to describe the data. The Anderson-Darling test is a quadratic one-tailed statistical hypothesis test. The goodness of fit between the EDF and the CDF for each probability distribution can be represented by a single number (the Anderson-Darling statistic, A^2). The Anderson-Darling test is considered the most robust goodness-of-fit test for both small and large samples and is widely used in commercial statistical software packages [21, 22]. The data set is ranked in ascending order and the Anderson-Darling statistic is calculated using Eq. 3 and then modified to take into account the effect of sample size using Eq. 4.

$$A^2 = -N - S \qquad (3)$$

$$A^2_{Adj} = A^2\left(1 + \frac{0.75}{N} + \frac{2.25}{N^2}\right) \qquad (4)$$

<u>Where:</u> N = sample size; S is given by Eq. 5 below; $F(Y_i)$ = CDF of probability distribution evaluated at observation Y_i; $F(Y_{N+1-i})$ = CDF of probability distribution evaluated at observation Y_{N+1-i}.

$$S = \sum_{i=1}^{N} \frac{2i-1}{N} \left[\ln F(Y_i) + \ln(1 - F(Y_{N+1-i})) \right]. \tag{5}$$

In the Anderson-Darling test, the null hopothesis states that the data comes from a population that follows a specific probability distribution model e.g. the null hypothesis is that the longitudinal tension strength of 11mm thick OSB panels produced by Manufacturer A follows a normal distribution. The A^2 value can be used to calculate a coresponding P-Value using sets of formulae derived by D'Agostino and Stephens [21]. The P-Value is the probability that the accepting the null hypothesis (i.e. the data comes from a population that follows the probability distribution being tested) is the correct decision. In other words, a high P-Value indicates a strong probability that the data set comes from a population that follows the probability distribution being tested. A level of significance (α) is normally chosen prior to performing the Anderson-Darling test. An A^2 value that produces a P-Value less than α leads to the immediate rejection of the null hypothesis i.e. the particular probability distribution currently being tested is poor at describing the data and should be rejected. A significance level of $\alpha = 0.05$ has been used throughout this study.

Fig. 5 and 6 show typical cumulative probability plots for the tension strength (f_t) and tension MOE (E_t) results, respectively, for the 11mm thick panels produced by Manufacturer A loaded in the longitudinal direction. The plots include the EDF for the sample results plotted on top of the CDF for normal and lognormal probability distributions. A summary table containing the sample size, the A^2 value and the corresponding P-Value is included on each chart. Visual inspection indicates that both probability distribution models describe the data quite well, making it difficult to make a decision based on visual comparison. However, in the case of the tension strength, the P-Value for the lognormal distribution is 0.8834 whereas the P-Value for the normal distribution is 0.5933, indicating that the lognormal probability distribution is the better fit. Likewise, for the tension MOE, visual inspection indicates that both probability distributions describe the data well but the P-Value for the normal distribution is 0.4783 as opposed to 0.3169 for the lognormal distribution, indicating that the normal distribution is the better fit. This process has been repeated for all panel types, thicknesses and material property directions and a summary is presented in Table 3.

Fig. 5 Probability Plots (Manufacturer A, 11 mm, Strength, Longitudinal)

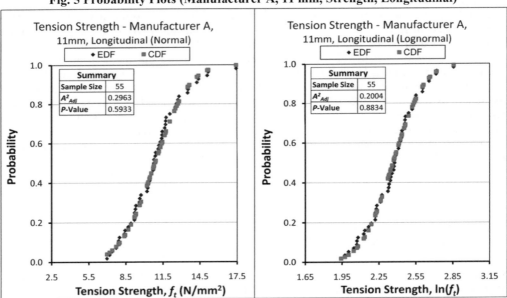

Fig. 6 Probability Plots (Manufacturer A, 11 mm, MOE, Longitudinal)

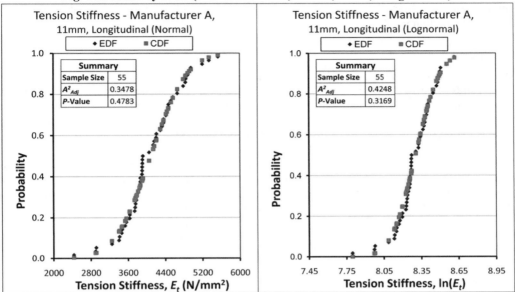

Table 3. Anderson-Darling Test Results

| | Results Set | Strength | | | | | Stiffness | | | | |
| | | Normal | | Lognormal | | Conclusion | Normal | | Lognormal | | Conclusion |
		A^2_{adj}	P-Value	A^2_{adj}	P-Value		A^2_{adj}	P-Value	A^2_{adj}	P-Value	
Longitudinal	A-11mm	0.2483	0.7502	0.1964	0.8894	Lognormal	0.2267	0.8167	0.2795	0.6462	Normal
	A-15mm	0.3343	0.5082	0.5141	0.1927	Normal	0.2850	0.6283	0.3373	0.5045	Normal
	A-18mm	0.7523	0.0466	0.6122	0.1041	Lognormal	0.2687	0.6822	0.3029	0.5744	Normal
	B-15mm	0.4101	0.3433	0.3462	0.4823	Lognormal	0.7311	0.0526	0.5988	0.1177	Lognormal
	C-15mm	0.5336	0.1723	0.7484	0.0477	Normal	0.4932	0.2169	0.5950	0.1204	Normal
Lateral	A-11mm	0.2956	0.5954	0.4743	0.2412	Normal	0.3935	0.3754	0.2022	0.8794	Lognormal
	A-15mm	0.3270	0.5194	0.3113	0.5525	Lognormal	0.4441	0.2851	0.3951	0.3722	Lognormal
	A-18mm	0.2110	0.8587	0.3694	0.4269	Normal	0.3005	0.5811	0.3657	0.4353	Normal
	B-15mm	1.0433	0.0088	1.0963	0.0065	Inconclusive	0.4016	0.3594	0.5607	0.1473	Normal
	C-15mm	0.4900	0.2208	0.4220	0.3218	Lognormal	0.5114	0.1956	0.4296	0.3087	Lognormal

A^2_{adj} = Anderson-Darling statistic adjusted to account for sample size; P-value = probability that the sample comes from a population that follows the probability distribution in question.

As can be seen in Table 3, the *P*-Values for the lateral tension strength for the 15 mm thick panels produced by Manufacturer B are less than 0.05 for both the normal and lognormal probability distribution. It is likely that the inconclusive result was a consequence of an insufficient sample size to fully capture the underlying probability distribution and further testing would eliminate this problem. In all other cases, *P*-Values for tension strength and MOE for both probability distributions are greater than 0.05 and it is therefore not possible to outright reject one or the other. Since a higher *P*-Value indicates a stronger probability that accepting the null hypothesis is the correct decision, it can be concluded that the probability distribution with the higher *P*-Value is the probability distribution that best describes the data. The conclusions columns in Table 3 summarise the chosen probability distribution for each parameter based on the *P*-Value.

The results summarised in Table 3 make it difficult to state definitively, for example, if tension strength always follows a lognormal probability distribution or if tension MOE always follows a normal probability distribution. However, visual inspection of the probability plots indicates that the sample results for strength and stiffness can be represented well by either a normal or lognormal probability distribution.

Conclusions

The experimental test program and statistical analyses of the results indicate that the short-term tension stress-strain behaviour of OSB can be described by a quadratic expression up to the point of failure. Linear and quadratic regression analyses were performed on the stress-strain data obtained from each test replication. Comparing the R^2 values indicated that a quadratic expression is more suitable to describe the short-term stress-strain behaviour up to the failure point. Furthermore, it has been shown using linear regression analyses that in the quadratic stress strain relationships ($\sigma = a\varepsilon^2 + b\varepsilon$), the coefficients a and b are negatively correlated to each other. Average stress-strain relationships have been established for each panel type, thickness and material property direction along with the associated 95% confidence intervals. The Anderson-Darling test has been used effectively to determine the underlying probability distribution for each set of results with a definitive conclusion been made in all but one case. Visual comparison of probability plots indicates that the tension strength and tension MOE can be reasonably well represented by either a normal or lognormal probability distribution.

References

1. BSI, *BS EN 789:2004 - Timber Structures - Test Methods - Determination of Mechanical Properties of Wood Based Panels*. 2004, London: British Standards Institute. 36.

2. BSI, *BS EN 300:2006 - Oriented Strand Boards (OSB) - Definitions, Classification and Specifications*. 2006, London: British Standards Institution. 24.

3. Taylor Steven E, T.M.H., Bender Donald A, Woeste Frank E, *Monte-Carlo Simulation Methods for Engineered Wood Systems*. Forest Products Journal, 1995. **45**(7/8): p. 43-50.

4. Hunt, M.O. and S.K. Suddarth, *Prediction of Elastic Constants of Particleboard*. Forest Products Journal, 1974. **24**(5): p. 52-57.

5. Wang, Y.-T. and F. Lam, *Computational Modeling of Material Failure for Parallel-Aligned Strand Based Wood Composites*. Computational Materials Science, 1998. **11**(3): p. 157-165.

6. Lam, F., Y.-T. Wang, and J.D. Barrett, *Simulation of Correlated Nonstationary Lumber Properties*. Journal of Materials in Civil Engineering, 1994. **6**(1): p. 34-53.

7. Wang, Y.-T., F. Lam, and J.D. Barrett, *Simulation of Correlated Modulus of Elasticity and Compressive Strength of Lumber with Gain Factor*. Probabilistic Engineering Mechanics, 1995. **10**(2): p. 63-71.

8. Clouston, P.L. and F. Lam, *Computational Modelling of Strand-Based Wood Composites*. ASCE Journal of Engineering Mechanics, 2001. **127**(8): p. 844-851.

9. Clouston, P.L., *Computational Modeling of Strand-Based Wood Composites in Bending*, in *Department of Forestry*. 2001, University of British Colombia: Vancouver.

10. Clouston, P.L. and F. Lam, *A Stochastic Plasticity Approach to Strength Modeling of Strand-Based Wood Composites*. Composites Science and Technology, 2002. **62**(10-11): p. 1381-1395.

11. Clouston, P.L., *Characterization and Strength Modeling of Parallel-Strand Lumber*. Holzforschung, 2007. **61**(4): p. 394-399.

12. Arwade, S.R., P.L. Clouston, and R. Winans, *Measurement and Stochastic Computational Modeling of the Elastic Properties of Parallel Strand Lumber.* Journal of Engineering Mechanics, 2009. **135**(9): p. 897-905.

13. Thelandersson, S. and H.J. Larsen, *Timber Engineering.* 2003, New York: J. Wiley.

14. Bodig, J. and B.A. Jayne, *Mechanics of Wood and Wood Composites.* 1993, Malabar, Fla.: Krieger Pub.

15. USDAFS, *Wood Handbook - Wood as an Engineering Material.* 1999, Madison, Wisconsin: USDA Forest Service Forest Products Laboratory.

16. O'Toole, C., *An Investigation Into the use of Irish Sitka Spruce in Timber I-Joists*, in *Department of Civil Engineering.* 2006, National University of Ireland: Galway.

17. Chui, Y., *Strength of OSB Scarf Joints in Tension.* Wood and Fiber Science, 2000. **32**(1): p. 7-10.

18. BSI, *BS EN 322:1993 - Wood-Based Panels - Determination of Moisture Content.* 1993, London: British Standards Institution.

19. Levine, D.M., P.P. Ramsey, and R.K. Smidt, *Applied Statistics for Engineers and Scientists: Using Microsoft Excel and MINITAB.* 2001, Upper Saddle River, N.J.: Prentice Hall.

20. Hayter, A.J., *Probability and Statistics for Engineers and Scientists.* 2002, Pacific Grove, CA: Brooks/Cole.

21. D'Agostino, R.B. and M.D. Stephens, *Goodness-of-Fit Techniques.* 1986, New York: Marcel Dekker.

22. Stephens, M.A., *EDF Statistics for Goodness of Fit and Some Comparisons.* Journal of the American Statistical Association, 1974. **69**(347): p. 730-737.

Key Engineering Materials Vol. 478 (2011) pp 64-69
© (2011) Trans Tech Publications, Switzerland
doi:10.4028/www.scientific.net/KEM.478.64

Generalized Maxwell Model as Viscoelastic Lubricant in Journal Bearing

M. Guemmadi[1, 2, a] and A. Ouibrahim[1,* b]

[1]Laboratoire d'Energétique Mécanique et Matériaux, Université Mouloud Mammeri, Tizi-Ouzou, Algeria.

[2]Departement d'Energétique, Faculté des Sciences de l'Ingénieur, Université M'hamed Bouguerra, Boumerdès, Algeria.

[a]e-mail : guemmadi_samah@yahoo.fr , [b]e-mail : ouibraah@live.fr

*Corresponding author : ouibraah@live.fr

Key words: Journal bearing, Lubrication, Maxwell model, Viscoelastic fluids, CFD.

Abstract

The hydrodynamic lubrication interest is still of great importance, so that more and more elaborated lubricants are considered. They, however, involve consequently more and more hydrodynamic complexity as a result of the rheological properties of the additives.

In our case, we consider lubricants having viscoelastic properties described by a generalized Maxwell model used in the case of journal bearing lubrication. The complexity of the coupled associated equations (momentum and constitutive) to describe the hydrodynamic prevailing in such a geometry requires numerical solutions. Using the commercial Finite Volume software Fluent 6.3 together with an appropriate developed computational code, via UDF (User Defined Functions), we determine the pressure distribution as well as the flow velocity profile and the stress field in the core, the load bearing capacity developed and the attitude angle; all together with the effects of the viscoelastic lubricant parameters (relaxation time and shear viscosity).

Introduction

The continuous development of brand new lubricants indicates that the hydrodynamic lubrication in journal bearing remains of great importance and interest in industrial applications as well as for theoretical research. Beginning with Newtonian film [1], then, several investigations have been performed using non Newtonian but purely viscous fluid [2]. Progressively, with the necessary evolution of brand new lubricants, assigned for different purposes such as performances improvement in the load bearing capacity [3 to 5], or enhancement of the cavitation initiation [6, 7], viscoelastic fluids have been then concerned.

Thus, different viscoelastic models have been involved such as Maxwell, PTT (Phan-Thien-Tanner) and Oldroyd B models [3-5, 8-10]. Moreover, the lubricant has been considered as suspensions of deformable particles [5]. Owing to the complexity of the associated hydrodynamic equations, numerical computation is widely used, involving different CFD (Computational Fluid Dynamic) analysis and programs [2, 4, 5, 8, 10, 11], compared to analytical approaches [12]. Besides the main interest in the hydrodynamic lubrication, heat transfer is also of great importance in journal bearing for Newtonian [13] and viscoelastic fluids [14].

As a whole investigation, we are studying the effect of viscoelastic lubricant in journal bearing, on lubrication, with generalized upper convected Maxwell model using the commercial Finite Volume software Fluent 6.3 together with an appropriate computational developed code by mean of User Defined Functions (UDF). As a first contribution, we determine here the pressure distribution, the shear stress field on the journal surface and the first normal stress difference all together with the effects of the viscoelastic lubricant parameters.

Rheological Model – Constitutive Equations

We consider here the generalized upper convected Maxwell model whose stress tensor components σ_{ij} are given by:

$$\sigma_{ij} = -p\delta_{ij} + \tau_{ij} \tag{1}$$

where p is the hydrostatic pressure, while τ_{ij} (the deviatoric part of the stress tensor) is defined by:

$$\tau_{ij} + \lambda \frac{D\tau_{ij}}{Dt} = 2\mu_p D_{ij} \tag{2}$$

λ and μ_p are the relaxation time and the viscosity of the viscoelastic lubricant respectively, while $\frac{D}{Dt}$ is the upper-convected time derivative or Oldroyd derivative [4, 5].

In the case of a Newtonian fluid, $\lambda = 0$, we have then obviously $\mu_p = \mu_s$ and the relation (2) leads to a purely viscous stress tensor τ_{ij}:

$$\tau_{ij} = 2\mu_s D_{ij} \tag{3}$$

in which D_{ij} are the components of the deformation rate tensor.

Application - Journal bearing

Hydrodynamic Equations

As an application, we now consider the above constitutive equations as representing a rheological model of a viscoelastic lubricant in a journal bearing. A schematic sketch of the associated geometry is illustrated in figure 1.

Journal bearing radii: R_j=5 cm and R_b=5.3 cm.
Clearance C= R_b-R_j.
Relative eccentricity ε=0.9
Journal rotation: Ω (rad/s).

$\vec{OM} = \vec{r}$: Fluid particle position in the core.

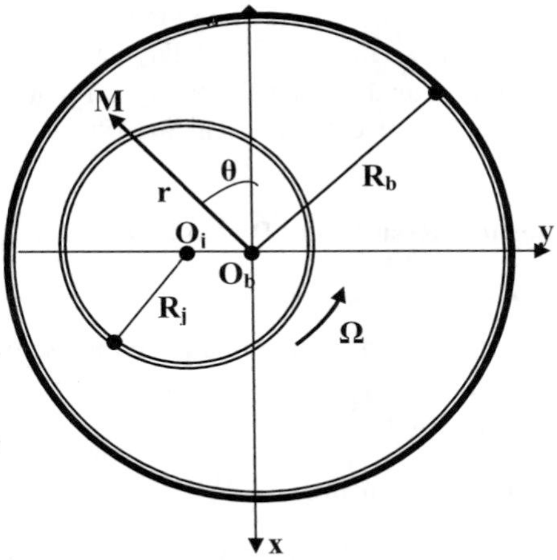

Fig. 1: Schematic of the flow geometry

With the above 2D flow dimensions, (Fig. 1), we consider the following conservative equations:

Continuity Equation: $$\frac{\partial u}{\partial x} + \frac{\partial v}{\partial y} = 0 \tag{4}$$

where u(x, y) and v(x, y) are the components of the flow velocity $\vec{V}(x, y)$

Momentum Equations: Assuming a stationary flow, we have then the following momentum equations:

$$\rho u_j \frac{\partial u_i}{\partial x_j} = -\frac{\partial p_i}{\partial x_j} + \frac{\partial \tau_{ij}}{\partial x_j} \tag{5}$$

where ρ is the volumic mass of the lubricant.

The above system of equations (4) and (5) is completed for τ_{ij} by the constitutive equations (2).

Boundary Conditions: We use of course the usual well known boundary conditions [1, 4, 5]:

a) for the velocity field:

$$y = 0 \implies u(0) = \Omega R_j \text{ and } v(0) = 0, \text{ while for } y = h(\theta) \implies u(h(\theta)) = v(h(\theta)) = 0 \tag{6}$$

$h(\theta)$ corresponds to a given fluid particle position in the core and is given [1, 4, 5] by :

$$h(\theta) = C(1 + \varepsilon \cos \theta) \tag{7}$$

b) for the pressure and the stress field: $p(r,\theta) = p(r,\theta + 2\pi)$ and $\tau_{ij}(r,\theta) = \tau_{ij}(r,\theta + 2\pi)$ (8)

Numerical Procedure

The above equations systems (2) to (5) together with (6) to (8) for given geometric and kinematic characteristics of this 2D flow, are numerically solved using the CFD package Fluent 6.3 completed by UDF. The pre-processor used for the grid generation is Gambit. The particularity of the problem examined here (the clearance size is very small compared to the journal diameter) requires to divide the area into three zones, using the bi-exponent mesh for the very small gaps and exponent mesh for the two other zones, while UDF has been defined [14] to compute the sources terms of the momentum equation and the three components of stress: τ_{xx}, τ_{yy} and τ_{xy}. The numerical procedure to handle the present numerical analysis is given in details in [14].

Numerical Results and Discussion

Newtonian Fluid

As a first step and a way to validate the use of the software Fluent, we test the generalized Maxwell model introduced in the software code via UDF and assign $\lambda = 0$ which corresponds then to a Newtonian fluid.

Pressure distribution

Figure 2 clearly indicates that the numerical pressure distribution along the core obtained is in quite good agreement with the analytical pressure distribution in the core for a Newtonian fluid.
For this calculation, we have considered the following: a moderate value of the clearance C=0.3 cm, for journal radii R_j=5 and 5.3 cm, a relative eccentricity ε=0.9, a journal rotation N=191 rpm (Ω = 20 rad/s), while the shear viscosity and the volumic mass of the lubricant are μ_s=0.02 Pa.s and ρ=820 kg/m^3 respectively.

In the case of a Newtonian fluid, the shear viscosity is the mean characteristic fluid parameter acting on the pressure magnitude as shown in figure 3. As a matter of fact, figure 3 shows an increase of the pressure magnitude with an increase of the shear viscosity μ_s.

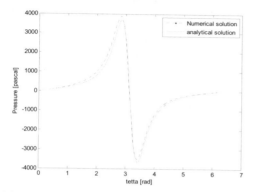

Fig. 2: Numerical and Analytical pressure distribution along the core for Newtonian Fluid.

Fig. 3: Effect of the shear viscosity μ_s on the pressure distribution for Newtonian fluid.

Shear stress and First Normal Stress Difference

For comparison purpose with the viscoelastic lubricant, we have also determined the shear stress τ_{xy} distribution in the case of a Newtonian fluid. Figure 4 exhibits a well known distribution of the shear stress along the core of the journal bearing for a Newtonian fluid. It is also shown in figure 4 that the values of the shear viscosity μ_s strongly affect τ_{xy}.

Calculating the first normal stress difference $N_1 = \tau_{xx} - \tau_{yy}$, we have found that $N_1 = 0$. This results in quite agreement for a Newtonian fluid; since it is well known that such a fluid does not exhibit any normal stress difference for this flow situation.

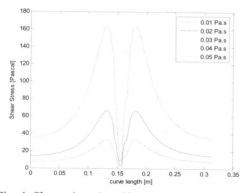
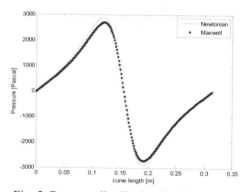

Fig. 4: Shear viscosity effect on the Shear Stress distribution along the core for Newtonian fluid.

Fig. 5: Pressure distribution for Newtonian and Maxwell fluids (μ_s=0.1 Pa.s; λ=1.2 10^{-4}s)

Viscoelastic Fluid – Generalized Maxwell Model

Pressure distribution

We use the same value of the shear viscosity for the Newtonian as well as the Maxwell fluids, that is to say $\mu_s = \mu_p = 0.1$ Pa.s. It is very interesting to note in figure 5 that the pressure distributions for these two fluids are practically the same, with just a small difference occurring at the maximum pressure. That is to say, the contribution to the pressure distribution is mainly viscous.

This is not the case for the shear stress distribution as well as the first normal stress difference.

Shear stress and First Normal Stress Difference

As a matter of fact, in figure 6, it is clearly shown that the Newtonian and the Maxwell (viscoelastic) fluid do not at all exhibit the same shear stress distribution even having the same shear viscosity μ_s and μ_p. There is obviously a viscoelastic effect on the shear stress in the case of the Maxwell fluid. This result is substantiated by the existence of the normal stress difference as indicated in Fig.6.

While the Newtonian fluid does not exhibit any first normal stress difference, figure 7 clearly indicates, for the Maxwell fluid, a first normal stress distribution along the core of the journal bearing. The magnitude of this first normal stress distribution is seen to increase with the increase of the shear viscosity μ_p.

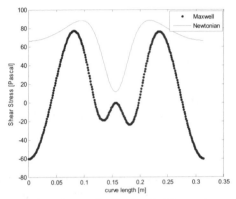

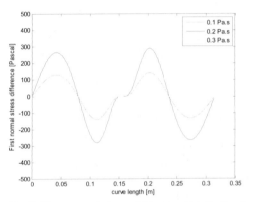

Fig. 6: Shear Stress distribution for Newtonian and Maxwell fluids ($\mu_s=\mu_p$ 0.1 Pa.s; $\lambda=1.2\ 10^{-4}$ s)

Fig. 7: First normal stress difference distribution for a Maxwell fluid for different values of μ_p ($\lambda=1.2\ 10^{-4}$ s)

Effect of the relaxation time

In order to analyze and appreciate the contribution of the elastic part in such a flow, we consider the effect of the relaxation time λ on the different distributions presented above.

It is easily shown in figures 8 and 9 that the value of the relaxation time does affect the pressure distribution, but slightly, and significantly in the case of the first normal stress difference distribution. They increase with the increase of the relaxation time.

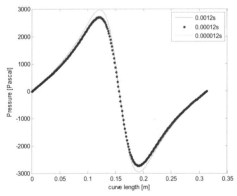

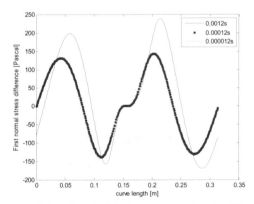

Fig. 8: Relaxation time effect on the pressure distribution for a Maxwell fluid (μ_p=0.1 Pa.s)

Fig. 9: Relaxation time effect on the first normal stress difference distribution for a Maxwell fluid (μ_p=0.1Pa.s).

The effects of the kinematic as well as geometric parameters have been also considered. They are described in details in a forthcoming publication. In the case of this contribution, we have mainly focused our attention on the viscoelasticity effects, phenomenologically and quantitatively, when we have to consider a viscoelastic lubricant instead of a Newtonian one.

Conclusion

The main challenge in this contribution is to analyze the effect of a viscoelastic fluid in journal bearing lubrication using a generalized upper convected Maxwell (UCM) model via commercial volume element software Fluent 6.3.

The first and main result is to have used (and adapted) for our calculations the Fluent software, not especially devoted for non Newtonian viscoelastic fluids.

Secondly, we have shown, by mean of this software, that viscoelasticity displays differences with a Newtonian fluid, especially for the shear stress and the exhibition of a first normal stress difference. It has been shown that the viscoelasticity enhances the magnitude of both the pressure and the stress fields on the journal surface. This means that viscoelastic lubricants affect the loading in the journal bearing system.

References

[1]   J. Frêne et *al*, *Lubrification Hydrodynamique, Paliers et Butées*, Edition Eyrolles (1990).

[2]   K. P. Gertzos, P.G. Nikolakopoulos, C. A. Papadopoulos, *CFD analysis of journal bearing hydrodynamic lubrication by Bingham lubricant*, Tribology International, Vol. 41 pp. 1190-1204. (2008).

[3]   G. W. Roberts and K. Walters: *On Viscoelastic Effects in journal-bearing Lubrication*, Rheologica Acta, Vol. 31, pp. 55-62, (1992).

[4]   M. Allouche et A. Ouibrahim, *Modélisation Numérique du comportement de Fluides d'Oldroyd B en Lubrification Hydrodynamique*, 3ème Colloque International de Rhéologie, Béjaïa, 12-14 Nov. (2005).

[5]   M. Allouche et A. Ouibrahim, *Milieux Viscoélastiques dans un Espace Confiné –Modèle B d'Oldroyd et Suspensions de Particules Déformables. (Partie 2 - Etude Numérique)*, 42ème Colloque du Groupe Français de Rhéologie, Clermont Ferrand, France, Oct. (2007)

[6]   A. Ouibrahim, D. H. Fruman et R. Gaudemer, *Cavitation dans des Espaces très Confinés*, Colloques Ecoulements Propulsifs dans les Systèmes de Transport Spatial, organisé par CNES, ONERA et CNRS, p 185, Bordeaux Septembre (1995).

[7]   A. Ouibrahim, D. H. Fruman and R. Gaudemer, *Vapour Cavitation in Very Confined Spaces for Newtonian and Non Newtonian Fluids*, Physics of Fluids, Vol. 8, N°. 7, p. 1964, (1996).

[8]   J. A. Tichy, *"Non Newtonian Lubrication with the Convected Maxwell Model"*, Transactions of the ASME, Vol. 118 pp. 344-348, (1996).

[9]   D. Rh. Gwynllyw, T. N. Phillips, *The influence of Oldroyd-B and PTT lubricants on moving journal bearing systems*, Journal of Non-Newtonian Fluid Mechanics, Vol. 150, pp. 196-210, (2008).

[10]   F. Talay Akyilidiz and H. Bellout: *Viscoelastic Lubrication with Phan-Thien-Tanner Fluid*, Transactions of the ASME, Vol.126, pp. 288-291, (2004).

[11]   D. Grecov and J. R. Clermont, *Numerical Simulations of non-Newtonian flow between eccentric cylinders by domain decomposition and stream tube method* Journal of Non-Newtonian Fluid Mechanics, 126, pp. 175-158, (2005).

[12]   Rong Zhang, Xueming He, Simon X. Yang and Xinkai Li, *Perturbation solution of non-Newtonian lubrication with the convected Maxwell Model*, Transactions of the ASME, Vol. 127 pp. 302-305. (2005).

[13]   R. Nebbali, *Propagation de la Chaleur dans un Arbre de Palier en Rotation en Présence d'un Ecoulement Laminaire Confiné*, Thèse de Magister , Université de Tizi-Ouzou, Juin (2002).

[14]   M. Guemmadi, *Convection Forcée de Fluides Viscoélastiques en Milieu Confiné – Cas de la Lubrification Hydrodynamique*, Thèse de Doctorat, Université de Boumerdès, (en cours).

Key Engineering Materials Vol. 478 (2011) pp 70-74
© (2011) Trans Tech Publications, Switzerland
doi:10.4028/www.scientific.net/KEM.478.70

Comparative Analysis of Vaporization Rates of 5456 Aluminum Alloying Elements during CO_2 Laser Welding

J.I. Achebo[a], O. Oghoore[b]

Department of Production Engineering
Faculty of Engineering
University of Benin, Benin City, Edo State, Nigeria
[a] josephachebo@yahoo.co.uk, [b] oviemuno2002@yahoo.co.uk

Key words: CO_2 laser welding process, evaporative energy loss, evaporative power loss, metal vapor rise, vaporization rate.

Abstract. In this paper, the vaporization rates of Mg^{2+} and Al^+ alloying elements of a 5456 aluminum plate were investigated using the CO_2 laser welding process. The models proposed and used by Block-Bolten and Eagar in 1984 and Zhao and DebRoy in 2003 were applied with experimental results generated from this study. The vaporization rate of Mg^{2+} ions and Al^+ ions using the equations proposed by Block-Bolten and Eagar gave 8.76 $\mu gs^{-1}cm^{-2}$ and 0.0465 $\mu gs^{-1}cm^{-2}$ respectively, whereas the equation proposed by Zhao and DebRoy gave 6.7 $\mu gs^{-1}cm^{-2}$ and 0.016 $\mu gs^{-1}cm^{-2}$ respectively. These values are within the reported values obtained by Block-Bolten and Eagar (1984). The heat transfer coefficient for Mg^{2+} and Al^+ ions were also obtained. The vapor bubble radius including the surface tension and buoyancy forces were examined. The evaporative power and energy losses as a result of these bubbles' collapse were calculated. The paper clearly shows the comparative analysis of alloying elements' vaporization process in the aluminum metal heating process.

Introduction

Evaporation is said to occur when atoms/molecules of any evaporants (the materials being evaporated) achieve sufficient energy to overcome the solid/liquid binding forces holding them together. To increase the evaporation rate the average energy has to be increased by raising the evaporant's temperature. This, however, increases the vapor pressure [1]. High temperatures necessary for laser welding, result in the evaporative loss of many alloying elements which have low vapor pressure, such as magnesium. Unfortunately this effect would reduce the strength of welds as their chemical compositions are permanently altered [2]. Therefore, alloying elements such as magnesium and zinc ions, which have low vapor pressures, reduce the suitability of these alloys for welding. These volatile ions are unsuitable in the sense that their early evaporative loss and consequent chemical composition alteration tend to decrease material thickness, so that problems occur especially during the welding of thinner sheets. The reason for this is that thicker sheets conduct heat more rapidly away from the weld point than thinner sheets would [3].

Several researchers have studied the evaporisation rates of alloying elements [4,5]. In this study, the vaporization rate determination models as proposed by Block Bolten and Eagar [4] and Zhao and DebRoy [6] were used. The radius of the vapor bubbles and the power and energy losses as a result of the bubble collapse were also investigated. The vaporization rates obtained were validated by the ones obtained by Block Bolten and Eagar [4].

Determination of Vapor Pressure of Alloying Element

In 5456 aluminum alloy, the concentration of zinc is very low, therefore, the vaporization of magnesium and aluminum only, are treated here. Brandes [7], Mundra [8]; and Zhao and DeRoy [5] proposed Eq. (1) and Eq. (2) for determining vapor pressures of aluminum and magnesium. These equations were deduced from the Clausius Clapeyron Equation [7].

For aluminum pressure, P (atm)

$$\log P = 12.36 - \frac{1.65 \times 10^4}{T} - 1.02 \times \log T - \log 760 \tag{1}$$

For magnesium pressure, P (atm)

$$\log P = 12.79 - \frac{7.55 \times 10^3}{T} - 1.41 \times \log T - \log 760 \tag{2}$$

Where T is the vaporization temperature.

Zhao and DebRoy [5] applied Henry's law for determining the activity of magnesium, (a_{mg}) in the molten pool as expressed in Eq. (3)

$$a_{mg} = 0.88 X_{mg} \tag{3}$$

Whereas, they obtained the activity of aluminum, (a_{Al}) using the Rault's law, expressed in Eq. (4)

$$a_{Al} = X_{Al} \tag{4}$$

Where X_{mg} and X_{Al} are the mole fraction of magnesium and aluminum in the alloy respectively. The diffusivity of elements aluminum and magnesium in helium gas (D_i) is considered here by Zhao and DebRoy [5] in Eq. (5) and Eq. (6)

Diffusivity of aluminum in He, D_{Al} (mm^2/s)

$$D_{Al} = \frac{-1.20 \times 10^2 + 0.39T + 2.09 \times 10^{-4} T^2}{P} \tag{5}$$

Diffusivity of magnesium in He, D_{mg} (mm^2/s)

$$D_{mg} = \frac{-1.10 \times 10^{-2} + 0.36T + 1.96 \times 10^{-4} T^2}{P} \tag{6}$$

However, the viscosity, μ of helium (He) gas (g/m.s) was determined as expressed in Eq. (7)

$$\mu = 2.20 \times 10^{-2} + 2.22 \times 10^{-5} T \tag{7}$$

The mass transfer coefficient, $h_{g,i}$ was calculated using the graphical results of Schlunder and Gniclinski [9] by Zhao and DebRoy [5] as expressed in Eq (8)

$$h_{g,i} = \frac{2 S_{ci}^{0.42} \, \mathrm{Re}^{0.5} \, D_i}{d} \left(1 + \frac{\mathrm{Re}^{0.55}}{200} \right)^{0.5}$$

$$\left[0.483 - 0.108 \frac{r}{d} + 7.71 \times 10^{-3} \left(\frac{r}{d} \right)^2 \right] \tag{8}$$

Where, d is the diameter of the gas nozzle in meters, r is the radial distance on the weldpool surface in meters, D_i is the average diffusivity of element i, in the shielding gas, Re is the Reynolds number at the nozzle exit and S_{ci} is the average Schmidt number.

The Reynolds number is defined by, $\mathrm{Re} = \dfrac{L V_i}{\mu}$ (9)

Where, L is the weldpool length in meters, V_i is the flow velocity in the weldpool in meters per second and μ is the liquid viscosity [10].

The average Schmidt number is defined by, $S_c = \sum\limits_{i=1}^{n} a_i S_{ci}$ (10)

Where

$$S_{ci} = \frac{V}{D_i} \tag{11}$$

Where D_i is the diffusivity of element i in the shielding gas in millimeters squared per second.

Determination of Rate of Vaporization

The rates of vaporization of the alloying elements used in this study were the ones suggested by Dushman and Laferty [11] for predicting the vaporization rate J_i from kinetic theory of gasses [4] as expressed in Eq. (12)

$$J_i = 44.331 P_i^o \left(\frac{M_i}{T} \right)^{\frac{1}{2}} \left(g.s^{-1} cm^{-2} \right) \tag{12}$$

Where M_i is the molecular weight of element i and $P_i^0 = P$ is the vapor pressure as determined in Eq (1) and Eq. (2).

Another equation proposed by Zhao and DebRoy [6] which is a modification of Langmuir equation for calculating the vaporation rates of alloying elements was also used and expressed in Eq. (13)

$$J_i = \frac{44.34}{K} a_i P_i^o \sqrt{\frac{M_i}{T}} \tag{13}$$

Where K is a correction factor = 7.5 but in this study K = 0.75 which is consistent with experimental results obtained by Block-Bolten and Eagar [4].

Theory of Metal Vapor Rise

The theory of metal vapor rise is based on the buoyancy force and the surface tension force. The equilibrium of these forces produces a radius R, obtained as [12],

$$R = \left[\frac{3\sigma}{2g(\rho_L - \rho_v)} \right]^{\frac{1}{2}} \tag{14}$$

Where R is the radius of the vapor rise, g is the acceleration due to gravity, ρ_L is the liquid density and ρ_v is the vapor density.

Evaporation Power Loss

The evaporation power loss, P_L was calculated using Eq (15) and related experimental results in Table 1. The power loss was due to the heat loss as a result of escaping vapor bubbles that move from hot regions to cool regions

$$P_L = J_i \left(L_i - \overline{\Delta H_i} \right) \left(Watt \; cm^{-2} \right) \tag{15}$$

Where, L_i is the heat of evaporation of pure element i and $\overline{\Delta H_i}$ is the partial molar heat of mixing of element i in the alloy

The evaporative energy loss, E_L, is given by

$$E_L = J_i \left(L_i - \overline{\Delta H_i} \right) t \left(Watt - cm^{-2} s \right) \tag{16}$$

Where t is time in seconds. In most cases, $\overline{\Delta H_i}$ is small compared to the heat of evaporation. If the element of interest is a solvent such as iron in steel or aluminum in aluminum alloys, $\overline{\Delta H_i}$ could be neglected because the values obtained would be too insignificant to make any real impact [4].

Results and Discussion

The vaporization rates of the alloying elements of 5456 aluminum alloy were investigated. Applying the equation proposed by Dushman and Laferity [11], and used by Block-Bolten and Eagar [4], the alloying element Mg^{2+} has a vaporization rate of 8.76 $\mu gs^{-1} cm^{-2}$, and Al^+ has one of 0.0465 $\mu gs^{-1} cm^{-2}$. The equation proposed by Zhao and DebRoy [6] was modified to suit the purpose of this study and used. The corresponding values for Mg^{2+} and Al^+ alloying elements were

6.7 $\mu gs^{-1}cm^{-2}$ and 0.016 $\mu gs^{-1}cm^{-2}$ respectively. The trends of these values are consistent with the ones suggested by Block – Bolten and Eagar [4]. The rate of vaporization of Mg^{2+} and Al^{+} respectively using the equation applied by Block-Bolten and Eagar amounted to about 13.2% and 48.8%, above that obtained using Zhao and DebRoy. Ordinarily, it is very difficult for vaporization rates of alloying elements to fall within specified ranges because of the high variability of welding technological conditions in general, such as the alloying element compositions, the welding gas, alloy heat treatment, and many others. The difference in vaporization rate could be specifically attributed to differences in these traits. However, when the weld metals used in this experiment were weighed, the difference was not as significant as expected, considering the potential for losses via evaporation. This shows that some elements must have been introduced from the electrode to the weld metal which compensated for the vaporized Mg^{2+} and Al^{+} elements.

Mg^{2+} is known to be much more volatile than Al^{+}. Therefore more heat is required to vaporize Al^{+} than is required to vaporize Mg^{2+}. This claim is confirmed by the heat transfer coefficient. The heat transfer coefficient required to vaporize Mg^{2+} was 62.5 $W/m^2\,°C$ whereas 1668.74$W/m^2\,°C$ was used to vaporize Al^{+} element. The high laser power which generated a high vapor temperature of 2537°C, was concentrated on the surface of the weldpool, and formed bubbles of metal films. Viscosity is significantly reduced as a result of the high temperature and a state of turbulence prevails in the weldpool, in short, the flow of the weldpool becomes turbulent. Its turbulent nature is determined by obtaining the Reynold's number. When Re>>1, the flow in the weldpool is considered to be turbulent. The Reynolds number, in this case was given as 530, which indicates that the flow in the weldpool was particularly turbulent at a maximum flow rate of 0.9m/s [13].

The continuous application of this high vapor temperature propagated a buoyancy force and surface tension force, calculated to be 0.44N, and 0.053N respectively. These forces collapsed the bubbles to form vapors rising above the weldpool. The average radius of the bubbles was calculated to be 0.01mm, with a density of 1333.68 kg/m³. This density value is lower than the measured density of the weldpool [14].

There is an expected heat loss due to evaporation. The evaporative power loss, which accounts for the fraction of the total input power lost in the evaporation process, was investigated. In this study the vaporization rate determined from using the Block-Bolten and Eagar equation was used to calculate for the evaporative power and energy losses. The reason for this procedure, is that the Block-Bolten and Eagar equation appears to be more potent and consistent with results from other investigators[4]. The evaporative power loss was calculated to be 41.15 W cm⁻² for Mg^{2+} ions and a corresponding value of 0.24 W cm⁻² was obtained for Al^{+} ions.

The energy expended that caused the power losses as a result of vaporization is known as the evaporative energy; being losses which occurred within the welding cycle, being 9.65s. The evaporative energy for Mg^{2+} and Al^{+} ions, were 397.10 Ws.cm⁻² and 2.32 Ws.cm⁻² respectively. Tables 1 and 2 show the parameters used for calculating the results in this study.

Table 1: Parameters used for calculation

Welding speed = 0.1m/s
Boiling temperature, T_b = 2482 °C = 2755K
Gas constant, R = 8314 J/mol.k
Width of keyhole = 0.44mm
Diameter of nozzle = 6 mm
Total welding cycle time = 9.65s
Partial heat of mixing for Mg in Al = 556J/g
Heat of vaporization for Mg = 5253 J/g
Heat of vaporization for Al = 10780 J/g
Density of heavy metal vapor = 1333.68 kg/m³

Table 2: Compositions and weight percentages of 5456 Aluminum plates [15]

Composition	Al	Mn	Mg	Cr
Weight %	93.9	0.8	5.1	0.12

Conclusion

In this paper, it has been shown that the equations proposed by Block-Bolten and Eagar [4] and Zhao and DebRoy [6] show great promise for calculating the vaporization rates of aluminum alloys. The vaporization rates of Mg^{2+} and Al^+ alloying elements were both consistent with the values obtained by Block-Bolten and Eagar [4].

It was found that Mg^{2+} ions are much more volatile than Al^+ ions, therefore, more heat was required to vaporize Al^+ ions than was needed with Mg^{2+} ions. The heat flow rate was found to be turbulent. The average vapor bubble radius was calculated, including the buoyancy force that is responsible for vapor rise, and the surface tension force that tends to sustain the vapor at the surface of the molten weld pool. The power and energy losses, which occur as a result of the vaporization process from a region near the heat source to a region further away from the heat source which is cooler in temperature, were also calculated and computed.

In this study the theory of the vaporization process of 5456 aluminum alloying elements has been investigated. This study has helped the researcher in selecting aluminum plates for manufacturing processes based on their chemical properties geared towards avoiding unnecessary loss of alloying elements, which if left uncontrolled would affect the quality of the welded plates.

References

[1]   Information on http://www.lesker.com/newweb/evaporation_sources/pdf/Evap_Technical notes_P2-3.pdf

[2]   Information on http://happyinmotion.com/jez/laser_welding_paper.pdf

[3]   Information on http://www.eaa.net/eaa/education/TALAT/Leactures/4300.pdf

[4]   A. Block–Bolten and T. W. Eagar: Metal Trans. B Vol. 15B (1984), p. 461 – 469

[5]   H. Zhao and T. Debroy: Met. & Mater. Trans. B Vol.32B (2001), p.163 – 172.

[6]   H. Zhao and T. DebRoy; J Appl. phys. Vol. 93, No.12 (2003), p.10090 – 10096

[7]   E. A. Brandes: *Smithells Metals Reference Book*, 6th ed. In association with Fulmer Research Institute Ltd., Butterworth and Co., London, (1983)

[8]   K.Mundra:The Pennsylvania State University, Univ Park, PA. (1994)

[9]   E.U.Schlunder and V. Gniclinski; Chem-Ing-Technol,Vol.39 (1967),p. 578 – 584.

[10]   M.H. Cho and D. F. Farson: Weld J. Vol.86 No.9 (2007), p. 257s

[11]   S. Duchman and J. M. Laferty, eds., 2nd Edition, Scientific Foundation of Vacuum Technique, John Wiley, NY, (1962), p. 691- 737and p. 15 – 21.

[12]   J.I.Achebo, in: A Multi-Parametric Analysis of Drift Flux Models to Pipeline Applications, edited by S.I.Ao and L.Gelman, volume 60 of Electronic Engineering and Computing Technology,Lecture Notes in Electrical Engineering, Chapter 56, Springer Science+Business Media B.V. Netherlands (2010)

[13]   J.I. Achebo: Int. J. Eng. Sci & Tech. Vol.2, No.6, (2010), p. 2034-2039

[14]   J.I.Achebo, and O. Oghoore: *Computational Analysis of Condensed Vaporized Alloying Elements of 5456 Aluminum Alloy* (Trans Tech Publications, Switzerland 2010).

[15]   Rong-Hua Yeh, Shih – Pin Liaw and Hong-Bin Yu: J. Marine Sci and Tech, Vol.11, No.4, (2003), p. 213 – 220.

Key Engineering Materials Vol. 478 (2011) pp 75-80
© (2011) Trans Tech Publications, Switzerland
doi:10.4028/www.scientific.net/KEM.478.75

Analysis of Chip Damage Risk in Thermosonic Wire Bonding

Christian Dresbach[1, 2, a], Georg Lorenz[1, b], Matthias Petzold[1, c]
and Holm Altenbach[3, d]

[1]Fraunhofer Institute for Mechanics of Materials, 06120 Halle, Walter-Huelse-Str. 1, Germany

[2]now at German Aerospace Center, 51147 Cologne, Linder Hoehe, Germany

[3]Martin-Luther-University Halle-Wittenberg, 06099 Halle, Germany

[a]christian.dresbach@dlr.de, [b]georg.lorenz@iwmh.fhg.de, [c]matthias.petzold@iwmh.fhg.de,
[d]holm.altenbach@iw.uni-halle.de

Key words: wire bonding, gold, copper, free air ball, micro-compression test

Abstract. In current highly integrated microelectronic devices including system-in-package and stacked-die solutions, system reliability is strongly influenced by reliability of the gold and copper wire bond interconnections. Especially in state-of-the-art ICs containing mechanically sensitive low-K dielectric materials, controlling the mechanical properties of the free air ball (FAB) is of utmost significance due to chip damage risks during the bond process. Because of an extreme change in microstructure when forming the FAB, the material properties change significantly. Consequently, it is necessary to determine the properties of the FAB itself, when analyzing chip damage risks via finite element simulations. We present a micro-compression test that allows the determination of the hardening behavior of typical gold and copper FABs with diameters between 45 µm and 75 µm. In this test a FAB is placed on a diamond support or a test capillary and loaded by a diamond flat punch in a microindenter. The hardening was determined from force/displacement behavior via parameter identification using finite element simulations. The identified yield stresses correlate very well with the microstructure which was determined by electron backscatter diffraction method; this means that the yield stress decreases with increasing mean grain diameter in analogy to the Hall-Petch correlation. Compared to unprocessed wires the initial yield stresses are 50% to 60% lower. Considering these material properties, the damage risk during bonding on complex bond pad layouts can be predicted more realistically. This can be shown by results of real bond structures.

Introduction

In more than 87% of microelectronic devices, the electronic connectivity of the chip is realized by wire bonding using gold or copper wires with diameters between 18 µm and 32 µm [1]. Even though this technology is well-established since many decades, there are new trends in technology which increase damage risk during wire bonding and show a lack in understanding the process affected material properties of the bonding wires and their resulting effects. Figure 1 shows the principle of a standard thermosonic wire bond process. Here, a thin bonding wire is carried through a bond capillary tool, melted and re-solidified at its end (a). The formed free air ball (FAB) is pressed on the bond pad of the chip and by applying additional ultrasonic power a permanent joint is formed (b). By moving the capillary tool, a bond loop is formed and the second joint is realized by applying a bond force and ultrasonic power (c). After breaking the wire at the second joint (d), the next connection can be formed in the same way.

The actual driving forces in microelectronics are a size reduction in all dimensions and an increase in system complexity. Both factors also increase the demands on wire bond interconnection. Firstly, a reduction in bond pitch is desired, which leads to decreased wire and free air ball diameter. Because of the increased yield stresses, which can be necessary in very small wire diameters (18 μm and smaller), the loading situation in the bond pad during wire bonding can become critical, especially when bonding on state-of-the-art ICs containing mechanically sensitive low-K dielectric materials. Secondly, due to cost reduction, industry is going to replace gold wires by copper wires. But because of the higher amount of hardening, increased bonding forces are needed to achieve sufficient bond quality. This can also increase damage risks during bonding on structured bond pads. For design optimization of robust structured bond pads and for establishing of alternative wire bond materials, finite element simulations can support the development process. For this, it is necessary to know the actual material properties of the free air ball. Up to now, the free air ball properties are unknown. But hardness measurements clearly indicate that a free air ball is significantly softer than the unaffected wire [2].

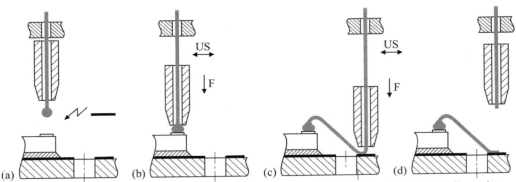

Figure 1: Principle of thermosonic ball wedge bonding after [3]: local melting of bonding wire (a); building of 1st contact by applying a load F and ultrasonic power US (b); forming of bonding loop and building of 2nd contact (c); breaking of the wire (d).

In this work we present results of a new test setup, the micro-compression test, for identifying the plastic hardening properties of free air balls. The flow curves of free air balls from three different wire materials (low doped gold, alloyed gold, copper) are determined by parameter identification using finite element simulation. We also demonstrate the effect of different material properties on unstructured bond pad layouts.

Determination of Hardening Behavior of Free Air Balls

The plastic hardening behavior of free air balls can be investigated using a new test setup called micro-compression test. Here, a free air ball is produced in a standard bond process, but not contacted on a chip. Instead, the wire is cut and the free air ball is placed on a flat diamond support. In this study we used free air balls with a diameter of 55 μm from standard bonding wires with 25 μm in diameter. But this methodology can also be applied on wires and free air balls with different geometries. The diamond support is fixed in the microindenter Shimadzu DUH202. By using a diamond flat punch, an increasing load is applied and the corresponding displacement is recorded, see Fig. 2. Mean curves with reduced data points are calculated from the measured force/displacement curves. A small correction of the force/displacement data is performed to consider the real point of contact by determining the point of highest slope in the force/displacement data and shifting the displacement by the intersection with the x-axis. The support compliance is also calculated from the slope of the unloading curve and considered in the force/displacement data.

Plastic material properties are calculated by parameter identification in combination with finite element simulations. The reduced displacement data is used for defining load steps in the finite element model in Abaqus 6.9 (Dassault Systèmes Simulia Corp., Providence, RI, USA) [4], see

Fig. 2. Plastic material properties for the simulation are defined in a parameterized Ramberg-Osgood hardening law [5]

$$\sigma_y = K_0 + K_y \, \varepsilon_p^{1/My}. \tag{1}$$

Here σ_y is the yield stress and ε_p is the equivalent plastic strain. The initial yield stress K_0 and the hardening parameters K_y and M_y are changed systematically by the optimization software optiSlang3.0 until the minimum of the error square sum between the force data from the experiment and the calculated data is achieved. As optimization strategy, an adaptive response surface methodology is used [6].

The hardening is assumed to be isotropic and applicable for finite strain simulations. The elastic properties are kept constant to achieve uniqueness in the optimization process. For gold free air balls a Young's modulus of $E = 77$ GPa and a Poisson's ratio of $v = 0.43$ are used. The elastic properties of the copper free air balls are chosen to be $E = 130$ GPa and $v = 0.34$. A friction coefficient of $\mu = 0.2$ is considered in the simulations [7].

Figure 2: Principle of micro-compression-test on free air balls (left). Deformed finite element model for identification of plastic material properties (right).

Stress/Strain Behavior Compared to Microstructure

The hardening behaviors of three different free air balls with a diameter of 55 µm were identified using the micro-compression test. The reduced data points and the corresponding standard deviations of the experimental force/displacement data are shown in Fig. 3.

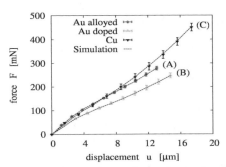
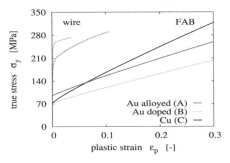

Figure 3: Comparison of experimental and simulated force/displacement curves for different FAB-materials (left). Identified flow curves compared to tensile test results of unprocessed wires (right).

It can be seen, that the deformation behavior of the alloyed gold FAB (A) and the copper FAB (B) are comparable in the first part of the loading curve. For deformations larger than 9 µm a higher force is needed for the copper FAB compared to the gold FAB. The doped gold FAB (B) is softer than the other FABs. For all materials, a very good agreement can be achieved in the optimization process.

The identified flow curves show significantly lower initial yield stresses of the free air balls compared to the unaffected wires, which were tested in tensile test experiments, see Fig. 3. The determined initial yield stress of the copper FAB and the doped gold FAB are similar, whereas the initial yield stress of the alloyed gold FAB is slightly higher. The hardening of the alloyed and doped gold FABs is similar, while hardening of the copper FAB is significantly higher.

The initial yield stresses correlate very well with the microstructure of the partially processed bonding wires. Lengthwise cross sections of additional non-tested free air balls were metallographically prepared. Final ion polishing was used for removing possible surface artifacts. The microstructure was analyzed in a scanning electron microscope by the electron backscatter diffraction (EBSD) method. The diffraction pattern of each scan point is used to determine the corresponding crystal orientation. Neighboring scan points with similar orientation can be clustered to grains. In Fig. 4 the microstructure of the partially processed free air balls in an inverse pole-figure color code can be seen. Here, the doped gold free air ball and the copper free air ball show very big grains and consequently low initial yield stresses. The grains of the alloyed gold free air ball are smaller, so that the initial yield stress has to be higher compared to the doped free air ball. The grains of the unaffected wires are very small, which is reflected in the much higher initial yield stresses of the unprocessed bonding wires.

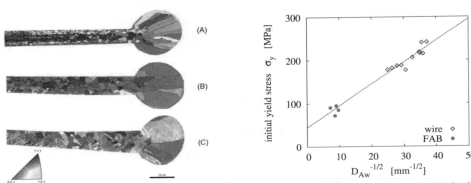

Figure 4: Microstructure of free air ball, heat affected zone and unaffected wire region (left) for an alloyed gold wire (A), doped gold wire (B) and a copper wire (C) shown in an inverse pole-figure color code. Hall-Petch plot for unprocessed bonding wires and free air balls (right).

For verification of the quantitative experimental results, the determined yield stresses of the gold free air balls and additional free air balls of other gold materials are compared to the Hall-Petch relation between grain size and initial yield stress determined in former investigations [7]. Here, the initial yield stresses of different unaffected gold bonding wires were determined by tensile test experiments. The mean grain size is calculated from EBSD measurements of up to five cross sections of each wire material. As mean grain diameter an equivalent diameter D_{Aw} is calculated from the area weighted expected grain area. In the Hall-Petch plot (σ_y - $1/\sqrt{D_{Aw}}$) the identified initial yield stresses of the FAB are in the range predicted from the values of the unprocessed bonding wires, see Fig. 4. So, the mean grain size is the dominating factor for defining initial yield stress and the presented methodology can be used for the determination of quantitative useful material properties for finite element simulations.

Loading Situation during Ball Bonding

For analyzing the stress situation and consequently the risk for crack initiation during bond process an axial-symmetric finite element model was build in Ansys 12.0.1 (Ansys, Inc., Canonsburg, PA, USA) [8], see Fig. 5. Pad structure, ball size and capillary geometry were parameterized so that different bond situations could be analyzed. Even though structured bond pads can also be investigated, we focused in this work on non-structured bond pads to analyze the effect of different FAB material properties. The influence of an elevated temperature of approximately 200°C during the wire bond process is regarded by lowering yield stress of gold and copper FAB by about 30%. This effect has been determined by comparing tensile tests of the unprocessed bonding wires at room temperature with tests at 200°C. Additional softening of the free air ball and additional mechanical loading due to ultrasonic energy are not simulated directly, but the joint formation is considered indirectly by an increased friction coefficient, like it is discussed in [9]. The bond capillary tool is considered as rigid body, while the bond pad is realized by a stack of oxides and a final aluminum layer. The oxides and the supporting silicon wafer are introduced as linear elastic material, whereas the aluminum is simulated as a bilinear elasto-plastic material. The material properties (Young's modulus and hardening parameters) were identified by nanoindentation experiments. Even though for bonding with copper wires higher bond forces are needed to achieve a good bond quality, we applied the same force on gold and copper FABs to compare the pure effect of FAB properties on the bond pad.

Comparing the 1st principle stress (σ_1) distribution in the critical oxide layer using gold and copper wires, significant changes can be observed, see Fig. 5. Regarding the bond simulation with a gold FAB, the middle of the contacted area is highly stressed, whereas for copper bonding additional stresses at the outer contact region appear. This stress situation will become even more critical, when applying the increased bond force, which is necessary. The determined highly stressed regions are in good agreement with real bond experiments which showed cracks initiated in these regions.

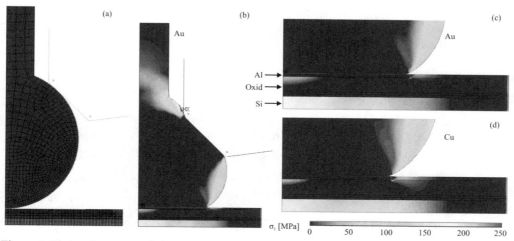

Figure 5: Finite element mesh for wire bonding simulation (a). Distribution of first principle stress during wire bonding with a 65 µm free air ball (b) of doped gold (c) and copper (d) at a bond force of 1 N and a friction coefficient of $\mu = 1$ (right).

The differences in stress distribution become even more evident when plotting the contact stress in wire direction. In Fig. 6, the evolution of contact stress during the load steps LS 1 to LS 6 show much higher stresses at the outer contact region when bonding with copper instead of gold.

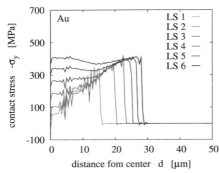 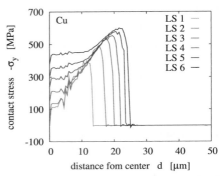

Figure 6: Contact stress between free air ball and bond pad at different load steps for gold (left) and copper (right) free air balls at a bond force of 1N and a friction coefficient of $\mu = 1$.

Additional simulations show that the stress distribution and the stress amplitude depend on the friction coefficient considered in the simulation. Therefore, for a quantitative analysis a meaningful suggestion of the friction coefficient is necessary. Additional experiments for identifying ultrasonic effects are still under investigation.

Summary

In this study we presented the results of a new developed micro-compression test for quantifying the hardening parameters of partially processed bonding wires. The determined initial yield stresses are in good agreement with the Hall-Petch relation determined on unprocessed bonding wires, so that the investigated material properties can be expected to be meaningful. Finite element simulations of a simplified bond process show a significant influence of the material properties of the free air ball on the stress distribution in the bond pad and consequently the risk for crack initiation. From these results it is concluded that replacing gold wires by copper wires can increase the damage risk during bonding, but a design optimization can be done by finite element simulations, like the one shown in this work.

References

[1] J. Eloy: *Overview of Packaging Technologies and Markets.* EMPC (2009).

[2] H. Knoll, J. Schischka, M. Petzold: *Bestimmung mechanischer Eigenschaften von Drahtbond-kontaktierungen mittels instrumentierter Eindruckprüfung.* Werkstoffprüfung (2004).

[3] W. Scheel: *Baugruppentechnologie der Elektronik.* Verlag Technik GmbH Berlin (1997).

[4] Abaqus: Theory Manual, Version 6.9. Dassault Systèmes Simulia Corp. (2009).

[5] J. Lemaitre, J. L. Chaboche: *Mechanics of Solid Materials.* Cambridge University Press (2002).

[6] Dynardo. optiSlang the optimizing structural language. Dynamic software and engineering GmbH (2008).

[7] C. Dresbach: *Ermittlung lokaler mechanischer Kennwerte mikroelektronischer Drahtkontak-tierungen.* PhD thesis, Martin-Luther-Universität Halle-Wittenberg (2010).

[8] Ansys. Ansys 12.0.1 documentation. Ansys, Inc. (2009).

[9] L. Zhang, V. Gumaste, A. Poddar, L. Nguyen, G. Schulze: J. Electron. Packag. Vol. 129 (2007), pp. 391.

Key Engineering Materials Vol. 478 (2011) pp 81-86
© (2011) Trans Tech Publications, Switzerland
doi:10.4028/www.scientific.net/KEM.478.81

Free Vibration Characteristics of Thermally Loaded Rectangular plates

Byoung-Hee Jeon[1, a], Hui-Won Kang[1,b] and Young-Shin Lee[2,c]

[1]Agency for Defence Development, Daejeon, Korea

[2] Corresponding Author, Department of Mechanical Design Egineering,

Chungnam National University, Daejeon, Korea

[a]jbh4506@add.re.kr, [b]jusin@add.re.kr, [c]leeys@cnu.ac.kr

Key words: Thermally induced vibration, Experimental modal analysis.

Abstract. This paper reports on experimental and finite element analysis of the free vibration analysis of three rectangular plates under thermal load. The materials of the three rectangular plates were steel, aluminum and stainless-steel, respectively. The dimension of the plate was 0.1 x 0.1 x 0.002 m. Halogen lamps were used for thermal loading. A PCS (Power Control System) electric control system and a scanning vibrometer (Poly Tech) for frequency response function's (FRF's) acquisition were used. The applied temperature conditions were from room temperature to 300°C in 50°C steps. The boundary condition was a free-free condition using bungee cord and one entire side of the plate was heated. ABAQUS was used for FEM analysis. At first, the heat transfer analysis was conducted for each temperature condition and the modal analysis afterwards. The FEM model was verified by comparing experiment and FEM analysis. The FEM model for the modal analysis of thermally loaded plates could be verified.

Introduction

The effect of temperature on the mechanics of solid bodies has highly increased because of rapid developments in space technology, high speed atmospheric flights and nuclear energy applications. Thermally induced vibration of plates and shells are of great interest in aircraft and machine designs and also in chemical, nuclear and astronautical engineering. The reason for this is that during the heating-up period of structures exposed to high intensity heat fluxes, the material properties undergo significant changes; consequently, the thermal effect on the modulus of elasticity of the material can affect the vibratory characteristics.

Many researchers have studied thermally induced vibration during the past several decades. Boley [1] and Boley and Barber [2] performed the first analytical investigation of thermally induced response of beams including inertia forces. They pointed out that this is a coupled problem of transient heat conduction and dynamic process of structures. Muge and Johnson [3] showed that the effects of thermal moment and thermal buckling on chaotic vibration of plates. Blandino and Thornton [4] showed that thermally induced vibrations of internally heated beams belong to the class of vibrations called self-sustaining oscillations. Kidawa [5] considers the problem of the transverse vibrations of a beam induced by a mobile heat source. The solution to the problem in analytical form is obtained by using the properties of the Green functions. Amabili [6] investigated large-amplitude (geometrically nonlinear) vibrations of rectangular plates subjected to radial harmonic excitation in the spectral neighborhood of the lowest resonances. Kong et al. [7] simulated the thermally-induced vibration phenomenon of a flexible thin boom structure of a spacecraft. The thermally-induced vibration was experimentally investigated at various thermal environments using a heat lamp. Ma and Lin [8] applied the amplitude fluctuation electronic speckle pattern interferometry (AF-ESPI) and laser Doppler vibrometer (LDV) optical techniques to investigate the transverse vibration characteristics of piezoceramic rectangular plates in resonance. Jeyaraj and coworkers [9] present numerical studies on the vibration and acoustic response characteristics of fiber-reinforced composite plates in thermal environment by considering the inherent material damping property of the composite material. Lee et al. [10] investigated by finite element analysis the thermal stress and vibration characteristics of an ATJ graphite disk under high temperature condition. The experiment under thermal heat was conducted using a CO_2 laser.

This paper describes thermally induced vibration characteristics of rectangular plates. The specimen's size is 0.1 x 0.1 x 0.002 m. The rectangular plates materials (Aluminum 6061, steel and stainless-steel) were used for the thermally induced vibration experiments in order to evaluate the thermal effect on the vibration characteristics. Finite element simulations were conducted and compared with experiments.

Experimental Procedure

Test specimen. The specimen used in the experiment was a rectangular plate. The materials of the rectangular plates were aluminum, steel and stainless-steel. The plate has a dimension of 0.1 x 0.1 x 0.002 m^3 as shown in Fig. 1.

Test configuration. The test configuration for this experiment consisted of three major subsystem as shown in Fig. 2. These included the heating system, the data acquisition system and the laser scanning vibrometer system. This paper intended to investigate the vibration characteristic of the specimen under thermal effects. The heating zone was one entire side of the rectangular plate. The free-free boundary condition was selected to minimize the complexity of the test setup. This type of boundary condition reduces the uncertainties associated with effects of heat conduction and thermally induced stress at the mounting frame interface. Fig. 3 shows thermocouple locations of the rectangular plate.

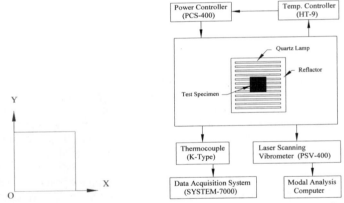

Fig. 1 Test specimen shape   Fig. 2 Test configuration of experiment

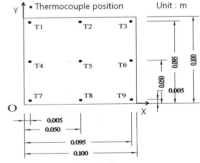

Fig. 3 Test specimen with heating zone and instrumentation locations

1) Heating system. The heating system used in this experiment was based on radiation-heating using quartz lamps. It consisted of 12 quartz lamps, a power controller and a temperature controller, as shown in Table 1. This system provided closed-loop temperature control of the rectangular plates. The specification of the heating system is shown in Table 1.

Table 1 Specification of heating system.

Unit	Specification
Quartz Lamp	- Power: 600 watts - Light length: 0.248 m - Voltage: 480 volts - Total length: 0.303 m
Power Controller	- Input: 480 volts (45-65 Hz) - Control: Input signal control - Cooling: Air cooling
Temperature Controller	- Input: 18 ch. analog - Output: 12 ch. analog, 4 ch. digital
Cooling Unit	- Air cooling system

2) Data acquisition system. For temperature measurements, there are thermocouples, RTD (Resistance Temperature Detector) and non-contact type thermometers available. We chose to use K-type thermocouples. To measure the temperature gradient, the nine thermocouples were attached as shown in Fig 3. The data sample rate was 10 Hz in the whole test and measured by System 7000 made by the Measurement Group (VISHAY, U.S.A.).

3) The vibration control system. Using a LDS 455 exciter, random vibrations were introduced to the rectangular plates and a Polytech Scanning Vibrometer (PSV-400) was used for data acquisition. The vibration control system used for the experiment operation, measurement and modal analysis was a PSV-400 [11].

Modal Test

The rectangular plate was uniformly heated from room temperature (25°C) to 300°C in 50°C steps on an entire side of the rectangular plate. The thermocouple readings were monitored to ensure that the rectangular plate was uniformly heated. Fig. 4 shows a photo of the experimental setup.

The measurement of the vibration characteristic of the rectangular plates followed. In total, 25 measurement points were evaluated. The sampling frequency band was 2.56 kHz, sampling time was 1.6 seconds. A frequency response function was averaged five times and the frequency resolution was 0.625 Hz. The total laser scanning time was approximately four minutes.

Vibration analysis

The vibration analysis was obtained by using the commercial finite element code ABAQUS [12]. The boundary conditions were the same as that of the actual test, which was uniformly heated from room temperature to 300°C in 50°C steps on an entire side of the rectangular plate. The analysis had two sequences: the first one is a heat transfer analysis and the second one is a modal analysis. Twenty-node, 3-D solid elements were used for the analysis and approximately 200,000 elements were used.

Fig. 4 Photo of experimental vibration test of thermally loaded rectangular plate

Table 2 Thermal properties of the rectangular plates [13]

Material	Young's Modulus (GPa)		Thermal Conductivity (W/m °C)	Specific Heat (J/kg °C)	Density (kg/m³)	Poisson's ratio
	Temp. (°C)	E				
Aluminum AL6061-T6	25.0	68.9	2163.4	1256.0	2712.5	0.33
	93.3	68.2				
	148.8	66.2				
	204.44	62.1				
	260.0	55.8				
	315.5	48.3				
Stainless-steel STS304	25.0	199.9	195.2	502.4	8027.1	0.27
	93.3	195.9				
	204.4	187.9				
	315.5	179.9				
Steel SM45C	25.0	213.7	311.7	460.5	8054.8	0.287
	93.3	209.4				
	204.4	203.0				
	315.5	193.4				

Results and Discussion

The verification and the validity of the finite element analysis are conducted through the comparison with the experimental results. Fig. 5 shows the mode shapes of the first four natural frequencies obtained from experiment and finite element analysis at 300°C. It can be seen that the experimental and computed mode shapes show a good agreement.

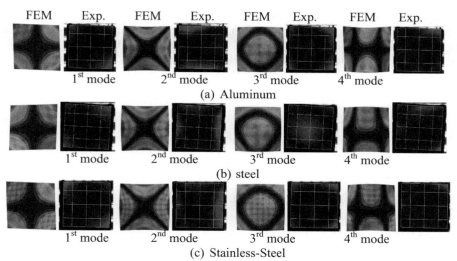

FEM   Exp.   FEM   Exp.   FEM   Exp.   FEM   Exp.

1st mode   2nd mode   3rd mode   4th mode

(a) Aluminum

1st mode   2nd mode   3rd mode   4th mode

(b) steel

1st mode   2nd mode   3rd mode   4th mode

(c) Stainless-Steel

Fig .5 Comparison of experimental and analytical mode shapes at 300°C

Fig. 6 shows the thermocouple data of the rectangular plates at 300°C. As shown in Fig. 6, the aluminum plate was uniformly heated from TC1 to TC9 but steel and stainless-steel plates reveal approximately a difference of 50°C from TC3 to TC8. Fig. 7 shows a comparison of finite element analysis and experimental frequencies for the rectangular plates heated at uniform temperature from room temperature to 300°C in 50°C steps. The trend shown by the data was that the frequency decreased as the temperature increased. The tendencies of the values from the two methods are similar within 5 % error range.

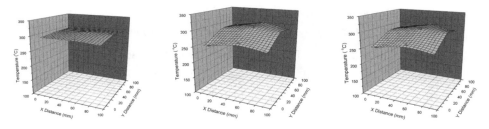

Fig. 6 Temperature distribution in the rectangular plates at 300 °C

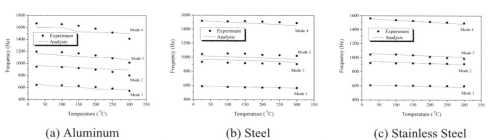

(a) Aluminum   (b) Steel   (c) Stainless Steel

Fig. 7 Comparison of experimental and analytical frequencies for the rectangular plates

Fig. 8 shows the decrease of the natural frequencies when changing the temperature from room temperature to elevated values. At 300°C, the first natural frequency decrease ratio of aluminum, steel and stain-less steel was 13.8 %, 1.7% and 3.7%, respectively. The natural frequency of the rectangular plate mode of aluminum showed the highest change.

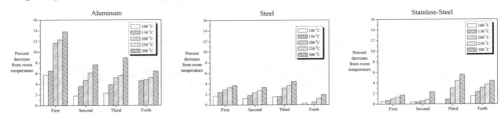

Fig. 8 Comparison of experimental frequencies changes

Conclusions

This paper reports modal experiments of rectangular plates under thermal loading when one entire side of the surface was heated from room temperature to 300°C in 50°C steps. Finite element analysis was conducted using the commercial software ABAQUS.

Comparisons between experiment and analysis showed excellent agreement on a variety of conditions. In all conditions, the natural frequencies were decreased during temperature increase. In the experiment of various thermal loading conditions, the first natural frequency decrease ratio of the aluminum plate revealed the largest change.

References

[1] B.A. Boley: Journal of Aeronautical Sciences Vol. 23 (1656), p. 179

[2] B.A. Boley and A.D. Barber: Journal of Applied Mechanics Vo. 24 (1957), p. 413

[3] Muge Fermen-Coker and G. E. Jonson: AIAA Journal Vol. 37 (1999), p. 1544

[4] J. R. Blandino and E. A. Thornton: Journal of Vibration and Acoustics Vol. 123 (2001), p. 67

[5] J. Kidawa-Kukla: Journal of Sound and Vibration Vol. 262 (2003), p.865

[6] M. Amanili: Computer and Structures Vol. 82 (2004), p. 2587

[7] Changduk Kong, Kyung-Won Oh, Hyun-Bun Park and Y.Sugiyama: Proceedings of SPIE Vol. 5649 (2005), p. 692

[8] Chien-Ching Ma and Hsien-Yang Lin: Journal of Sound and Vibration Vol. 286 (2005), p. 587

[9] P. Jeyaraj, N.Ganesan and C. Padmanabhan: Journal of Sound and Vibration Vol. 320 (2009), p. 322

[10] Young-Shin Lee and Jae-Hoon Kim et al.: International Journal of Modern Physics B Vol. 20 (2006), p. 4105

[11] User Guide for PolyTech V400M (2000)

[12] Dassautt Systems Simulia Corp.: *ABAQUS/standard User's Manual*, (Version 6.8-2) (2008)

[13] Department of Defense Handbook: *Metallic Materials and Elements for Aerospace Vehicle Structures* MIL-HDBK-5J Superseding MIL-HDBK-5H (2008)

Key Engineering Materials Vol. 478 (2011) pp 87-92
© (2011) Trans Tech Publications, Switzerland
doi:10.4028/www.scientific.net/KEM.478.87

Structure-Property Relationship of Burn Collagen Reinforcing Musculo-Skeletal Tissues

Yan Ling Yeo[1, a], Kheng Lim Goh[2,b], Liao Kin[1,c], Huijuan Wang[1,d],
Anne Listrat[3,e], Daniel Bechet[3,f]

[1]School of Chemical & Biomedical Engineering, Nanyang Technological University, Singapore

[2]School of Engineering, Monash University Malaysia, Selangor 41650, Malaysia.

[3]Institut National de la Recherche Agronomique, 63122 St Genes-Champanelle, France

[a]sherrill.yeo@gmail.com, [b]goh.kheng.lim@eng.monash.edu.my, [c]WANG0441@e.ntu.edu.sg, [d]anne.listrat@inra.fr, [e]daniel.bechet@inra.fr

Key words: Burn, Connective Tissues, Strength, Stiffness, Structure.

Abstract. An investigation has been conducted on burn ligaments, addressing the specific conditions in burn arising from dehydration and heating, and how these affect the structure-property relationship of collagen for reinforcing the tissue. Collagen fibres were isolated from a sheep's anterior cruciate ligament, i.e. our model for this study, and divided into six groups. The first group was designated as control; the second (D) group was dehydrated without exposure to elevated temperature. The remaining (DH) groups were dehydrated followed by heating at 120°C for 30 minutes, 2, 4 and 24 hours, respectively. Tensile test to rupture was carried out to derive the fibre modulus of elasticity (E), maximum stress (σ), strain at maximum stress (ε) and strain energy density to maximum stress (u). Electron micrographs of the ruptured ends reveal a mixed mode of fibril pull-out and rupture: fibril pull-out dominates in the control group but fibril rupture dominates increasingly in the other groups, i.e. with increasing exposure time to elevated temperature. Apart from ε, there is significant increase in E, σ and u in the D and DH groups with respect to the control group but there is no evidence of variation among the D and DH groups. The results of this study implicate (1) the removal of water in the hydrated proteoglycan-rich matrix, leading to shrinkages at micrometer length-scale during dehydration, and (2) the alteration of the collagen organisation arising from the underlying changes in the crystallinity and denaturation during heating, on the mechanical properties of burn collagen fibres.

Introduction

Over the years, many studies have been carried out to understand how thermal damage changes the biochemical nature [1] and ultra-structure of ECM [2,3] and how these insights were used to understand the alterations in the mechanical properties of skin [4]. This has led to significant advancement in surgical techniques for repairing burn skin, e.g. transplantation following debridement, after burn injury, enhancing the survival of the burn victim [5,6]. However, in cases where extensive full-thickness burn occurs, i.e. from 54°C to 148°C (categorises as third degree burn [6]), the heat affected zone extends beneath the skin into deeper connective tissues of the musculo-skeletal system such as ligaments [6]. Unfortunately little is known about how burn affects the mechanical integrity of these tissues. Here, we present a report describing our investigation on burn ligaments, to gain an understanding of how burn affects the ultra-structure of collagen which is responsible for maintenance of the tissue micromechanical properties.

Materials and Methods

Tissue preparation Collagen fibres were obtained from the anterior cruciate ligament (ACL) of a fresh, unfrozen sheep knee joint purchased at the local market. Of the caudolateral and craniomedial bundles which make up the ACL, only the the craniomedial bundle was used as it yields longer collagen fibres (hence easier to handle). Sixty fibres were teased off from the bundle using tweezers; these fibres were divided into six groups. The fibres were divided into six groups. One group acts as control; another group (designated as 'D') was dehydrated without exposure to elevated temperature (i.e. zero heating exposure duration). The remaining four groups (designated as 'DH') were dehydrated followed by heating at 120°C for 30 minutes, 2, 4 and 24 hours, respectively. For the D and DH groups, each fibre was air-dried for 24 hours. Thereafter, the DH group were placed in a vacuum oven (TVO-2, Cascade TEK), maintained at a pressure of 30 Hg. To investigate full-thickness thermal damage heating was carried out at 120°C, which is considered close to the upper limit temperature where skin burns. The fibres in the sixth group were designated as controls, which were kept hydrated in phosphate buffer saline solution (pH 7.4) before and during mechanical testing.

Structure-property testing A small-scale horizontal tensile rig, designed and built in-house, was used for mechanical tests [7]. Each fibre was mounted onto a template using cyanoacrylate adhesive; then grip plates were used to secure the fibre (at its ends) on the rig. The rig was placed onto the stage of an inverted microscope (TS-100, Nikon) for sample observation during the test. A displacement rate of 0.067 mm/s was applied to stretch the sample until the tissue ruptured [8,7]. The load-extension data were used to derive the stress-strain plot. The fibre stiffness (E), strength (σ), strain at maximum stress (ε) and toughness (u) were determined from stress-strain plots. Here, stress is defined as the ratio of the load to the nominal cross-sectional area of the sample; strain is the ratio of the change in the sample length to the length described by the grip-to-grip distance. By fitting an appropriate polynomial equation to the data points on the plot, from stress = 0 to the maximum stress (which is defined by σ), the point of inflexion was identified. The gradient at this point parameterised E [7]. From the area under the stress-strain curve, the strain energy density (u) up to σ was evaluated to determine the energy needed to cause fibre fracture. A field-emission scanning electron microscope (FESEM; JSM-6390LA, JEOL) was used to provide further details on the fracture morphology of the fibrils that made up the fibre. Here, specimens for FESEM imaging were coated with platinum, applied over 60 seconds at 20 mA, using an auto fine coater machine (JFC-1600, JEOL).

Statistical analysis One-way analysis of variance (ANOVA), complemented by Tukey's test, was carried out to test for evidence of a difference, i.e., variation in E, σ, ε and u among the different treatment groups. The null hypothesis of no difference in the mean values among the different age groups was tested against the alternative hypothesis. Significant difference was accepted if the p value was less than 0.05.

Results

Fig. 1 Light microscopy images of collagen fibres showing (A) the micrometer crimp patterns from a control specimen (×40), (B) morphology of a control specimen (×10) and (C) morphology of a D specimen (×10). Scale bar represents 100 μm.

When viewed under a light microscope, collagen fibres from the control group reveal wavy lines at varying interior depth in the relaxed state; this waviness is also known as the micrometer crimp

(Fig. 1A; [9]). These lines are highly paralleled, running continuously along the axis of the fibre (Fig. 1B). The hierarchical structure of collagen fibres implies that each of these lines are, in turn, made up of bundles of smaller fibrils [9]. In comparison, fibres from the D group, as well as DH groups, are more opaque, revealing fewer lines of fibril bundle (Fig. 1C); here we note that the bright and dark patches reflect the different degree of constructive and destructive reflection (in addition to the attenuation of light) characteristic of the undamaged and denatured collagen, respectively [10]. In addition, the gross shrivel running along the dehydrated fibre could be attributed to a combination of transverse distortion and axial shrinkage in the fibres.

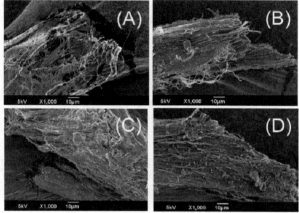

Fig. 2 Electron micrographs of collagen fibres from (A) control, (B) D, (C) 2-hour and (D) 24-hour DH groups.

Mechanical test results reveal that all fibres ruptured at the region in between the grip plates. FESEM micrographs of the fractured fibres reveal a mixed mode of failure attributed to fibril pull-out and fibril rupture (Fig. 2A to D). Presence of single fibrils with coiled ends, isolated from the bulk in the vicinity of the fracture site, suggests failure by fibril pull-out; a distinct cleaved edge at the fibre end indicates that fibrils around this edge have ruptured. In particular, it is observed that pull-out appears to dominate in the fractured fibres from the control group (Fig. 2A), as well as the dehydration group. However, a gradual decrease in the number of fibril pull-outs is observed in fibres from the 30-minute (Fig. 2B), 2-hour (Fig. 2C) 4-hour and 24-hour (Fig. 2D) DH groups.

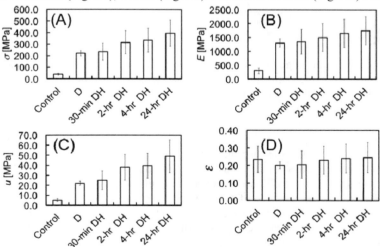

Fig. 3 Bar-charts of the mean ± SE of (A) σ, (B) E, (C) u and (D) ε versus the control, D and 30-minute, 2-hour, 4-hour and 24-hour DH groups. The vertical error bars are used to indicate the standard error.

From the results of ANOVA, it is observed that the p value of E is less than 0.05; we reject the null hypothesis in favour of the alternative that not all the mean value of E (Fig. 3) from the control, D and DH groups are equal. Similar results were also obtained for σ and u. However, the p value of ε is greater than 0.05; in this case we have not rejected the null hypothesis that the mean values of ε are the same. Tukey's test yields, for each mechanical parameter, five sets of multiple comparison confidence intervals (CI's). In the case of E, the mean value of the control group is different from those of the D group and the DH group because all CI's fall outside 0. However, among the D and the DH groups, the comparison reveals that none of the mean values of E are different because all CI's include 0. Similar results are also obtained for σ and u. (As for ε, Tukey's test shows that none of the mean values of ε are statistically different because all CI's include 0).

Discussion

From mechanical engineering point of view, mammalian connective tissues, such as skin, tendons and ligaments, are biological composites comprising collagen fibres, strong and stiff in tension, reinforcing a weak proteoglycan-rich (PG) gel-like extra-cellular matrix (ECM) [11]. Thus the collagen fibres in the skin are arranged in a mesh-like random manner, enabling the tissue to take up load acting on it in more than one direction; in tendons and ligaments, the collagen fibres are highly paralleled structures so load-bearing is only effective in one direction, i.e. along the fibre axis [11,12]. Unfortunately, collagen is susceptible to denaturation when heat is introduced [1,13]; in burn skin, the tissue dehydrates as water is also set free [4]. This underlies a transition process involving the transformation of the highly crystalline collagen to a random, gel-like state [1,4] (Fig. 4) and the alteration in the chemical bonds of collagen [14,15].

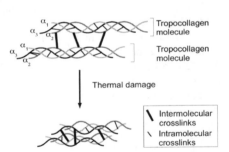

Fig. 4 Schematic of changes in crosslink density in collagen (adapted from Wright & Humphrey [1] and Xu & Lu [4]).

To the best of our knowledge this is the first report detailing how dehydration and heating affect the ultra-structure and biomechanical properties of collagen fibres of the ACL. Our results show that in the normal state, collagen fibril pull-out dominates in the fractured fibres. However, collagen fibril rupture dominates as the heating time increases. The mechanical test data reveals that only σ, E and u are altered as a result of dehydration and heating; ε was not affected by dehydration and heating. Previous report has indicated that the influences of dehydration and high temperature on the ultra-structural properties of tissues are significant when the heat exposure is long-term, i.e. over a period of several hours to days [2]. It is also interesting to note that the average stiffness within the large stretch-ratio regime (uni-axial tests) decreases rapidly as temperature increases from 37 to 80 °C [4]; the stress at large stretch-ratio of 1.8 also decreases rapidly with increase in temperature [4]. Here, our investigation on E and σ showed otherwise. Clearly, compare to a single collagen fibre, skin is an organ possessing a greater complexity of structural hierarchy and composition [4]. Thus, any increase in the stiffness and strength of collagen fibres embedded in burn skin would be offset by large-scale and extensive changes in the ground substances, i.e. removal of water molecule, around the collagen fibres and, consequently, the mechanical stiffness and strength of skin decrease.

It is important to note the different underlying mechanisms governing dehydration and heating. Dehydration addresses the removal of water molecules from the PG-rich matrix and collagen fibrils as the fibre shrinks [16]. Consequently, the interaction (arising mainly from van der Waals forces) between glycosaminoglycans (GAG's; on collagen-bound PGs) at adjacent fibrils increases. Heating addresses a structural phase change in collagen; Wess & Orgel [2] speculated that the key alteration involves the molecular tilt of collagen molecular chains in the gap region. The fundamental periodicity of collageneous tissue, i.e. 67.2 nm in the wet state, may be shorten to 65.1 nm by dehydration hence indicating the beginning of the collapse of the gap-overlap. However, heating yields a further structural phase change by reducing the periodicity. Wess & Orgel [2] noted that periodicity of 61.8 nm was observed at 24 hour; over long heating duration, the reduction in periodicity reflects tilting of chains over the 'gap' region. The structural phase change could be attributed to a change in the character of amino acids of the collagen chain associated with cross-linking [2]. These are the intermolecular bonds (or cross-links) formed between the carboxyl and amino groups on adjacent amino acid side chains [4]. There are two categories of cross-links; one category (known as divalent) links two collagen molecules whereas the other (known as trivalent) links three collagen molecules; Lepetit [15] pointed out that the latter category has a high resistant to degradation when heated while the former category is susceptible to heat and are destroyed when heated to 73 °C. The change in periodicity contributes partly to the overall shrinkage; it also implies that more energy is required to overcome the molecular tilt in the gap region and the remaining cross-links, in order to cause the fibril to stretch for a given deformation. The net effect of dehydration and heating must manifest in the increase in E, σ and u. However, we have also found that the values of E, σ and u among the D and DH groups were not significantly different, suggesting that the changes in the mechanical properties during dehydration are not appreciably offset by the effects due to heating.

In an elevated temperature environment, collagen molecules in a fibre undergoes the 'helix to coil' transition [14,15]. Assuming that the mechanical behaviour of collagen is governed by the theory of rubber-like elasticity, we present a simple argument to predict shrinkage at a local level for implicating changes in the underlying nature that is associated with inter and intra-molecular interactions (Fig. 1). According to the kinetic theory of elasticity [17], the total entropy changes per unit volume of ECM may be modelled by a thermal-mechanical relationship [14] which yields an expression for E as follows,

$$E \sim NRT \qquad\qquad\qquad (1)$$

where T is the temperature at which the mechanical test is carried out (i.e. 300 K), R (= 8.31 J/atom/K) is the universal gas constant, N is the number of moles of collagen chains in the network per unit volume. Eq. (1) predicts that shrinkage from dehydration and heating of the fibre yields an overall increase in N and correspondingly an increase in E. Next, we represent the number of moles of collagen chains in the network per unit volume for the control, D and DH groups by N_c, N_D and N_{DH}, respectively. A comparison of the four DH groups with the control group yields values of N_{DH}/N_c that fluctuate between 5.3 and 6.7; there is no appreciable trend with increasing treatment duration. For the D group, we find $N_D/N_c \sim 5.0$. This simple model implicates that both D and DH treatment yield an appreciable increase (five fold increase or more) in the number of moles of collagen chains in the network per unit volume. According to Lepetit [14], N is related to $\mu\varphi$, where μ is the number of cross-links per unit volume and φ is the cross-link functionality (defined as the number of chains meeting at the junction [17]). Thus μ decreases when the collagen fibre is heated since an increasing heat treatment would progressively destroy the cross-links (see earlier argument in this section). According to this relationship, i.e. $N \sim \mu\varphi$, we argue that the change in φ has to be greater than the corresponding change in μ so that the nett values for N from the D and DH groups are larger than that from the C group (hence the five-fold to six-fold increase as predicted by N_D/N_c and N_{DH}/N_c). In addition, between the DH versus D groups, we further argue that the change in φ is also much greater than the corresponding change in μ. Overall, this simple model implies that both D and DH treated tissues yield an appreciable change in the cross-link functionality.

To summarise, this study has shown that dehydration and heating alters the ultra-structural properties of the collagen fibres and this, in turn, increases σ, E and u. While it is not clear how these could be linked to deleterious effects the analysis implicates a fail-safe measure for collagen reinforcing the burn tissue. These findings suggest that any surgical repair of burn sites by transplantation or grafts should consider the possible gross mismatch in the micromechanical properties of fibres between the transplantation (or graft) and the burn sites and the underlying causes.

Acknowledgement

This project was funded by a research grant (AcRF 34/06). This manuscript is dedicated to Dr Jacques Lepetit in memory of his generosity for sharing his understanding of ECM with us.

References

[1] N.T. Wright, J.D. Humphrey: Ann. Rev. Biomed. Eng. Vol. 4 (2002), p. 109

[2] T.J. Wess and J.P. Orgel JP: Thermochimica Acta Vol. 365 (2000), p. 119

[3] G. Cox, P. Xu, C. Sheppard and J. Ramshaw: Proc. SPIE Vol. 4963 (2003), p. 32

[4] F. Xu and T.J. Lu: Adv. Appl. Mech. Vol. 43 (2008), p. 147

[5] M.J. Muller and D.N. Herndon: Lancet Vol. 343 (1994), p. 216

[6] S. MacNeil: Nature, Vol. 455 (2007), p. 874

[7] K.L. Goh, D.F. Holmes, K.E. Kadler, Y. Lu, P.P. Purslow and T.J. Wess: ASME J. Biomed. Eng. Vol. 130 (2008), 021011-1

[8] K.A. Derwin and L.J. Soslowsky: ASME J. Biomed. Eng. Vol. 21 (1999), p. 598

[9] A.K. Diamant, E. Baer, M. Litt, G.C. Arridge: Proc. Roy. Soc. Lond. B Vol. 180 (1972), p. 293

[10] M.C. Pierce, R.L. Sheridan, B.H. Park, B. Cense and J.F. deBoer: Burns, Vol. 30 (2004), p. 511

[11] K.L. Goh, J.R. Meakin, R.M. Aspden and D.W.L. Hukins: Proc. Roy. Soc. Lond. B Vol. 272 (2005), p. 1979

[12] K.L. Goh, J.R. Meakin, R.M. Aspden and D.W.L. Hukins: J. Theor. Biol. Vol. 245 (2007), p. 305

[13] K. Pietrucha: Intl. J. Biol. Macromol. Vol. 36 (2005), p. 299

[14] J. Lepetit: Meat Sci. Vol. 76 (2007), p. 147

[15] J. Lepetit: Meat Sci. Vol. 80 (2008), p. 960

[16] J. Lepetit, A. Grajales and R. Favier: Meat Sci. Vol. 54 (2000), Vol. 239

[17] J.E. Mark and B. Erman, *Rubberlike elasticity a molecular primer*, John Wiley and Sons, New York (1988)

Key Engineering Materials Vol. 478 (2011) pp 93-102
© (2011) Trans Tech Publications, Switzerland
doi:10.4028/www.scientific.net/KEM.478.93

Femur Design Parameters and Contact Stresses at UHMWPE Hip Joint Cup

H. Fouad[1, 2, a] and S.M. Darwish [3, b]

[1]Department of Applied Medical Science, RCC, King Saud University, P.O. Box: 28095- 11437 Riyadh Saudi Arabia

[2]Helwan University, Faculty of Engineering, Biomedical Engineering Dept. Egypt

[3]Department of Industrial Engineering, College of Eng., King Saud University, P.O. Box: 800-11421 Riyadh Saudi Arabia

[a]menhfefnew@hotmail.com, [b]darwish@ksu.edu.sa

Key words: FE, femur, Cup Dimensions, UHMWPE, FGM, SS, Ti, CoCrMo.

Abstract. The contact stress that occurs in the ultra-high molecular weight polyethylene (UHMWPE) hip joint cup has been shown to be correlated with the implant wear rate. The wear of the hip joint is considered as one of the main factors that affect the long term performance of the implant. The contact stress that occurs in the UHMWPE hip joint cup is affected by the implant dimensions and materials. In this study, four different femur materials and geometries were used to investigate the effects of femur design parameters on the resultant contact stress on the UHMWPE cup. The results of the finite element (FE) simulation show that the contact stresses at the UHMWPE cup decreases dramatically with increasing the femur diameter. Also the results indicated that the contact stresses on the UHMWPE cup decrease significantly when using functionally graded (FG) femur with low modulus of elasticity. The presence of metal backing results in a slight reduction in the UHMWPE cup contact stresses especially for small femurs. Finally, the presence of a gap between the UHMWPE cup and the femur results in a remarkable increase in the cup stress especially for a small femur. The hip joint femur dimensions and materials are thought to play an important role in the transition of load in the implant and should be taken into consideration during the design of the hip joint.

Introduction

The total hip joint arthroplasty has been recognized as a successful technique for the enhancement of the quality of patient life. The artificial hip joint arthroplasty involves the replacement of the femoral head by a ball made of metallic alloy or ceramic material, and the acetabulum by a polymeric hemispherical lining [1]. The long-term behaviour of the total hip joint replacement is dependent on obtaining a low wear rate within the hip joint polymeric cup [2-7]. The hip joint polymeric cup is usually made of UHMWPE due to its good mechanical properties and excellent biocompatibility [8-13]. In some designs, in order to stiffen up the UHMWPE cup, metal backing has been used. This also produces a more even distribution of contact stresses over the entire surface of the UHMWPE cup that is in contact with the femoral ball [14-16].

According to the clinical results, however, there still exist a lot of reasons to cause artificial hip joints failure. These include the infection, dislocation, stem fracture and loosening, etc. Among them, loosening due to wear of polymeric cup has been one of the main factors that affect the long-term stability of the total hip arthroplasty. It is believed that the production of wear debris may induce adverse tissue reaction that may lead to extensive bone loss around the implant and consequently osteolysis and implant loosening [7, 14]. Therefore, several attempts have been made to improve the wear properties of the polymeric cup with the aim of improving the long term performance of the total hip joint prostheses [4, 7-9].

It is known that the wear rate of a polymeric hip joint cup, which contributes to aseptic loosening, has been shown to correlate with the contact pressure on the polymeric cup. An increase of the contact pressure at the polymeric cup has shown to increase the cup wear rate leading to total hip joint loosening [17-20]. Past theoretical work focused upon that the femoral head diameter, material and ball/cup clearance were identified as the most important factors influencing the resultant contact pressure on the hip joint cup [21-24]. Therefore, over the past 50 years, different artificial hip joint designs have been demonstrated to modulate implant survival [25-27]. However, the combined effects of the hip joint design parameters on the resultant contact pressure on the polymeric cup are still unclear. For instance, the hip joint design parameters such as femur dimension and material, polymeric cup thickness and material, radial clearance between cup and ball and metal backing shell stiffness may modify the resultant contact pressure at the polymeric cup. The parameters that reduce the contact pressure on the polymeric cup may also reduce the cup wear rate and diminish the risk of hip joint loosening. Therefore, this study uses 3D finite element modeling in order to investigate the effect of femur head dimension, material and radial clearance between ball and cup at the same instance on the resultant contact pressure at the hip joint cup. Also, the effect of the presence of a metal backing shell on the UHMWPE contact pressure is studied. The main aim of this study is to reduce the contact stresses at the UHMWPE cup that is thought to play an important role in the long term clinical performance of the artificial hip joint prostheses.

Finite Element Model

The proposed finite element study was considered to highlight the effects of femur head dimension and material, presence of a metal backing shell and the clearance between cup and femur on the predicted contact stresses at the UHMWPE cup. In the present study, the 3D finite element models of the hip joint components were generated using the finite element code ANSYS v12. Four different femur head geometries are considered. The choices of femoral heads have expanded from 22 mm to include sizes up to 46 mm in diameter. The dimensions of femurs, UHMWPE cups and metal backing shell are tabulated in table 1. The dimensions of the femur head, UHMWPE cup and metal backing are similar to the standard sizes that are normally used in the clinic [28]. Figure 1 shows schematically the hip joint models, consisting of femur, UHMWPE cup, metal backing and finally the pelvis bone.

Table 1

Hip joint dimensions (mm)

Femur Head	UHMWPE Cup Inner Diameter	UHMWPE Cup Outer Diameter	Metal Backing Thickness
22	22, 22.1, 22.2	39	0, 3
28	28, 28.1 , 28.2	41	0, 3
32	32, 32.1, 32.2	51	0, 3
46	46, 46.1, 46.2	59	0, 3

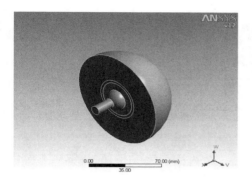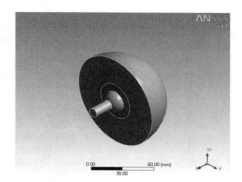

Figure 1 Hip joint model (a) metal backed and (b) non backed design

In the first model that is shown in Figure 1a, the artificial hip joint contains the pelvic bone, the femur with different materials and dimensions and their corresponding UHMWPE cups. The second model is similar to the first model except that a metal backing shell covers the UHMWPE cup as shown in Figure 1b. For all models, a radial clearance of 0 mm, 0.1 mm and 0.2 mm between the femurs and UHMWPE cups have been taken into consideration. The dimensional geometries of femurs, UHMWPE cups, bone, and metal backing shell are all constructed with CATIA software V5R19 and then imported to the ANSYS code as IGES files. A 3-D 20 node solid element (tetrahedron Solid 95) is chosen for modeling the hip joint assembly. This element is defined by 20 nodes having three degree of freedom at each node. This element has quadratic displacement behaviour and is well suited to model irregular meshes.

Material Properties

four different materials are used in the present finite element simulation: titanium alloy (Ti 6AL 4V), cobalt chromium (Co Cr Mo), stainless steel (SS) and Function Graded Material (FGM) which are used to simulate metallic femur due to their high strength and sufficient biocompatibility in clinical conditions.

Functionally graded material (FGM) may be characterized by the variation in composition and structure gradually over volume, resulting in corresponding changes in the properties of the material. The materials can be designed for specific function and applications. There are many areas of application for FGM. The concept is to make a composite material by varying the microstructure from one material to another material with a specific gradient. This enables the material to have the best of both materials. If it is for thermal, or corrosive resistance or malleability and toughness both strengths of the material may be used to avoid corrosion, fatigue, fracture and stress corrosion ,
UHMWPE is selected to represent the cup material due to its relatively good wear resistance while SS is used also as the metal backing shell material due to its high strength. Finally, the pelvis which is represent as a cortical bone. The materials of the hip joint components are assumed to be homogenous, isotropic and linearly elastic. The values of elastic modulus and Poisson's ratio of the hip joint materials are summarized in table 2 [21, 22, and 27]. The FG material is assumed to have an elastic modulus of 110 GPa at the core of the femur and decreases linearly to 50 GPa at the outer

surface of the femur head. The FG material is assumed to have a constant Poisson's ratio of 0.3. The femur is assumed to be rigid since its elastic modulus equals from 40 to 200 times that of the cup material.

Table 2

Hip joint material properties

Material	Elastic Modulus GPa	Poisson's Ratio
Titanium alloy	110	0.3
Cobalt Chromium Alloy	230	0.3
FG Material	Changes linearly from (50 to 110)	0.3
Cortical Bone	17	0.3
SS	210	0.3
UHMWPE	1.2	0.4

Application of Loads and Constrains

The hip joint model is fixed superiorly at the ilium and a fixed load of 3 kN, which corresponds to 3-6 times body weight, is applied at the femur neck as shown in Figure 2. This resultant load is based on the assumption that the body weight is 70 kg. The other initial conditions like sex, age, activity, etc. are neglected [22]. The contact interface between UHMWPE cup, metal backing, shell and pelvic bone is represented by completely bonded surfaces. On the other hand, the interface between the femur and the UHMWPE cup is simulated as a frictionless contact.

Figure 2 loading and boundary conditions of the design

Results and Discussions

Effect of Femur Diameter and Material

It is known that the short and long term performance of the total hip joint replacement is dependent on obtaining optimal stress distributions within the implant. The distribution of stresses at the hip joint is mainly related to the structure, dimension and material of the implant. The present research focused on investigating the effects of femur dimensions, material, presence of metal backing and clearance between femur and UHMWPE cup on the von Mises stress at the UHMWPE cup at static loading conditions.

The distribution of the maximum stress on the UHMWPE cup for different femur diameters and materials is shown in Figure 3. This figure shows the variation of the maximum von Mises stress at the UHMWPE cup with different femur geometries and materials. From this figure it can be remarked that the maximum von Mises stress on the UHMWPE cup decreases significantly with increasing the femur diameter up to 32 mm femur. After that, the reduction in cup stress changes slightly with increasing the femur diameter up to 46 mm. For the CoCrMo femur, the stress at the cup decreases by 60% when a femur of 32 mm diameter is used instead of 22 mm femur. Also, for FG femur, the stress at the cup decrease by

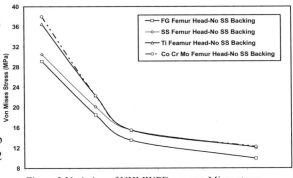

Figure 3 Variation of UHMWPE cup von Mises stress with femur diameter for different femur materials

54% when a femur of 32mm diameter is used instead of 22 mm femur. The significant reduction in UHMWPE cup stress due to using of large femur diameter can be referred to the increase in the contact area between the femur and the cup. However, the larger contact area between the cup and head induced lower contact pressure at the cup.

For a 22 mm femur, the values of maximum von Mises stress on the UHMWPE cup are 38 MPa, 36.5 MPa, 30.5 MPa and 29.1 MPa for CoCrMo, SS, Ti and FG femurs, respectively. These values are higher than the yield strength of the UHMWPE material [28]. The presence of such higher stress zones in the UHMWPE cup will result in an increase in the cup wear rate, which contributes to aspect loosening. For a 32 mm femur, the maximum values of von Mises stress in the UHMWPE cup are 15.5 MPa for CoCrMo, SS and Ti femurs, and 13.5MPa for FG femur. In this case, the values of the resultant Von Mises stresses in the UHMWPE cup are lower than its yield strength. This reduction in the contact stresses in the UHMWPE may lead to reduction in the material wear rate and then improve the short and long term performance of the hip joint implant [17-20]. For a 42 mm femur, the maximum von Mises stresses at the UHMWPE cup decrease by 21% for CoCrMo, SS and Ti femurs when compared with 32 mm femur. Also, the maximum von Mises stresses at the UHMWPE cup decrease by 27% for a FG femur when compared with a 32 mm femur.

The effects of femur material on the resultant von Mises stresses at the UHMWPE cup are also shown in Figure 3. This figure indicates that for a 22 mm femur, the resultant von Mises stresses on the UHMWPE cup decrease by 4%, 20% and 24% when SS, Ti and FG femurs are used respectively instead of CoCrMo femur of these materials. This reduction can be referred to the large variation in the femurs Young's modulus. According to Figure 3, it can be found that for the femurs of greater modulus of elasticity, the resultant von Mises stress at the UHMWPE cup is higher than that for the low modulus femurs. However, the FG femur with modulus equal to 50 GPa at the outer layer can be deformed more than the CoCrMo and SS femurs that have a modulus of about 220 GPa.

Effect of Metal Backing

In order to stiffen up the UHMWPE cup, a metal backing has been used to cover the polymeric cup. This metal backing can assist in avoiding the loosening of the artificial acetabulum that may be caused by the creep of the UHMWPE layer. This metal backing also results in a more stress homogeneous distribution over the entire surface of the UHMWPE cup. The distribution of these stresses reduces the total stress on the UHMWPE cup and improves the implant performance.

Figure 4(a-d) shows the variation of the resultant von Mises stress at the UHMWPE cup as a function of the femur diameter for metal backed and non backed implants. The results indicate that the metal backing results in a slight reduction in the UHMWPE cup von Mises stress up to femur diameter of 28 mm for all the femur materials. For the implants with a femur diameter higher than 28 mm, the resultant contact stress at the UHMWPE cup is nearly unchanged due to the presence of 3 mm SS metal backing. However, the presence of metal backing results in a uniform distribution of von Mises stresses at the UHMWPE cup. The unremarkable effects of the presence of metal backing on the UHMWPE von Mises stresses for the implants with a femur diameter higher than 28 mm can be referred to that at this case, the UHMEPE cup contact area is large enough to carry the implant load.

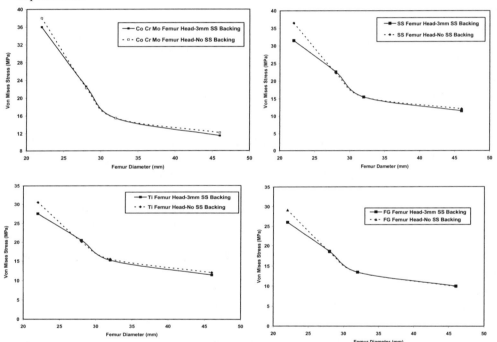

Figure 4 Variation of UHMWPE cup von Mises stress with femur diameter for different femur materials for SS metal backed and non metal backed designs

Effect of clearance

It is known that the radial clearance between the femur and cup results in a reduction for both wear rate and fraction coefficient in the hip implant. Therefore, many hip joint designs include a radial clearance between the femur and the cup [17, 30]. Figure 5(a-d) shows the effects of the presence of a gap between the UHMWPE cup and the femur on the resultant von Mises stress on the cup

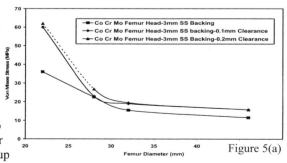

Figure 5(a)

for different femur dimensions and materials. For a CoCrMo femur with a 22 mm diameter, the cup stress increases from 36 MPa to 62 MPa due to the presence of a 0.2 mm gap. These values decrease to 19.5 MPa and 15.5 MPa when using a CoCrMo femur with a 32 mm diameter.

Figure 5b shows the variation of UHMWPE von Mises stress for SS femurs in the presence of a gap between femur and cup. Again, the cup von Mises stress increases by 48% due to the presence of a 0.2 mm gap for a 22 mm femur. This value reaches 20% for a 32 mm femur.

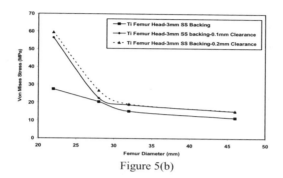

Figure 5(b)

Figure 5(c-d) shows that the Ti and FG femurs have also similar trends as these of the CoCrMo and SS femus. The von Mises stress increases due to the presence of a gap especially for small femurs dimensions. For all femurs that start from 32 mm diameter, the presence of the gap increases the UHMWPE cup von Mises stress by a value of about 20% for all femur dimension and materials. The increase of UHMWPE cup Von Mises stress due to the presence of a gap can be regarded to the reduction of the UHMWPE contact area that carries the joint load and hence the peak contact von Mises stresses increase.

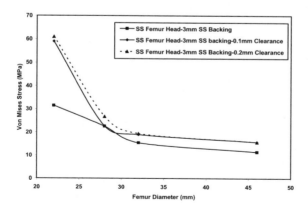

Figure 5 (c)

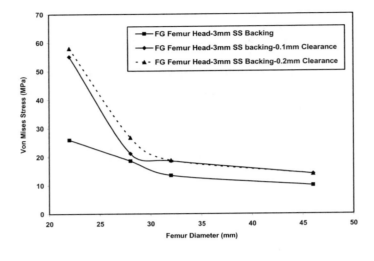

Figure 5 (d)

Figure 5 Variation of UHMWPE cup von Mises stress with femur diameter for different femur materials for metal backed implant with different value of clearance between the femur and cup

Stresses at Bone

The relation between the resultant stress at the bone and femur dimension and material is shown in Figure 6. From these results, it can be remarked that the stress at the bone decreases with a increase in the femur diameter due to the change in contact area. Also, the results show that the FG femur results in low stress at the bone especially for large femur diameters. The presence of metal backing also results in low stress at the bone especially for a small femur dimensios. The reduction in bone stress due to the presence of metal backing can be referred to the fact that the metal backing carries a part of the
load that is transmitted from the UHMWPE cup to the bone. Generally, for all femur materials and dimensions, the stress at the bone has a value lower than its yield point [31].

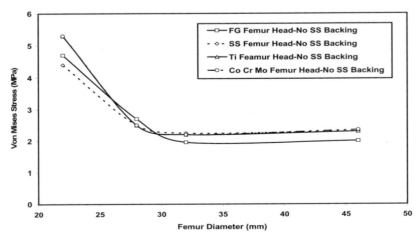

Figure 6(a)

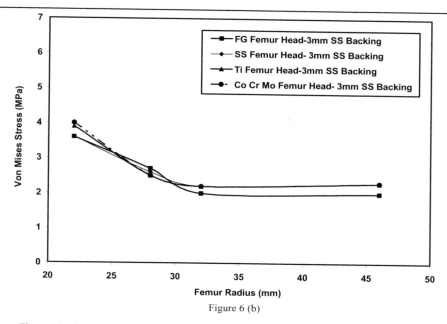

Figure 6 (b)

Figure 6 Variation of bone von Mises stress with femur diameter for different femur materials for SS metal backed and non metal backed implants

Conclusion

In the present study, the Finite Element results showed that the femur dimension and material, and the presence of radial clearance between the cup and the femur have significant effects on the resultant von Mises stress at the polymeric cup. Using a FG material as a femur instead of CoCrMo results in a reduction in the UHMWPE cup von Mises stress of about 36% for the metal backed implant. Also, Using a large femur dimension results in a significant change in the cup stresses. The using of a femur with a 32 mm diameter instead of a 22 mm femur results in a reduction of the UHMWPE cup stress by 57%, 51%, 44 and 48% for CoCrMo , SS, Ti and FG femurs respectively. The Finite element results also indicate that the metal backing results in lower stress at the UHMWPE cup only for small femur dimensions and generally gives better stress distribution on the implant. The presence of a radial clearance results in a significant increase in the stress at the UHMWPE cup especially for small femur dimensions. Generally, the hip joint femur dimensions and materials are thought to play an important in the transmission of load in the implant and should be taken into consideration during the design of the hip joint.

References

[1] S.H. Teoh,W.H .Chan and R. Thampuran: Journal of Biomechanics Vol. 35 (2002), p. 323

[2] S.Vesa and S.Ming: Wear Vol. 268 (2010), p. 617

[3] A. Unsworth, S. C. Scholes, S.L. Smith,A.P.D. Elfick and H.A. Ash : Tribology and Interface Engineering Series Vol. 38 (2000), p. 195

[4] L.V. Wilches, J. A. Uribe and A. Toro: Wear Vol. 265 (2008), p. 143

[5] T. Ilchmann, M. Reimold and W.Müller-Schauenburg: A simple access to geometrical concepts. Medical Engineering & Physics Vol. 30 (2008), p. 373

[6] B. Lowry, D. David, R. Scott Corpe, N. Satya, C. Michael and T. Irina: The Journal of Arthroplasty Vol. 23 (2008), p. 56

[7] S. Affatato , G. Bersaglia , M. Rocchi , P. Taddei , C. Fagnano and A.Toni: Biomaterials Vol. 26 (2005), p. 3259

[8] W. Qingliang, L. Jinlong and G. Shirong: Journal of Bionic Engineering Vol. 6 (2009), p. 378

[9] F. Jevan, A. Martin, B. Sonny, A. Seth Greenwald, H. David, P. Brad, R. Michael and P. Lisa: Biomaterials Vol. 30 (2009), p. 5572

[10] H. Fouad: Materials & Design Vol. 31 (2010), p.1117

[11] A-HI. Mourad, H. Fouad and E. Rabeh: Materials & Design Vol. 30 (2009), p. 4112

[12] H. Fouad, A-HI. Mourad and D. C. Barton: Polymer Testing Vol. 24 (2005), p. 549

[13] H. Fouad, A-HI. Mourad and D.C. Barton: Plast Rubber Compos Vol. 37 (2008), p. 346

[14] S. Griza, A.N. Cê, E.P. Silva, F. Bertoni, A. Reguly and T.R. Strohaecker: Engineering Failure Analysis Vol. 16 (2009), p. 2036

[15] C.W. Ray, J.J. Joshua, A. Barrington and E.R. Harry: The Journal of Arthroplasty Vol. 20 (2005), p. 914

[16] S.C. Frank, E.D.C. Paul, A.K. Ashay, F.L. Jen, H.F. Victor, A.S. Steven and D.Z. Joseph: The Journal of Arthroplasty Vol. 13 (1998), p. 867

[17] R.K. Korhonen, A. Koistinen , Y.T. Konttinen , S.S. Santavirta and R. Lappalainen: BioMedical Engineering Online Vol. 4 (2005), p. 32

[18] E. Rixrath, S. Wendling-Mansuy, X. Flecher, P. Chabrand and N. Argenson: Journal of Biomechanics Vol. 41 (2008), p. 1137

[19] T. Bertram, H. Anton, K. Johan, K. Veronika, F. Gunnar, V. Nico and D. Ron: Journal of Biomechanics Vol. 41 (2008), p. 100

[20] P.S.M. Barbour , D.C. Barton and J. Fisher: Wear Vol. 181-183 (1995), p. 250

[21] J. Hai-bo: Journal of Bionic Engineering Vol. 4 (2007), p. 123

[22] B. David and G. Tarun: Materials & Design Vol. 29 (2008), p. 45

[23] S.D. Marianne, W. Luc, D. Siegfried and S. Kai-Uwe: Medical Engineering & Physics Vol. 30 (2008), p.1186

[24] L. Kang, A.L. Galvin, Z.M. Jin and J. Fisher: Proceedings of the Institution of Mechanical Engineers, Part H (Journal of Engineering in Medicine) Vol. 220- H1 (2006), p. 33

[25] G.B. John, K.D. Thomas, A.W. Paul and C.C. Ian: The Journal of Arthroplasty Vol. 23 (2008), p. 1090

[26] P.D.E. Alistair, M.H. Richard, M.P. Ian and U. Anthony: The Journal of Arthroplasty Vol. 13 (1998), p. 291

[27] S.M. Darwish and A.M. Al-Samhan: J. of Materials Science and Engineering Technology Vol. 40 (2009), p. 218

[28] K.M. Orhun, R.B. Charles, O'C. Daniel, S.P. Rebecca, M.E. Daniel, J. Murali and H.H. William: The Journal of Arthroplasty Vol. 16 (2001), p. 24

[29] H. Fouad: Materials and Design Vol. 31 (2010), p. 1117

[30] A. Wang, A. Essner and R. Klein: Proceedings of the Institution of Mechanical Engineers, Part H: Journal of Engineering in Medicine Vol. 215(H2) (2001), p. 133

[31] J.D. Currey: The Journal of Experimental Biology Vol. 202 (1999), p. 2495

Key Engineering Materials Vol. 478 (2011) pp 103-111
© (2011) Trans Tech Publications, Switzerland
doi:10.4028/www.scientific.net/KEM.478.103

Biomechanical Characterization of a Cervical Corporectomy using Porcine Specimens, following an Experimental Approach

L.H. Hernández-Gómez[1a], J.A. Beltrán-Fernández[1b], G. Urriolagoitia-Calderón[1c], A. González-Rebatú[2d], M. M. Galán Vera[1e], G. Urriolagoitia Sosa[1f]

[1]Instituto Politécnico Nacional. ESIME. Unidad Profesional Adolfo López Mateos, Edificio 5, 3er Piso. Colonia Lindavista. 07738, México, D. F. México.

[2]Hospital Regional ISSSTE 1° de Octubre, Av. Instituto Politécnico Nacional. Núm. 1669, Col. Magdalena de las Salinas, 07760, México.

[a]luishector56@hotmail.com, [b]jbeltranf@hotmail.com, [c]urrio332@hotmail.com, [d]janosclub@hotmail.com, [e]mmgave@hotmail.com, [f]guiurri@hotmail.com

Key words: Cervical plate, porcine vertebrae, displacements, corporectomy, bone graft.

Abstract. In this paper, the interaction among cervical vertebrae, a cervical plate and a bone graft implant, which is developed in a Corporectomy, is analyzed in an experimental form. In the case of specific damaged vertebra, its replacement is one of the alternative solutions. However, the displacement between the vertebral adjacent facets and the bone graft is a critical parameter which has to be evaluated in order to ensure the stability of the spine. Besides, it is advisable to make a precise evaluation of the structural integrity of the arrangement. For this study, porcine cervical vertebrae (C3-C5) were instrumented in order to replace a damaged C4 vertebra. This arrangement was tested under compression. The experimental observations were complemented with a numerical model. The displacements between the vertebral facets and the bone graft were measured. They are lower than 3 mm in order to develop stability in the spine. Besides, the proposed arrangement has structural integrity and the surgical procedure is simplified, as no wires are used.

Introduction

A damaged vertebra is removed, when it fails completely. Adjacent surfaces are prepared and a bone graft, previously conformed, is fixed. In a Corporectomy, it is necessary to include a cervical plate, and a wire is used on the posterior side of the spine. Besides, the patient has to use a collar, which supports and prevents movements of the damaged zone. During the therapy period, several X-Ray plates are taken in order to study the behavior of the bone graft, wire or cervical plate. If an adjustment is required, other surgical operations will be carried out. Reports indicate that a patient needs around 4 - 6 operations [1].

In fact, the structural integrity and the stability of rehabilitation arrangements, which are used in the treatment of damaged cervical vertebra, have attracted attention. Several proposals have been reported in the open literature. As an example, the results of Hakalo et al. [2] can be mentioned. They analyzed three arrangements: cage alone, cage with a plate and a plate cage. For this purpose, cervical porcine vertebrae were tested. They concluded that the use of plates is useful, because the arrangement is stiffer. The descent of the bottom observed was around 1.6 mm. On the other hand, when the case was only used, this parameter was 3.1 mm.

A static analysis of C3-C5 cervical section of a human spine was analyzed with the Finite Element Method [3]. It was proposed to avoid the use of wires. It was assumed that C4 was completely damaged and has to be replaced. Therefore, a bone graft was installed between the anterior side of C3 and C5. Besides, a cervical plate of 55 mm. was fixed at the same side with 4 expansive screws. The analysis was focused on the bone graft. Encouraging results were obtained. Structural integrity was observed and the displacements between the graft and the adjacent vertebrae were less than 3 mm. It is in accordance with the concept of spine stability after Müller [4].

The stability and mechanical behavior of the cervical plate of this arrangement was evaluated with a numerical model in [5]. The results showed that stresses in the elastic range on the plate and fixation screws were developed. Healthy bone conditions were considered and the results show that the integrity of the screw implant-vertebrae system is not compromised. In this paper is reported the experimental analysis of a cervical C3-C5 section of porcine specimens. The previous numerical observations were considered. The behavior of intact specimens is compared with those instrumented with a bone graft and cervical plate. The stability of this arrangement is evaluated.

Materials and Methods

Specimens were taken from Duroc-Jersey pigs, which were 18 months old. It is equivalent to human specimens which are 50-55 years old. The cervical porcine section C3-C5 was analyzed. Six intact specimens were prepared, and other six were instrumented, as is shown in Fig. 1. Regarding the instrumented specimens, the damaged C4 was replaced with a bone graft and a cervical plate (55 mm) made of a titanium alloy (Ti6A14V).

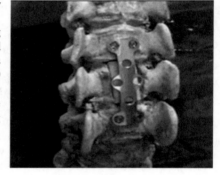

All the specimens were tested under compression, using clamps designed for this purpose. They were manufactured with aluminum. Cast plaster was used to fix the specimens on the clamps. Its compression strength is around 390 kg/cm^2 [5]. In this way, the displacement between the vertebral bodies and the clamps is restricted (Fig. 2). The mechanical properties of the main elements of the testing arrangement are shown in table 1.

Fig. 1. Porcine specimen with the bone graft
and a cervical plate

The yield stress of the cervical plate is 827 MPa [8] and the compression strength of the bone graft is 15 MPa [9]. Porcine specimens were used because there are geometrical and mechanical similarities with the human vertebrae in the range of C2-C7 [10]. Besides, the range of movements of a human and a porcine head, the structure of the ligaments, the stiffness and the orientation of the union faces are very similar.

Table 1. Mechanical properties of the elements of the testing arrangement

Element	Young´s modulus [GPa]	Poisson´s ratio	Reference
Cortical bone	12	0.2	[6]
Trabecular bone	466	0.3	[7]
Cervical plate and screws	102	0.3	[8]

Experimental Analysis

After the bone graft and the cervical plate have been attached on the specimens, a LVDT SDP-50C was installed with a linear range of measurement between 0 mm and 100 mm.

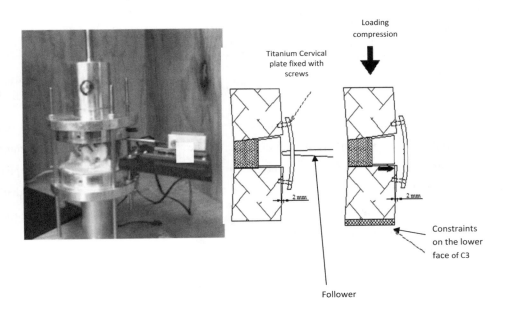

Fig. 2. Testing rig
a) Experimental rig b) Schematic draft of the bone graft and phidget

The follower of this transducer was on permanent contact with the lateral surfaces of the bone graft (Fig. 2). It is important to keep in mind that there was 2 mm space between the anterior surfaces of the C3 and C5 vertebrae and the lateral surface of the bone graft, in such way that the instruments can measure the resultant movement of the bottom face of the bone graft and the upper surface of C5.

The LVDT was connected to Phidget card (RS-6200). They communicated via a USB with an API (Interface Program Application), which is compatible with Visual Basic. All this arrangement was complemented with a linear potentiometer. All the instruments were mounted on a plate fixed to the lower clamp (Fig. 2). Besides, this arrangement was previously calibrated in order to identify its linear response range.

All the compression tests were carried on an Instron 8540 machine. The maximum compression load applied on the tests was 6374.5 N with a load speed of 1 mm/min. The testing temperature was 20°c and the data was collected every 2 s. The compression load was applied monotonically until failure. Three cases were studied. The first one corresponds to the head weight (35.31 N). In the second case, it is assumed that the average patient weight (637.5 N) is supported by those vertebrae, while in the last one; the compression load failure (6374.5 N) is applied on the vertebrae.

Numerical Analysis

A 3-D Scanner ZCorp 700 was used for this purpose. Beltrán-Fernández et al. [11] discussed the advantages and limitations of this procedure. In general terms, it is possible to digitalize the irregularities of the geometry with a high resolution (Fig. 3). The finite element mesh has 543362 tetrahedric elements and 891106 nodes. Special care was taken when assembling the shared nodes. In this way, a correct load transfer is developed. All the nodes on the bottom surface of C5 were fixed.

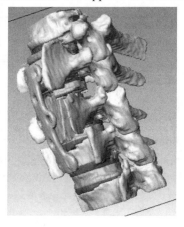

Fig. 3. Instrumented numerical cervical porcine specimen

Results

Experimental Results. The relationship of the applied compression load with the lateral movement of the vertebral body and the vertical movement of the crosshead of the testing machine is illustrated simultaneously in Fig. 4. The purpose is to get an idea of the influence of compliance over the testing arrangement, as C3-C5 section has some degree of flexibility. Also, note that the range of this graph is between the normal loading conditions (the region close to the origin) and extreme conditions (right side of the graph).

The vertebral bodies move in the transversal direction. As the load starts to grow almost monotonically, the initial displacements were registered until the specimen underwent an 800 N compression load. Bellow a load of 1 kN, such movement is less than 1 mm. When a 5 kN load was applied, the transversal lateral displacement was around 2.149 mm. However, the transversal displacement of cervical vertebrae of a patient in a rehabilitation process is always smaller. Also, these results show that the intact specimens have lateral movements lower than 3.5 mm, under normal loading conditions. All the tests continue until failure takes place. In this case, the lateral movement is around 4.5 mm. Regarding the vertical displacement of the crosshead, it is 5 mm when a 5 kN load is applied.

The results of the instrumented specimen are shown in Fig. 5. The graph was developed under the same considerations mentioned above. It can be observed that the load and the displacements grow monotonically until the initial break of one of the vertebra. This takes place when the load is around 2.45 kN.

Fig. 4. Relation between displacement and load on intact specimens.

It can be said that the bone graft is stable when the load range is between 0 and 2450 N. The maximum resultant displacement is 3 mm. When the maximum compression load (11200 N) is applied, the associated lateral displacement is between 6 and 8 mm. This is the case of specimens 2 and 4, respectively. In a rehabilitation process, damaged cervical vertebrae are never subjected under such compression load. Regarding the lateral displacements, they are lower than 3.5 mm, when the applied load is around 780 N.

Regarding the vertical displacement, it is around 11.5 mm at the break condition. The compliance of this testing arrangement is bigger than the case of the intact specimen.

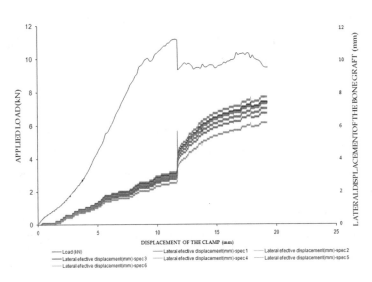

Fig. 5. Relation between displacement and load on instrumented specimens

Numerical Results. The experimental and numerical evaluations of the displacements are compared in table 2. In the first loading case, the experimental results show that no displacement is registered and the numerical evaluation gives a small figure. In the second loading case, the experimental displacement is bigger than the numerical value. These cases may be considered as the range of movements, which are observed in those patients, who are returning to their normal activities. On the other hand, the third case is an extreme situation. All these displacements take place in the opposite direction toward the medullar channel. Moreover, in the last loading condition, a vertebral failure is expected.

Table 2. Comparison of the numerical and experimental evaluation of the displacements between the bone graft and the vertebra.

Loading Case	Numerical evaluation [mm]	Experimental evaluation [mm]	Absolute difference [mm]
Weight of the head (35.31 N)	0.000439	0.0	0.000439
Average weight of a Mexican patient (637.5 N)	0.0042	0.01	0.0058
Maximum compression load over a vertebrae (6374.5 N)	0.0483	1.67	1.6217

Numerical results are shown below the experimental figures. It seems that the numerical model is stiffer and it is not taking into account some other compliance characteristics of the testing rig. This can be explained by the vertical movement of the crosshead of the testing machine, which is reported in the horizontal axis of Figs. 4 and 5. In all the cases, the range of displacements is bellow the criterion established in[4]. Therefore, the vertebral column is stable when it is instrumented with a cervical plate and a bone graft.

As the bone graft is made of a ceramic material, the maximum principal stress has to be evaluated in order to avoid its fragile fracture. When a 35.31 N compression load is applied, a 0.124 MPa maximum stress is developed. This parameter is increased up to 0.986 MPa when a 637.5 N compression load is applied. In an extreme condition (6374.5 N), the maximum principal stress is 9.867 MPa. In order to complement the analysis, the relation between the displacement of the bone graft and its maximum principal stress is shown in Fig. 6. The displacement increases as the load increases. Nonetheless, such displacements are small. This is in line with the experimental observations. Also, it is important to mention that in all the analyzed cases, the bone graft does not move toward the medular channel.

The maximum principal stress is bellow 15 MPa. In this way, the structural integrity of the bone graft is guarantee. In accordance with [12, 13], it is supposed that 60% of the load is taken by the cervical plate and the other 40% is carried by the bone graft. This load is transferred through the cervical plate screws and the bases of the bone graft. Clearly, the stiffness of the instrumented specimens have increased, for this reason it is possible to apply higher loads as 11200 N. However, a patient with this instrumentation never develops compression loads higher than 2450 N during the rehabilitation phase.

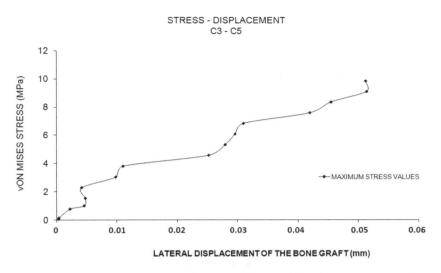

Fig. 6. Relation between the lateral bone graft displacement and its maximum principal stress.

Discussion of Results

The small displacements observed, when lower loads are applied, suggest that the use of a Philadelphia collar can be avoided, because the implant is stable and the patient makes careful movements. Nonetheless, the criterion of Allen and Ferguson [14] has to be considered in order to get a better understanding of the failure mechanism.

Once the plate is fixed to C3 and C5, there is a stress concentration. This depends on the torque applied to tight the screws and the mechanical quality of the bones. The last situation is important, when there is a certain level of decalcification. This situation has to be evaluated carefully in the case of elderly adults. Fig. 7 compares the numerical and experimental observations.

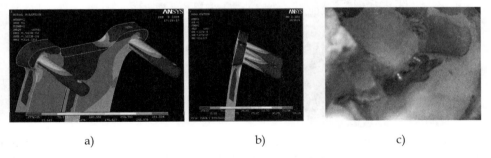

a)   b)   c)

Fig. 7. Numerical and experimental observations of the mechanical behaviour of the screws under compression loading. (a and b) numerical results, (c) Experimental results

An analysis of the resultant stress field is carried on when the maximum compression load is applied. It was observed in the experimental analysis that the apophysis was broken. This is in line with the numerical analysis, in which a stress concentration was obtained in the same area (Fig. 8a). Besides, the vertebral body was broken in three points, which corresponds to the place in which peak stresses are developed (Fig. 8b). The numerical results show that there is a uniform stress distribution among C3, C5 and the cervical plate. However, there is a stress concentration around the lateral face of the bone graft. Around the place in which the bone graft is supported, small physical effects over the surfaces are observed (Fig. 8c).

Clinical Point of View

One of the problems that have to be faced is the stability of the spine. A detailed evaluation has to be taken in order to avoid a wrong installation of the bone graft. Under this scenario, such bone graft can move in different directions. If it moves toward the medullar channel, tetraplegy can be caused.

In a correct instrumentation, stability takes place and the arrangement is stiff. As a result, the use of wires on the posterior side is avoided. Besides, the time of use of the Philadelphia collar is reduced up to two weeks, which is the minimum period in which a cicatrization of a suture is developed. Fusion of the vertebral body can be obtained without the permanent use of such collar and the number of operations is reduced, as adjustments of the wires are not required. This can be done with commercial shapes of bone graft can be used. When the bone graft is not of the correct size, there is column instability. Spaces among the elements of the instrumentation are developed and fatigue loads are generated, which will cause failure of the cervical plate or the screws.

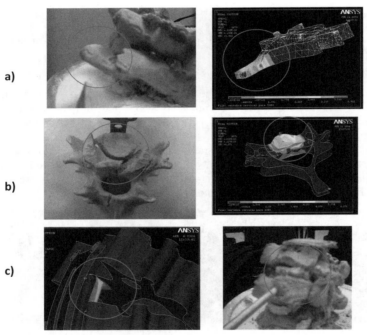

Fig. 8. Comparison of the points of failure observed experimentally and determine with numerical analysis. (a) Apophysis failure, (b) Peek stress points, (c) Damage around the base of the bone graft.

Injury mechanisms, as those discussed by Allen et al. [14], can be analyzed in the evaluation phase with the Finite element Method. Besides, the numerical analysis can be helpful in the determination of the correct geometrical parameters, which have to be in accordance with the patient characteristics (age, weight and bone quality, among others). This improves the required instrumentation and a better quality of life of the patient will take place.

Conclusions

Experimental observations show that the transverse displacements of the bone graft are lower than the limits established by Müller [4]. This takes place in loading conditions that are developed in the rehabilitation phase. The proposed instrumentation gives stability and stiffness of the vertebral column. It is considered that a patient with this sort of surgery can return to its normal activities in a short period. The trabecular tissue is regenerated over the surfaces of the bone graft and the adjacent vertebrae during the repose period. In accordance with these results, the use of wires on the posterior section of the cervical vertebrae can be avoided.

Acknowledgements

The support given by the Instituto Politécnico Nacional, COFAA, Hospital 1° de Octubre of ISSSTE and CONACyT for the development of this work is kindly acknowledged.

References

[1] L. T. Holly, D. F. Kelly, G. J. Counelis, T. Blinman, D. L. Mc Arthur and H. G. Cryer : Journal of Neurosurgery: Spine Vol. 96. No. 3 (2002), p. 285

[2] J. Hakalo, C. Pezowicz, J. Wronski, R. Bedzinski and M. Kasprowicz: Journal of Orthopaedic Surgery. Vol. 16. No.1 (2008), p. 9

[3] J. A. Beltrán-Fernández, L. H. Hernández-Gómez, R. G. Rodríguez-Cañizo, G. Urriolagoitia-Calderón, G. Urriolagoitia-Sosa, A. González-Revató and M. Dufoo-Olvera: Applied Mechanics and Materials Vols. 7-8, (2007), p. 101

[4] Müller, W.: *Manual of internal fixation.* 3rd ed, Científico-Médica (1992)

[5] J.A. Beltrán-Fernández, L.H.Hernández-Gómez, R.G. Rodríguez-Cañizo, E.A. Merchán-Cruz, G. Urriolagoitia-Calderón, A. González-Rebatú, M. Dufoo-Olvera and G. Urriolagoitia-Sosa: Applied Mechanics and Materials Vols. 13-14 (2008), p. 49

[6] J. A. Beltrán Fernández. Ph. D. Thesis. SEPI-ESIME Zacatenco, México (2005)

[7] C. M. T. Jeremy et, Si-Hoe Kuan Ming, E. L. K. Justin and H. T. Swee: Clinical Biomechanics Vol 21. No. 3 (2006), p. 235

[8] Ortosintese. Catalog of products (2006) Brasil

[9] D. C. Moore, M. W. Chapman and D. Manske: J. Orthop. Res. Vol. 5 (1987), p.356

[10] V. R. Yingling, J. P. Callaghan, S. M. McGill: J.of Spinal Disorders & Techniques Vol. 12. No. 5 (1999), p. 415

[11] J.A. Beltrán-Fernández, L.H. Hernández-Gómez, G. Urriolagoitia-Calderón, A. González-Rebatú and G. Urriolagoitia-Sosa: Applied Mechanics and Materials Vols. 24-25 (2010), p. 287

[12] T. Miura, M. M. Panjabi and P. A. Cripton: Spine Vol. 27. No. 1 (2002), p. 43

[13] T. Miura, M. M Panjabi, P. A. Cripton, in: Proceedings of the 2001 Cervical Spine Research Society. Rosemont, IL: CSRS, p. 55

[14] B. Allen Jr., R. L. Ferguson, T. R. Lehmann and R. P. O´Brien: Spines Vol. 7 (1982), p. 1

Keyword Index

Author Index

ABOUT THIS BOOK

People-Shaped is about creating a beautiful, new and positive world for all.

People-Shaped, Tales and Tricks of a Human Centred Designer is primarily aimed at leaders, practitioners and students of product, service and brand design.

But it is also for anyone else who is curious about learning about new ways to bring novel forms of experience into existence.

As such, it is directed at all people involved in making the "next new thing" – business innovators, entrepreneurs and business strategists too.

People-Shaped is a book about design, thinking and striving to be innovative in a human centered way. It offers a fresh and invigorating perspective on what design practice could, and should be in the 21st century.

It is an intentionally short book - hopefully something you can read in just a few hours.

Writing from a firsthand experience perspective, Matt Marsh shares ten case studies from over 30 years of practice, revealing the inner workings of what *really* happens on design innovation projects.

And as part of each of these case studies, he illustrates ten "tricks" he learnt along the way to address the challenges that he encountered.

These are ten tricks that every designer should know.

He begins the book describing the evolution of human centred design by covering the ethic behind it, where it came from, what's going on now, and what we can expect to confront next.

This is then followed with the ten "tales and tricks" that are alluded to in the title.

Appropriately, Matt Marsh finishes the book with a manifesto for change. In the 21st century, all business must be people-shaped – or die!

It is a generous book; honest, non-judgmental, brutally frank and very useful to boot!

The paperback version contains all the images and frameworks in full colour. The digital version is available only in black and white.

Matt is keen to receive your feedback about this book, and to hear your thoughts about human centred design.

So, if you do have a moment, please do share your thoughts about People-Shaped either directly with Matt, or leave a comment or review from wherever you got it.

You can contact Matt Marsh at Matt.Marsh@Firsthand Experience.net.

Thank you.

THANKS AND ACKNOWLEDGEMENTS

To Tania Rodrigues, for sticking with me, helping me to start this project, and for the hours of invaluable proof reading. Without her, there would simply be no point.

To Jane Fulton Suri, who gave me the break I needed right back in the beginning. Without her belief in me, everything would be nothing.

To Dodger Phillips, who through hours of text-doctoring helped me find my voice without leaving any footprints.

To Nick Durrant, Steve Heron, Kathleen Holman and Eddie Obeng for being so generous to allow me to share their ideas.

To James Alexander for being there whenever I needed help, giving me encouragement to give it all a try, and lending me the wisdom I needed to avoid disaster along the way.

To Mat Clum for ensuring that the photos and frameworks are legible.

To Kyle and Aidan, for the help on the cover design and for being my future.

To Jim and Charmian. Good job, and thank you!

And last, to all those who remember being part of these stories, I thank you all.

Matt Marsh

MAKING NEW STUFF? TRICKY, ISN'T IT.

Bain and Company surveyed 362 firms and their customers.

80% of the organisations believed that they were delivering a superior experience to their customers.

But when the customers were asked, only 8% said that the organisation was delivering a superior experience compared to their competitors.

Most companies assumed they were delivering what their customers wanted.

Usually, they were kidding themselves.

INDEX

Matt Marsh

Matt Marsh

PEOPLE SHAPED – SO, WHAT'S IN A NAME?

People-Shaped means shaped by people, for people.

It's a simple phrase with far reaching implications – especially for innovators, entrepreneurs, and designers. Innovation is, by definition, about bringing new forms of experience into existence - and this exposes those doing inventive things to all sorts of risk.

People-Shaped is a response to this challenge.

People-Shaped is about reorienting *what* we make and *how* we choose to make it, around championing people's real needs, desires and aspirations.

At its heart, People-Shaped works by enabling practical and early dialogues between the people who make new things and the people who will use them - thereby creating a win-win situation where everybody benefits from the results.

But "People-Shaped" is about more than just consultation. It goes beyond the empty promises and tired clichés of getting closer to your customer.

It builds on the ideas of the human centred innovation process, and the techniques of user centred design practice, to create something entirely new – an ethos about how to create value for people in a compassionate, empathetic and gratifying way.

As such, there is much satisfaction to be derived from adopting this People-Shaped approach.

After all, it is nice to know that the fundamental problem was correctly identified, that the development process was rich and rewarding for your colleagues, that the limits of what was thought possible were reached and perhaps exceeded, and that someone's investment in innovation was spent wisely.

Of course, it is most satisfying when you get to witness people appreciating your effort.

There is a paradox here. Because if you have genuinely been successful at being People-Shaped, then there should be nothing left that irritates or disappoints.

In fact, you are most successful at being People-Shaped, when your work is all but invisible to the end user. They will just be getting on with using, enjoying and telling other people about how good it is.

People-Shaped. Shaped by people. For people. To delight people.

But without costing the Earth.

Matt Marsh

IS THIS BOOK FOR ME?

"You can please some of the people all of the time, you can please all of the people some of the time, but you can't please all of the people all of the time."
John Lydgate
(British Poet – 1370 to 1451)

The goal of this book is to demystify human centred design, make it accessible, easy to adopt and apply, and to offer arguments to those who need to get permission from their managers and funders to do it.

This book is definitely not for everybody involved in what is loosely called design. So let's just lance this boil right away.

The word "design" is used to describe many types of creative endeavor – from "fast" fashion, to building a road or creating a completely new form of public service. And everything else, within and between.

In many ways DESIGN is an unhelpful term. I have worked on and off for fifteen years for various parts of the UK Government, and it has been an almost reoccurring obsession to try and "define" it. In some ways it is a laudable goal – how to "bottle it up" so it can be replicated, adopted and embedded in order to positively stimulate the UK economy.

But in my view, defining design has always been a hopeless task. There are so many approaches to creating value or "making stuff" – so it is entirely appropriate for different practices of design to use entirely different processes that befit a specific sector, industry type, or, kind of experience that is to be brought to life.

Here's an example of the limits of applying a human centered approach. While working at the BBC it was totally appropriate to utilise user centered creativity and design approaches to try and make their web and digital propositions more compelling; make shows easier and quicker to search and find; to make content more useful based on context such as location.

But I knew we had the lost the plot when we were asked to help develop new comedy and entertainment propositions. This requires an entirely different set of creative skills and type of genius that isn't based on understanding user needs.

Therefore, I believe that human centred design is an approach that is best applied to solving problems relating to product, service and brand design. Things that assume mass-production. It tends not to be a good approach for arts-based creative practices like writing a play, painting or composing a new song!

I strongly believe that one size rarely fits all needs. In fact, for me, this is one of the key tenets of adopting a human centered approach. As such, it is quite possible that you will find that only some parts of this book are relevant to you.

If so, that's fine. This isn't meant to be some kind of "take it all or leave it" dogma. Please take the bits that you find useful, build, refine and improve on the parts that seem to make sense - and then put the other bits away for another day.

This book is for people who are interested in how to bring novel and innovative products, services and brands to life in a human centred way.

It is for people who are tasked with launching the next new thing, the things that people haven't seen before. And, as mad as this might seem, it is for people who are interested in doing the revolutionary, rather than the evolutionary.

So, if your thing is tweaking the colour or shape, applying a template style sheet, or putting the same old gunk in a new bottle and calling it "game changing", then this book is probably not for you.

Never Give Up, Art Installation. The Boom Boom Club. PunchDrunk at The Old Vic Tunnels 2011. Authors photograph

This is for people who enjoy doing difficult stuff. By difficult, I mean things like:
- Creating a completely new product that didn't exist before (like Red Bull energy drinks did)
- Transforming an entrenched service category with a totally new and differentiated offer (like Apple iPhone did)
- Totally replacing a whole business sector with something much, much better (like Tesla cars is doing)

I'm not sure if there is an agreed definition of what human centred or user centred design means. Some people use the terms "user centred" and "human centred" interchangeably.

Contemporaries feel "human centred" implies taking a more holistic humanitarian perspective, while the term "user centred" infers a more transactional viewpoint. But I'm pretty relaxed about all of this. In the end, as long as practitioners are *thinking* about the person in the first place, I think we are heading in the right direction.

Now it's generally thought that human, or user, centred design is all about doing usability trials and measuring performance at the end of the process. These are important parts of the process, but they are certainly not the most important reasons for using human centred design approaches.

Focusing on users and their needs can be so much more helpful than that. It can tell you things like:
- What is the right development process to use?
- What is the best way to spend your innovation pounds and dollars?
- What is the right leadership approach to take?
And critically
- How can you mitigate the risk of ending-up making something that the world neither wants nor needs?

This book is divided into three parts.

Matt Marsh

The first chapter aims to give some useful context and background about the practice of human centred design. It covers why there is a pressing need for human centred design today, what the ethic behind human centred design is, and also attempts to provide some historical perspective.

The second chapter of the book shares ten stories from my involvement with human centred design projects. They aim to bring to life some of the challenges associated with being a human centred designer.

Each of these chapters consists of a different case study, and twinned with each case study is a mechanism – or trick - that I learnt on the job for solving the design problem described. Together, these are the tales and tricks I allude to in the title of this book.

The intention of sharing these tales and tricks is provide you, the reader, with (a) something to empathise with so you don't feel alone, and (b) a way that you can solve similar problems.

Within these chapters, I have selected ten case studies that address the tricky questions I so often get asked by my students, clients and colleagues.

Specifically:
- Why is getting it right for the user always tricky when you are creating something that the world hasn't seen before?
- Why does the human centred designer need to work early in the process to be most effective?
- Why is it critical to select the right research technique so that it matches the type of design challenge being undertaken?
- Why do different types of project need to be led in different ways?
- Why do you need to design a complete path to participation when creating novel services?
- Why does putting the user at the centre of thinking help a team coordinate it's thinking?

Finally, chapter three of the book is a manifesto for change. It serves to inspire and act as a call for action towards the adoption of human centred design practice in all business innovation programs.

Perhaps, one day, all forms of product, service and brand innovation will have successfully embedded human centred design practices so firmly into everyday development that this book and the manifesto will no longer needed.

Genuinely, I hope that happens sooner rather than later.

The vision? In the 21st century all business and organisations will be people-shaped. Bring it on!

Matt Marsh, June 2017

CHAPTER ONE – PEOPLE SHAPED: A TANGLED PATH

Matt Marsh

THE ETHIC

"If you think you can't make the world a better place with your work, at least make sure you don't make it worse."
Herman Hertzberger
(Dutch Architect – born 1932)

Since I first entered the world of innovation consulting, I have been bothered by the arbitrariness and thoughtlessness with which too many things are produced and brought to the market. I would even go as far as to describe much of what goes on within the design and innovation world as irresponsible.

I have encountered so many irresponsible innovation programs; not only in the sector of consumer goods and technology, but in architecture, and in advertising too. None of us are untainted.

As a profession, we need to use our intellectual resources differently. We as makers and designers need to be less wasteful. We have to move away from the throwaway habit. Things can, and must, last longer. They must be designed so that they can be reused.

But it is more than taking care of our environment. It means thinking about how we build our cities, and of course, the opportunities we cast for our fellow human beings now, and into the future.

If this is true, then today, the creators of original products, services and brands, have to work to a higher standard. And that higher standard is, in my view, about being human centred right from the earliest stages of design, through conceptualization, delivery and finally post-usage.

Authors own image. Montage.

If you are in broadcasting this human centred approach is frequently called being audience centred. In product design, the term is customer centred. In digital design, people speak of being experience centred. But, this human centred-ness is, right now, the essential oxygen of success when it comes to creating novel products, services and brands.

We desperately need to bring a new design era to life. And to embrace this era, the design practitioner must commit to two responsibilities. First, a willingness to genuinely empathise with the people you are designing for; their preferences, their idiosyncrasies, their attitudes, their behaviours, and of course, a willingness to understand their needs.

And second, a desire to understand what the whole customer journey (or as I prefer to call it, the path to participation) must be; from stimulating initial appeal, encouraging engagement and adoption, supporting use, and finally nurturing the creation of user advocates.

Matt Marsh

There are lots of things that an organisation *could* make, but what it is critical to know is what they *should* make before they get started on actually mass-producing and manufacturing it. Good design is often about knowing what to take away or omit, before you consider adding something new.

And knowing "what we should make" is best achieved if:
-       An unmet user need has been correctly identified
-       A coherent user experience across the whole customer journey has been created
-       And, the skills within your organisation have been correctly harnessed to make these happen.

For me, this is the future of design; to take responsibility, think ahead and anticipate the consequences of what we do. If we don't, I'm not sure what the future will hold for us.

Matt Marsh

A BRIEF HISTORY

"We should work on making our world understandable and not make it more confused."
Gunter Behnisch
(German Architect – 1922 to 2010)

It is my belief that most designers have always been – and always will be - fundamentally and intuitively interested in people and the idea of "human fit".

After all, its BETTER that clothes fit. Books ARE more useful if they are legible and readable. Advertisements work better if people CAN understand them. Tools MUST be suitable and effective. Designers know that in the end, it's people – of some sort – who will reap the benefit and enjoy their creative enterprises.

It's hard to argue that human centred design even existed during the early days of industrialisation of production – when humanity discovered mass markets for the first time.

At the mid-point of the 19th Century machines were designed to optimise production, with little or no thought given to the needs of the people who were using them. If you look at industrial machinery from the second half of the 19th Century, you will be amazed at how badly they were designed from a human centred perspective.

Controls are placed too far apart to be comfortable to use. Sightlines require people to lean into a machine's most dangerous parts. Let alone the noise, and filth that people were regularly exposed to. Thinking about people really wasn't part of the mix then!

It all began to change, at the beginning of the 20th Century with something called industrial psychology. And, ironically, as is so common in human centred design, it was primarily due to a military initiative (big sigh!).

During the First World War, there were things called munitions factories. They made bombs and other armaments.

Because of the TNT that they had to handle, it turned the women who worked in these munitions factories, and their unborn babies, literally yellow (no health and safety there then!). By the way, they were called "Canary Girls". Unbelievable, but true!

But the top brass were worried for another reason. The problem they identified was, what if someone dropped one of these munitions while on the production line? Well, the whole place would go up in a chain reaction.

Women workers with shells in Chilwell filling factory 1917. Nicholls Horace. Q 30040. Imperial War Museum

Matt Marsh

So someone started thinking about the design of work processes – how to design tasks to avoid errors, and especially catastrophic errors. As far as I know though, they still didn't care too much about the caustic environment and the health of the "canary girls".

Fast-forward another 50 years, and human centred design got another boost from the military, and this time, particularly the air forces. As the jet age emerged, pilots needed to do more things, faster, better and smarter. Something called human factors emerged, also known as ergonomics in the UK.

This new discipline was all about the study of work, and how products and equipment needs to fit the human, rather than the other way around. It was initially deployed in areas where there was potential for high consequence from errors – for example, in aeroplanes and other safety critical environments such as nuclear power stations.

It wasn't long before car designers and office furniture manufacturers adopted ergonomics and human factors principles to make their products safer, more comfortable and easier to use. It was largely viewed as a human science and many experiments were conducted to develop standards and metrics that aimed to improve human performance.

The next wave of human centeredness came in the late 1970's and 1980's when computing became a, erhm, consumer proposition. The problem was that these new fangled computer things hid all the working parts in software code. You couldn't see how a computer worked by just looking at it, and thinking, "oh, that flywheel turns the piston, that makes the car go along". It was all invisible.

And this meant people couldn't develop a conceptual model about how it all worked. And this made it hard to learn how to use. You needed a manual, to learn all sorts of commands that were written literally in an alien language, to get it to do anything. Boy, it was frustrating! And it made computers hard to sell too.

So computer engineers started to do some interesting things. They used metaphors and new ways of showing what the bits and bytes inside the computer were doing. They invented the graphical user interface at Xerox Park in Menlo Park, CA to show you what was going on.

They invented the desktop metaphor to help you understand what you were doing. You knew that in the real world you had a desktop, you had documents and you put them inside things called folders, and then those folders were stored inside a filing cabinet. And, if you wanted to throw something away, you put it something called a trashcan (well, in the US anyway).

What the graphical user interface did was replicate these real-world models in a digital environment. They re-introduced the idea of being able to "see" what you were doing, just like you could, in the old days, see mechanical linkages, and understand how cause and effect worked. Bingo!

This was called What You See Is What You Get or WYSIWYG. And the whole point was so that people didn't have to read all those tricky manuals and learn all those alien languages. People just had to do the same things that they did on their real desktop, and they could work a computer.

The buzzword for human centred designers at this time was trying to make things "intuitive" – you just knew what to do. And this was, and still is, a laudable goal for all human centred designers.

But what next? What does human centred mean for today and the future? Well, that's the next few sections in this chapter.

Matt Marsh

WHAT'S GOING ON?

"Think well to the end, consider the end first."
Leonardo da Vinci
(Sculptor, Painter and Inventor – 1452 to 1519)

Thanks to a democratisation of influence – mainly through the advent of social media - we now live in an era of unprecedented customer (or user) voice. As a person responsible for crafting and making new products, services and brands, this means you are in a "tight spot".

Now, if your design delivers a rubbish user experience, everyone knows about it more or less immediately.

Organisations of all types – corporates, charities, and governments - now have almost instant metrics about how well their new proposition is doing. They know what consumers are saying, what they are looking at, for how long and what their engagement is.

This is a tricky new reality for all of us - designers, marketers, engineers, etc. – who are tasked with spending the hard earned product or service innovation Dollars, Pounds, Won, Yen or Euro's of the organisations paying us to build new business propositions. After all, they are expecting us to do it in a responsible and effective way.

Gone are the days where you could you could simply invent a new technology, market the hell out of it, and assume that people will buy it. This approach, favoured for the last half of the 20th Century is frankly obsolete in this new digital age. Because if you make something that no one actually buys and loves - what is the point?

Unfortunately, when it comes to launching innovative products or services, there is rarely the chance to tweak things, and have a second crack at it. The money is spent, the brand goodwill is dissipated, and the well-informed and fickle consumer has already gone somewhere else. There is no second bite at the cherry.

A notable case study in getting it "wrong" was the HP TouchPad. According to Channel Insider (and others), HP spent $1.2 Billion to acquire Palm for their web Operating System to use on their HP tablet product range. Unfortunately, it was a product that just didn't take off.

Whether it was the apps, the storage, the WiFi connectivity, or the choice of services that came bundled with it, something didn't quite captivate the audience. Perhaps HP was just too late to the market and couldn't catch up with already well-established competitors.

Research record shot. Authors own photograph

Matt Marsh

None the less, just seven weeks after the launch of the HP TouchPad, HP unexpectedly gave up and ended development for good. This is a definitive "direct to landfill" innovation story.

As such, we are now part of a world where the making process must result not just in the creation of purchasers, but in the creation of positive end-user advocates as well. And by end-user advocates, I include not just people who are customers, but people who are partners and employees too.

Doesn't matter if your client is a loaded Silicon Valley behemoth, or a charity in a neglected community, or a start-up working out of their kitchen. They need us – all of us involved in bringing "the next new thing" to life - to make sure we get it right for all the different "users" first time around.

Now, when most people hear the words human centred, they typically think about the notion of usability. And that is OK. But this book aims to show a new way to think about the idea of being human centred.

And this new way doesn't mean shifting doing a few focus groups from the end of the process, to the beginning. This doesn't work – primarily because users generally don't know what they want next. They are still dealing with the vast array of choices they have right now. So asking them when you are at the beginning doesn't work. More on this later!

But what you can do is work to understand underlying consumer behaviours by putting people at the centre of your thinking, accurately identify what their unmet needs are, and rapidly prototype complete customer propositions, expose them to people and learn what works, and what doesn't.

So lets demystify this human centred way of doing things. Let's make it accessible, and demonstrate that it isn't rocket science. Let's see how adopting a human centered approach mitigates financial risk, protects the reputations of those who do the crafting and the funding, and stimulates more opportunities for creativity and innovation - all at the same time.

Bold claims! Stick with me – it's fun!

Matt Marsh

A NEW ERA

"Our prime purpose in this life is to help others. And if
you can't help them, at least don't hurt them."
Tenzin Gyatso
(The 14th Dalai Lama of Tibetan Buddhism)

Being human centered is not a new idea. But it is constantly evolving,
and it is as far as I'm concerned the best way of bringing complicated
and new stuff to life. Now we are in the Internet era – and human
centred design is morphing again.

And for human centred designers, in some ways it's getting more
complicated. We use a range of different devices to access information,
communication and entertainment - all integrated by web based "cloud"
services that we can't see, touch or fully comprehend. And by using
these services, we generate LOTS of personal data along the way.

I have a hunch that the next big battleground for human centred design
will surround the use of this personal data for profit. We have had a
preview of the kind of battle to expect– history tells us about the
behaviours of the railroad barons, followed by the steel barons, the oil
barons and then the media barons. By no means did everyone behave
badly - but some certainly did!

And I'm certainly not saying that all companies that trade in data are
bad. Far from it – there are some fine instances of where data is being
used to help people and, for example, work to eradicate poverty.

But the picture isn't clear. It is hard to tell who is behaving well - and
who isn't at the moment. Brand messaging clearly says one thing, but
the behaviours exhibited say something quite different. It's all
becoming rather confusing again.

When you look at how some isolated parts of Silicon Valley are behaving now, the last thing you could argue is that they are human centred, even though they promote the idea that they are. Arguably, they are the very opposite. They are wolves dressed up in human centred clothing. They equate making things convenient with being human centred.

Human centeredness is being appropriated by digitally enabled corporations and blurred to mean the same as customer centred. When an on-line store says they are customer centred, because they say that "the customer is king", that doesn't mean they are treating their staff correctly, using the planet's resources responsibly, or have even got humanities' best interests at heart.

If they steal your data, sell it on to people you don't even know, don't look after it properly or responsibly, then they aren't being human centred. Nor are they human centred if they use environmentally dubious distribution systems and, to add insult to injury, treat their workforce as little more than machines by tracking their employees by the second and offering them zero hours contracts with no job security.

Watch out – customer centred and human centred are not necessarily the same thing. You may have recoiled at the idea of Canary Girls in the 19th Century. But this lack of human centeredness is still the reality for many organisations today – it just looks different. Profit trumping people is BACK big time.

In December 2013, the German Deutsche Post AG tested a microdrones md4-1000 for delivery. 6 January 2014 by Frankhöffner This image is licensed under the Creative Commons Attribution-Share Alike 3.0 Unported license.

In fact, when it comes to dealing with new data based technologies and services, the buzzword of the moment is "disruptive" – as in "this technology is going to be totally disruptive".

What does this "being disruptive" mean for a human centred designer? Does it mean, "hooray, we've invented something new that the world actually needs"? It certainly used to mean this before 2006.

But today it seems to mean, hooray, we have put lots of people out of work. Or perhaps, hooray, we've catalysed social upheaval. Or more ominously, hooray, we've seduced people into being monitored, manipulated and digitally mugged.

I think we need to think about these things - carefully.

In some ways, disruptive is my least favourite term of the moment because it currently implies the opposite of positive invention and trying to make things better for people. Too often "disruption" seems to be subtext for how can we automate, and how can we the few, make more money for OURSELVES.

We still have a long way to go. And if this book creates just one more future convert to the human centred design cause, then my job is done.

Matt Marsh

A POLITICAL ACT ?

"I'm trying to find a way of working which reduces the number of layers of assholes between me and the public."
Tibor Kalman
(US Graphic Designer - 1949 to 1999)

I come across three predominant and typically toxic attitudes towards making novel products, service and brands all the time. They are;

(i)   The "new-ness" of the technology is placed at the centre of decision-making,

(ii)   Making the most money is placed at the centre of decision making, and

(iii)   Personal ego is placed at the centre of decision-making.

In natural conversation, it comes out something like this: "Are you asking me to ****ing focus group my idea?" "Just leave me alone and I'll show how it works later", or "I'm paying for it, so just do what I tell you".

Unfortunately, each of the above three quotes (these are real quotes I've heard more than once from some of the most celebrated designers and makers I've worked with) speak to a version of the world where makers are adopting a "let me build it, and the world will come" approach.

Authors own image. From People Shaped lecture in Krakow 2011

My problem with this approach is that it far too often results in something that pleases the individual maker, but rarely the end user.

And because it doesn't please the end user, it isn't adopted and then dies an ignominious death shortly after manufacture and launch. These are "designed direct to landfill" solutions.

And it's not an approach I like. It puts personal assumptions ahead of data and evidence. It puts the needs of the few and privileged ahead of the many and deserving. It places irresponsibility ahead of designed intent.

Apart from that, it is plain selfish and lazy. Creating things requires considerable resources to bring them to life. To state perhaps the obvious, making innovative products, services and brands takes a lot of people. These sorts of creative endeavor are notoriously complex and risky to pull off.

And apart from requiring large teams, they also usually require complicated and highly sophisticated fabrication and use up a lot of natural resources – things like, energy, mining raw materials, building factories, running data centres.

It is important not to forget, that making something that the world ends up <u>not</u> needing or wanting - is WASTE. Creating things that end up going straight to landfill - well, that bastardises the idea of positive creation.

So, if you are that sort of designer that worries about how we treat our planet, struggles with thinking about how you can work to best improve humanities' lot, is tormented by the possibility that we as makers have a responsibility to our fellow terrestrial occupants - then you are already thinking like a human centered designer.

People-shaped means designed for people, by people. It is as much an ethos as it is an approach or a process to create new value. It assumes that the role of the designer is to act with informed intent. Yes, it's for people who think that design is, gosh, a political act (that's a small "p" not a party political big "P").

This is the heart of people-shaped. You serve as a custodian for bringing a new product, service or brand to life. And that you can choose how you and the team go about it.

That means sometimes saying NO! This thing shouldn't come to life. That sometimes, the cost - ethically, socially, financially – just isn't worth it.

You can be part of the solution - or abdicate those responsibilities. That is what choosing to be a human centered designer forces you to confront.

As such, you won't be surprised if I share with you that the human centered designer is sometimes an unloved person. You get in the way of big egos and the person looking for the fast buck.

Your job is to ask the tough questions, seek out evidence, and help a complex and fast moving team make the right decisions. Human centered design is for people that think that designing and making new stuff is a craft that comes with great responsibility.

Now read on and hear some stories, some tales of human centred design challenges and the tricks I learned along the way to address them.

I hope you find them useful and that they provide you with the ammunition to change the way we think about creating value while we invent exciting and new products services and brands.

Onwards, my human centered brothers and sisters!

Matt Marsh

CHAPTER TWO – TALES AND TRICKS

Matt Marsh

DIRTY LAUNDRY

"Zero invites the imagination, but small numbers
invite questions about whether large numbers will
ever materialize."
Eric Ries
(Author of The Lean Start Up)

In the land of innovation, some people seem to take the words of US president John F Kennedy almost as a mantra - "we don't do these things because they are easy, but because they are hard".

Well Ok, if you are building the first rocket to take people to, and then back from the moon, and keep them alive too. But if you are tasked with making something for regular people, that's meant to make their lives easier, and that's meant to turn a profit too. Well, that needs a totally different approach (quite literally, it's not rocket science!).

In the mid-nineties I experienced for the first time what I have come to recognise as being a "technology-push project", a project defined by the idea of "we'll build it, and the world will come".

The concept seemed sound enough. Bring dry-cleaning into the American consumers home. De-Stink your jacket from cigarette smoke (you could still smoke in bars then!), spruce up your business clothes for the next days critical meeting, look sharp every Sunday (or Friday if you preferred).

The idea was to bring some home convenience to the chore of dealing with clothes that needed dry cleaning – in the same way that the home washing machine had liberated people from having to traipse down to the laundrette.

Design research record shot. Authors own photograph

The opportunity was to obviate the need of having to drop your special clothes off in the morning at a dry cleaner's, then pick them up at some point later on – and not have to shell out a pile of cash in the process. But could this really be delivered in a practical home appliance?

So, by placing people at the centre of our thinking, we set out to determine whether it was even possible to engineer this idea, and if it was, what exactly would the device need to deliver to make it a truly compelling proposition compared to the current model of outsourcing it to an expert.

We went into people's homes, observed and interviewed dry cleaning firms, spoke to experts in fabric care, and, consulted with some of the leading chemists around at the time. We worked hard to understand where the value of the outsourced dry cleaning service lay, where inconvenience existed and what technical challenges needed to be overcome.

Matt Marsh

What became apparent very quickly was that - apart from actually getting the dirt out of your clothes - it's the 'finishing' that people really appreciate. Getting back a well-pressed suit is what counts for the customer when evaluating if they got great service. Nice creases, nice folds, crisp edges are the tell-tale signs of a job well done.

In fact, the idea of "freshening" your clothes, rather than actually cleaning them was pretty unattractive to people. And, we found out that people had other workarounds at their fingertips if freshening was all they were looking for.

A great way to de-stink and de-wrinkle your clothes is to hang them next to your shower while you get spruced up. It really works pretty well! Or you can liberally spray them with fabric freshener.

So to fulfil the promise of equivalent "home" dry cleaning, you not only need to rinse out the odours (and stains!), but you need to press the garment, de-tangle the fibres, and fold it or seal it up as well.

But there was another challenge too. People were concerned about the chemicals dry cleaning used. On the one hand, people found it reassuring that their clothes came back smelling of "dry cleaners". But on the other hand, many people found that the chemicals impregnated in their clothes gave them a headache – so much so that it was typical to air their clothes before bringing them into the home's living area.

So the chemistry required to perform dry cleaning was a clear consumer concern. These chemicals are, perceived to be, totally toxic. And according to the chemists we spoke to, they were right. In short, there was a reason why people choose to outsource this task to professionals – the professionals were equipped and know how to handle these chemicals properly.

These chemicals are something you simply can't be casual with - the seas would be dead next week if people just, er, disposed of them down the drain.

So to truly replace the role of the outsourced dry cleaner, the device would have to clean, fold, regenerate the fabric and protect the completed garment. To achieve this was going to require a complicated and expensive device. Initial prototypes suggested such a device would cost a minimum of $650.

It's a lot easier to make a "clothes-refreshing" device – no cleaning and no pressing – but the value to the consumer to do this was small. In fact, there was already a range of devices that delivered quite a lot of the benefits associated with refreshing clothes – beyond hanging them in the shower or spraying them with freshener. It is called a hand-steamer and (at that time) cost about $45 plus the replaceable scented solvents.

So, based on all this evidence - the benefit of "refreshing" was already valued at around $45. The cost of doing full home dry cleaning started at $650 - but the finishing probably couldn't match what you got at the dry cleaning store. And there was the small issue that consumers had to find a large space in the home to install it.

You can see where I'm going here. Sure, it's probably technically possible to make a true home dry cleaning device - but it's pretty hard to make it practical and affordable.

You would think at this point that common sense would prevail and this project would be gently killed off. But oh no! The technical challenge was just to damn "fun". No amount of common sense was going to stop our own little lunar vanity programme.

Despite my best efforts, $250,000 of development money, one experience prototype, a series of cross-country focus groups later, the client accepted that there was no demand for a $650 device that would take up half your bedroom wardrobe and do a poor job compared to your local dry cleaner.

It was an "interesting" learning experience for me. Honestly I was incensed - why not give a quarter of a million dollars to a deserving charity instead. After all, the writing was on the wall from the very get-go.

So how did this happen? Too much tech-push, not enough market pull. The team refusing to listen to evidence, and putting personal passion in front of adopting a truly human centred approach and clearly user stated preferences instead.

A TRICK . . .
To help a team find where the sweet spot of a new proposition lies – if it exists at all !

FINDING WHERE THE SWEET SPOT OF NEW PROPOSITION LIES

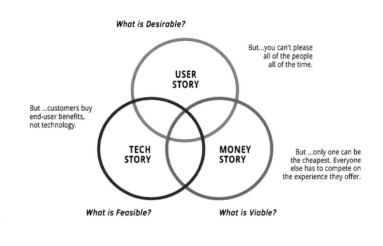

This framework can be used at any point in the development process - when planning a project, writing a proposal, during concept development or even at the end when you need to validate a design.

I first came across it when I was at IDEO, a San Francisco based design and innovation company. Some people also attribute it to Illinois Institute of Technology, and others seem to think it can be traced back to the Romans. So, I'm not exactly sure who came up with it for the first time. None the less, it is a rather good framework and very useful!

You should use it if you are concerned that perspective from the technology, marketing or financial teams is missing or out of synch.

Matt Marsh

The beauty of this framework lies in its simplicity. The first circle represents the user story - what is desirable. The second circle represents the technology story - what is feasible. And the third circle represents the financial story - what is viable.

Success lies when all three stories collide – when viability, desirability and feasibility are in perfect balance.

You need to bear in mind the following. People don't think in terms of buying technology, they buy benefits. Only one player can be the cheapest - the rest have to compete on the quality of the experience they deliver.

It is important for the team to know what their strategy is moving forward – is it to compete on the basis of offering features that no one else can? Or is it to provide an essentially equivalent and indifferent offer compared to everyone else's, but do it cheaper. Or is it to seduce the market by offering something genuinely more compelling, exciting and delightful. Each has its merits.

The challenge therefore is find out where this sweet spot exists. You can do this by bringing the whole team together, drawing this framework up on the wall, and then asking the team to share the data, insight or evidence they possess relevant to each part of the Venn diagram.

Working with Post–it notes can be very effective at this stage. Each person can write down everything that they think might be relevant on the Post It notes – and attach them to the relevant circle of knowledge – business, technology or user factors.

You can then work together to discuss and debate which parts of that evidence or data are critical for this particular business proposition. If you photograph what you have mapped, you can then repeat this process and compare it to previous iterations so that you can work as a team to slowly home-in on the sweet spot over time.

It is almost like using a compass to navigate across an open and uncharted sea – keep checking as you go. This way you have a tool that can help calibrate whole-team thinking, make trade-offs and seek compromises, and ultimately find where business proposition optimisation lies.

TEMPER TANTRUMS

"Nothing reveals humanity so well as the games it
plays."
David Hartley
(18th century philosopher)

The thing about being human centred is that it is rarely about doing the easy thing – for example recruiting the most obvious participants, asking the most obvious questions, completing the most obvious tasks.

Even though I have always been interested in involving end-users in the design process, and using their feedback to improve the design, I, like everyone else, needed to learn this lesson first-hand.

A few years into my career I really discovered why it was important to "stretch" the participant group to include the extremes of the user population, and reflect actual usage contexts beyond the limitations of the usability lab or focus group.

It was the early 1990's, and I was lucky to be working at the beginning of the explosion of the computer games industry. This was when dedicated gaming consoles were being developed for the home and when "proper" gaming was moving on from just being played on arcade type devices down the pub.

I was designing the hand controllers. Prior to this, controllers tended to be small slabs of plastic, with infuriating little buttons that stuck, were uncomfortable to hold – and were being criticised for causing all sorts of repetitive strains injuries (which was kind of justified – one of our team was a keen player and had the most awful lump on his thumb from playing as a teenager!).

Authors own image. In home design research study

So we started our user research. We went into the client's game development and testing studios to watch, interview and analyse the behaviours of their testing team, while they went about their business of finding flaws in the game code by playing hour upon hour of new games.

We reached out and consulted with experts in medical biomechanics, and discussed hand injuries with hand surgeons, human factors experts and physiotherapists.

By the way – and this is important to this story - while we doing all this, it was awkward to mention that I was interested in preventing repetitive strain injuries during gaming.

Matt Marsh

Why? In truth I was worried about the possibility of the client being exposed to future litigation. An admission of interest in avoiding these sorts of issues, could, potentially be seen as an admission of failure of design intent.

Wow, that being the case, how do you go about doing the right thing? Well, I came up with a work-around. The human centred designer's best friend! I organised some trials of my own, isolated from the client and their direct employees. I didn't invite any of them in to take part.

I recruited a broad range of gamers from my own network of friends and colleagues and invited them into the studio to play a few games. The trick I used was asking each person recruited to bring a friend along as his or her "play" partner.

The only requirement was that they had to have prior history of playing with their friend over months to be eligible to participate. We spent some additional time designing the recruitment qualifier to make sure of this – hey, less rush, more integrity!

And the results were a revelation. What people did at the games test centre bore no relation to what people "actually" did. Real play was far more frantic, intensive and occurred for longer. Making mistakes was a far more serious deal than when a paid employee was simply "assessing" a game for coding errors.

And players were far less forgiving of poor hand controller design. The design studio had never heard such fruity language in a user trial until one of our test participants experienced unresponsive buttons that didn't bounce back fast enough.

And then there was the revelation about play-based aggression and frustration. We invited a few pairs of brothers and sisters to play – and it was then that we really discovered what standard of engineering these hand controllers really had to exhibit.

When you see one sibling lose to another, and the controller gets flung to the floor in sheer anger, then you know what the notion "design requirements" really means from a human centred perspective. The device needs to be really strong, the electronics well protected – and its best it doesn't have any sharp edges too!

The learning? If you really want to know what goes on when people use products, services or experiences, then you need to replicate REAL usage contexts – who is playing, why they are playing, include them when they are tired, and when personal pride is at stake. And this takes work on the part of the designer.

It is so easy to go through the motions of being "customer centred". But unfortunately going through the motions usually doesn't reveal much that actually matters.

Being lazy, making it convenient or cutting corners when choosing whom to include in your design research and where you do it, means that you become part of the problem. Worse than that – you ARE the problem.

A TRICK . . .
To convince a team to include end users which represent the extremes of the target market - if you really want to find new and important information.

BALANCING THE SAMPLE TO INCLUDE EXTREMES & THE TARGET MARKET

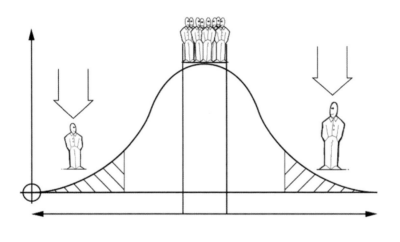

This framework helps the human centred designer to explain why including extremes of the user population in a design research program not only makes sense, but is often critical - especially if you intend to offer something new, fresh and different compared to everything else that is on the market.

The shape of this curve is frequently described as a binomial distribution. These sorts of curves don't have to be symmetrical – if the peak is offset to one side or the other; it is called "skewed".

None the less, the essential principal is that the binomial curve describes the distribution of an attribute, compared to the number of occurrences of that attribute within a specific user population or sample (known as the frequency).

This binomial distribution can be used to describe a range of human characteristics – for example, height, weight, eyesight, etc. etc.

So, you can describe the differences in people's shoe sizes in this way. There are fewer adults with very small shoe sizes, as there are few people with very large shoe sizes. The majority of people have shoe sizes somewhere in the middle.

And with a bit of, erhm, creative latitude, you can use it to describe differences in human behaviour or preference too. For example, describing people's propensity to try out new and emerging technologies, products or services.

At one end of the curve might lie people frequently described as "early adopters". At the other end might be the "laggards", who might wait for a few years before trying a new technology or product. Again, like the shoes, the majority of market lies somewhere in the middle of the curve.

Typically, people developing any product or service want to optimise their business proposition to where they think the majority of their future customers are. And then they refine the proposition - not just in terms of choosing the features or benefits to offer - but things like their distribution and sales strategy as well.

This is perhaps why, with the average (UK) shoe size at around 9 to 11 for men, that the shoe size that high street stores carry the most of is 9 to 11. It is also why there are specialist shops that cater for the larger gentleman or woman – they are choosing to focus on a special part of the binomial curve.

What it's important to understand from a design research perspective is that the most interesting and inspiring things are frequently found in the extremes of user population – because this is where the work-arounds and improvisations tend to take place.

What we try to do is include the extremes of the user population in the research sample, and then learn from what those people do to improve the design for those in the middle of the distribution – where, remember, the big money tends to be!

An example is when a design company was designing a new potato peeler. They went and observed people with arthritis and learnt how these people improvised getting better grip by using rubber bands on the metal handle.

This insight informed a re-design of the handle of their potato peeler by using neoprene - a material that not only conformed to support different kinds of gripping, but also provided a high friction surface that improved control and safety.

By looking at an extreme user population for inspiration, they discovered a way to improve the design of the potato peeler for all.

Matt Marsh

DOING THE MASHED POTATO

"I think constraints are very important. They're positive because they allow you to work off something."
Charles Gwathmey
(American Architect - 1938 to 2009)

When you set off to do something novel or innovative, whether you end up being successful or not, lies in correctly understanding what the REAL problem you are trying to solve is, AND what constraints you are operating within.

Unfortunately, there is often a paradox here. The sponsor of an innovation project doesn't want to constrain the team – after all that is why they are bringing you in; to get new thinking and ideas. So the client is often reluctant to tell you what success looks like, or, dictate what you can or cannot do.

On the other hand, you as the creative on the project need to operate within some boundaries. Otherwise, the temptation is to indulge yourself. This is what I used to euphemistically call "code word Barbados". You know? "We need to ship the team out to Barbados for, oh, say three months, to work together in an isolated place where creative juices can really flow".

Now that sounds like fun work if you can get it! But will it actually solve the problem you've been tasked with? Do you know what the problem is that you're trying to solve?

My point is, we as the innovation team, need to work hard early on in the program to discover what the limits of the problem statement are – not too constrained, but not too nebulous either; we need to find out what is out of bounds, deemed to be dull, old hat, or business as usual.

Authors own image. In home design research study

Matt Marsh

It sounds easy doesn't it? But, so often it isn't. My first experience of this dilemma was when I was working on what I thought was an innovation program to "re-invent, reposition and rejuvenate" the enticing staple known as dehydrated potato products.

The context. A massive, global food company had noticed that people weren't buying dehydrated potato products any more. This convenience foodstuff consisted of a sachet of dehydrated potato, and a sachet of dehydrated garnish and flavourings, in the same package. Market share, and total sector sales were DOWN, DOWN, DOWN.

So my first question to the sponsor was this. "Do you eat you own product?" Predictable answer. "OMG, No". Not altogether surprising. It was basically gloop with added vitamins, flavour and colour . . . what many would consider to be a culinary disaster.

Deferring judgement as far as humanly possible, we went out to talk to people who (a) were self identified buyers of dehydrated potato products, and (b), people who were keen consumers of convenience cooking products (like pizza, frozen food, ready meals, etc.).

And we discovered some really interesting stuff. One guy said that he used the dehydrated potato product, but didn't have any in at the moment. So we asked him to show us his pantry (larder to you Brits). And sure enough, there on the top shelf, tucked at the back was a packet of potato product covered in dust.

"Damn", he said. "That must have been left there when my wife divorced me five years ago!" Hmmm, interesting. But more interesting was the fact that on the same shelf he had seven (yes SEVEN) large bags of pasta. Enough to feed him for months!

Why did he have so much pasta in the house? "Well," he replied, "I go to the shops, and I can never remember what I have in the cupboard back here – so I just buy another one". That tells you a lot. He had no idea what was in his pantry.

Then we went to see a bunch of other people who lived the "convenience meal lifestyle" and asked them to act out how they made their shopping list. There was a pattern across seemingly very different people.

First, they would draw from their memories, and start to make a list. Then they would go to the refrigerator, and look to see what they were low on. More OJ, more milk, eggs, etc. etc. Then, they would go to the cupboards - cupboards that were hard to look into, poorly lit and hard to reach. And make a GUESS.

Hey presto, they have a shopping list - and off they would go to the store!

And the point here is . . . people DO know what is in (or isn't in) their refrigerator, but they tend to have no idea what is in the pantry or deep in their cupboards. Makes sense though. The refrigerator does a really fine job of presenting things to the consumer with its clever shelving, bright lighting and massive opening doors.

So we realised the problem. Dehydrated potato products are stored deep in the pantry where they become all but hidden away. And because they are hidden, you forget that you've got them, and therefore don't use them. The opposite happens to products that are kept in the fridge.

What needed to be done is to have a presence in the fridge. This could be neatly achieved by splitting the dehydrated potato bit from the garnish / flavour bit – and making the garnish reside where it was well lit and visible (and where the fresh food was).

This way the consumer would get a nice little reminder each time they opened their fridge – that dehydrated potato was an option. And also by calibrating quantities of garnish and gloop, then people would know when they needed to re-stock.

We were ready to play back to the client. The message - you need to claim a presence in the consumer's fridge, go for freshness with the garnish, allowing them to dump the horrible additive E-number stuff that was previously part of the dehydrated potato product of old.

I was expecting a pat on the back and a "hey, Mr Marsh, that's brilliant". I was brought crashing back to earth. Their response; "Mr Marsh, are you suggesting that we move our product into the fresh food section?" "Yes" I said.

"Don't you realise Mr Marsh that our whole business model is based on occupying aisle 13, second shelf. We have done deals with all the supermarkets to get our product on that shelf. We own that shelf! We are NOT going to compromise THAT."

Damn. They weren't in the dehydrated potato market at all. They were in the "filling aisle 13, second shelf" market. They were a DISTRIBUTION company – not a food company.

They had no desire to get a presence in the fresh or refrigerated part of the supermarket – even if it would lead to more sales. What they wanted was a product to sit on aisle 13, second shelf.

So, I had totally missed seeing what the key constraint governing the project was. But don't worry; I got there in the end. We invented a new range of potato-based snacks for them instead – what became the next generation of crisps.

A TRICK . . .
To help a team discover early on in the development process what constraints exist – and avoid making something that the client doesn't actually want.

NARROWING DOWN THE CONSTRAINTS PRIOR TO IMPLEMENTATION

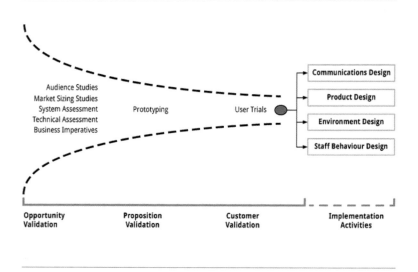

The purpose of this framework is to help an interdisciplinary team, early on in the development process, to recognise what constraints exists, how they might shape a program going forward, and to discover some foresight about ways to best deal with them.

The framework uses the model of a cone to describe the act of cross-disciplinary perspective gathering. At the beginning - when things are vague - it is used to ask broad and fundamental questions that will determine whether you successfully understand the brief.

For example, you need to gain an understanding of the business imperatives, the system design, the audience needs and segmentation studies, as well as the technical risks. Initial answers to these questions can be achieved through desk research, prototyping and modelling activities.

By going through this process of research, prototyping and modelling, the range of opportunities becomes narrower. However, it is critical to document the decisions that are made, to circulate these discoveries broadly, and to seek consensus about what the implications and action items are – even if this means logging them as "we don't yet know".

As the cone narrows and the range of opportunities and constraints become more defined, the next step is to develop an informed range of proposition prototypes and to then test those with end users to find out what is working, and what isn't working.

The goal is to seek evidence about not only what end-users find compelling, and perhaps confusing, but what other stakeholders think too. For example, it is important to reach out to other decision makers within the client organisation, their partners or their suppliers too.

By creating these proposition prototypes, you are making it much easier for people to constructively critique what is being proposed because you are "making something real, before it is real" – and by doing this it is easier for people to perceive how this new idea might impact them in the future.

This stimulates a further narrowing down of the range of possibilities to a workable sub-set. It is now possible to build a small number of experience prototypes to test out the complete concept in near-real usage situations with actual users, stakeholders or partners. In my experience, three to five variants of experience prototypes are sufficient to gain good perspective.

If necessary, the constraints can be more deeply explored through formalised user trials where performance measures can be determined, and validation sought.

The endpoint of this reductive process is an accurate definition of the customer's requirements, in tandem with the generation of a clearly articulated user experience brief. This documentation might include making models, drafting usage-scenarios, sketching personas, crafting wireframes or creating detailed sketches.

These materials can then generate a "hymn sheet" from which the implementation agencies – communication design, interaction and product design, environmental design and training design – can all work from.

This makes sure that all the implementation work that is about to be initiated is perfectly aligned with each and every other piece of work going on, and that nothing needs to be repeated or reinvented late in the process.

This way all the implementation agencies know whom they are designing for, why they are designing this particular concept, and what success should look like. It also clarifies the constraints that have been discovered along the way, and why they are important.

Collectively, this ensures the business proposition is one that will make sense for the client, and customers alike.

CROSSED WIRES

"We are stuck with technology when what we really
want is just stuff that works."
Douglas Adams
(Author of The Hitchhikers Guide to the Galaxy - 1952
to 2001)

It was the summer of 2005, a few years after WAP phones had begun to be heavily promoted, and when WAP traffic was doubling every year. WAP was the first generation of phones that enabled you to "surf the web" (as it was then called!).

So there was a lot of pressure at mobile phone companies worldwide not only to reap the benefit of this thing called the "mobile web", but also to be known for delivering the best customer experience too.

The experience is an important criterion here – because the WAP experience was in all honesty pretty crappy. Bear in mind, the broadband revolution was taking place simultaneously – apparently in 2002, there were fewer than 200,000 UK broadband users. Four years later, there were 13 million.

So people knew what using the mobile Internet *should* feel like, because their expectations were being formed via their broadband connections. The problem was that the mobile experience didn't go anywhere near the quality of experience they were getting at home or at work using their cabled connections and big desk-top screens.

But the mobile Internet was different – context and location made a big difference to what you wanted to do, and get done. You wanted access to stuff that made sense based on where you were, where your friends were, what you wanted to do NOW!

The mobile Internet needed to serve different needs. And the race was on to see who could get there and serve these emerging needs first.

Mobile Internet. Ethnographic "shadowing" research. Authors own photograph

And because so much change was going on, civil war was happening in Telco companies all over the world. Marketing was yelling at the engineering teams asking them to give them "something new" to sell, and engineering would respond – just as forcefully - by asking "what is it exactly you want us to invent?"

As you can imagine, meetings in Telcos at this time were pretty poisonous. Accusations were being made, frustrations aired, and the "wheels of the service innovation project bus" falling off.

And it was into this arena at one Telco that we were brought in to try and arbitrate these warring parties, and then formulate some sort of strategy for moving forward.

Matt Marsh

So, as you might expect, our starting point was to understand what it was that the user actually wanted and needed from the next generation of mobile devices and services. By the way, there was a new web service that people with their ear to the ground were talking about – "the face book" or "facebook" as it had just become.

Believe it or not, but at that time people were calling it the "social internet" or Web 2.0 and what they meant (well, we thought anyway) was real time responsive interaction over the web. So, two things were happening simultaneously; mobile access to the web and totally new social behaviours.

We started our research on the West coast and East coast of the USA to learn more. East coast because it was still the media capital of the United States. West coast because it was the technology capital.

We also went to Korea because it had, beyond doubt, the very best mobile connectivity anywhere in the world at that time – always on and always connected, whether on the subway or in the 'burbs. "On demand" was the phrase of the day.

And we found out probably what every other vaguely respectable design research agency had found out. That we were in a new era of what we called "the attention economy".

People didn't want to just do something online, and then have to wait ages for a response. It was about staying up to date with what was going on, right blooming now! And that meant that from a user's point of view, the rules of interacting on-line via a phone had changed. It had to be super easy - and super fast. It had to be media rich too! And WAP simply didn't cut the mustard!

We found out a bunch of other important stuff too – but that is another story. So we went back to report and share our findings.

We showed the team the evidence of new user behaviours, we sketched out compelling customer journeys and interactions, and we created personas that matched product formats to different user types. We showed what a post-WAP display needed to do, what the ensuing implications for interaction design were, and laid out what the technical engineering challenges were.

We thought that providing all this end user insight would bring these two siloed teams together, and help them agree what to work on next, and then they would naturally be able to prioritise and coordinate their different development goals.

And this is when it went decidedly pear-shaped. Instead of responding by saying, "Oh, that's a simple set of ideas that we can all work on", the internal warfare simply intensified. They just couldn't think of themselves as one team working together because they had very different ideas of what constituted success.

The engineering team still wanted space to be left alone and to invent the next greatest thing, whilst the marketing team still wanted something that was going to lead to an immediate "techno hit" and a dramatic improvement in sales.

What they couldn't recognize was that actually there was a lot of agreement between them about what to do. But their different ideas about how to go about it, and when, just made them more combative, and to be honest, occasionally a bit paranoid.

We finished the project frankly a little depressed. And shortly after that my colleague Nick Durrant (currently of Plot) came up with a brilliant framework that would have really helped rectify this dysfunctional situation – how to get the marketing and engineering teams to listen to each other and work to a set of common goals.

If only we had it six months earlier.

Oh, and an aside. Precisely one year later after we had left with our tail between our legs, Steve Jobs announced the iPhone in January 2007. A new user interface, new engineering technology, new social applications. It made getting on the mobile Internet easy!

A TRICK . . .
To help marketing and engineering teams work together – and stop them banging their heads against each other, and then go home sobbing.

COORDINATING DEVELOPMENT ACTIVITY TO MATCH USERS NEEDS

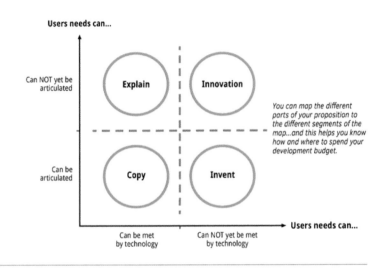

I like to call this "Durrant's Diagram" after Nick. Nick likes to reference Hamel and Prahalad as an inspiration for it – but honestly, in my opinion, his version is much more useful and clearer.

This powerful framework helps align the creative activities of the engineering and the marketing teams.

Both the X and Y-axis - horizontal and vertical - are labelled the "user needs can..."

Matt Marsh

On the Y-axis, either the "user needs can be articulated", or, the "user needs can NOT yet be articulated". The X-axis is labelled, "user needs can be met by technology", or "user needs can NOT yet be met by technology".

If the user needs can be articulated and they can be met by technology, then probably something similar already exists. Therefore, the challenge is to emulate (er, copy!) what has already been done and to build on what has already been set as a precedent. There is no point in reinventing the wheel.

If the user needs can be met by technology, but can NOT yet be articulated by the end user, then the challenge is to explain to them what it is that you are planning to offer them. As such the emphasis of the challenge needs to be around communicating that this need exists – and that you have something that can meet it.

If the user needs can be articulated, but can NOT yet be met by technology, then the challenge that the team faces is to invent something new which fulfils this challenge.

If the user needs can NOT be articulated and can NOT yet be met by existing technology, then the team is in genuine innovation space – you are in uncertain territory. Which can be rather exciting for the human centred designer.

What it is important to note is that most product, service or brand design programs involve a mix of copy, explain, invent and innovate within them. It is important that the team recognises which parts of a program are which, and then determines what distribution of resource should be allocated to reflect the different activities.

By mapping the different parts of your proposition proportionally to the different segments of this framework helps you know how and where to spend your development budget.

It is interesting to note that the question of whether the user needs can be met by technology, or can NOT yet be met by technology, is usually the domain of engineering.

Whereas, whether user needs can be articulated by the user, or can NOT yet be articulated by the user, is usually the domain of marketing.

What tends to happen in innovation programs is the following. The marketing department asks the engineering department to invent something new to capture the zeitgeist. The engineering department (reasonably!) responds by saying, "yes, but tell me what it is that you want me to invent".

Or vice versa. The engineering department says, "We've invented something, go sell it!", and marketing says "But no one knows what it is or what it is for". And this is where so many internal innovation teams stumble. It turns into two teams bashing their heads together!

The beauty of this framework is that it provides a mechanism for these two domains to come together - to understand that some parts of a new business proposition require a measure of copying, a measure of explanation, a measure of invention, and others require a determined measure of exploration in "innovation space". Success comes in correctly identifying the mix – just like a great cocktail.

And it is this trick that this framework so elegantly pulls off. It provides a recipe from which the team can collectively work out how to properly allocate money and resources in an effective way to achieve a shared – and doable - result.

Cheers, Nick!

IT'S MY PARTY (AND I'LL IGNORE YOU IF I WANT TO)

"It's easy to design for yourself. It's just when other people get involved that it gets tricky."
Bill Moggridge
(Founder of IDEO and all round good bloke - 1943 to 2012)

While there is much chatter about the merits of alternative development approaches – for example, agile, gated, lean, funnel, double diamond, etc., etc. – there is, in my view, far too little honest conversation about the different leadership styles that the human centered designer needs to master.

I didn't learn this skill 'till far too late in my career. I wish I had understood it better earlier. I did know the basics. For example, that a designer frequently wants a different kind of input to the engineer. One might want inspiration and insight to riff off, whereas the other might like to know exactly what the acceptable parameters are. You have to know to whom you are talking and deliver the right kind of input for the right person.

Part of taking on the role of being an effective human centered designer is to learn how to provide the right techniques, support, evidence and, critically, leadership style – at the right time - to help another part of the leadership team transition through these very different stages of design development.

For example, I was lucky and I met a guy called Eddie Obeng. He is frankly a genius when it comes to helping people tune-up their leadership skills, and he currently runs a firm called Pentacle as well as being a renowned TED speaker. You should really check his TED talk out – you won't be disappointed!

He explained to me that projects require different types of leadership style as they go through different phases; from the more abstract to when they become more concrete.

Authors own image

I was asked in to help a healthcare company that was developing two radically new – and potentially - life saving devices. One of the devices was in the later stages of development and needed more tactical human factors input; legibility, interaction design, usability, instructions design, etc.

Matt Marsh

The other device was at a much earlier stage. It provided a similar life saving function, but for an entirely different application and usage context. For this second device, the fundamental business proposition was not yet well understood, and the team hadn't determined what the user requirements were. They didn't really know who their end users were or whether any unmet needs actually needed resolving. As such, it wasn't really clear whether for this application the world actually needed it or not.

On the client side, the same person was in charge of both programs and applying the same leadership style to both. He was stuck in 'command and control' mode for both. This approach had served him well when he was the lead clinical researcher inventing the potentially life saving technology.

Unfortunately this leadership approach didn't lend itself to any type of product or service development. It was a style based on preserving status and control, and celebrating his own genius.

I should have known better, but I didn't realise that I had to "turn on a dime" when working with him.

Having been asked to assess the first device (the one that was in the final throws of development), I had successfully delivered a set of design recommendations and next steps. It was all very tactical. Do this, Do that. And, if you do this, then you stand a good chance of getting through the Federal Drug Administration's assessment process.

But when it came to working on the other device, I stupidly remained in "do this, do that" mode by mistake. And unsurprisingly, it was a disaster. He became defensive, frustrated, and he pretty much shut down the conversation. He didn't want to be told what to do, he didn't want direction, and he definitely didn't want to be challenged.

As a result of my clumsy leadership style, the development of the device went on in the absence of any external perspective – whether it was end users, clinicians, purchasing people or marketing and communications teams.

And because of this, the final design was indeed "a dogs breakfast", a "dog's breakfast" that needed endless last minute and expensive iterations, where the budget went up and up, and which remained fundamentally unappetizing to the market.

So I failed. I should have made it clear how different the two programs were, how we needed different approaches to running the two different teams, to have laid out options to choose from, to talk about questions that needed answering rather than tasks that needed doing.

I should have been in problem share mode, not problem solve. I should have been offering him room to develop some foresight, reflection and reaction time. I should have been showing him alternative ways to move forward, rather than telling him what I thought must be done. All wrong, wrong, wrong!

I learnt that I needed to improve my listening skills, to be more patient, and to think really carefully about how fragile innovation programs can be - and think much more about the feelings of those who lead them.

It's about needing to be as empathetic with those who are running an innovation program, as you are empathetic about the end user. Unless you are doing both, then quite frankly, you are not doing your job right.

Matt Marsh

A TRICK . . .

To help a team leader adopt an appropriate leadership style – and prevent a team giving up and mutinying instead.

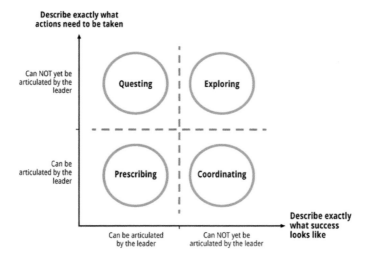

CHOOSING THE RIGHT LEADERSHIP STYLE

Typically, what one tries to achieve, as a human centred designer is to provide the team leader with evidence to help them recognise, and then select, the right leadership style needed for different stages of a project.

If the team is getting blocked, distracted or is conflicted, this framework describes how the human centred designer can modify their leadership style depending on the nature of the challenge that they face.

It is important to understand that one's leadership style may need to change over time, and as a business proposition becomes more refined and better defined. Eddie's original model labelled the axes Goal and Means, and populated the quadrants with paint by numbers, movie, quest and fog. But over my years of teaching, I've discovered that a slight modification of his model helps people recognise the leadership behaviours a bit better.

The X-axis – horizontal - is labelled DESCRIBE EXACTLY WHAT SUCCESS LOOKS LIKE; the team leader possesses an understanding of what it is that the team is trying to achieve, i.e. the desired end point!

The Y-axis - vertical - is labelled DESCRIBE EXACTLY WHAT ACTIONS NEED TO BE TAKEN; the team leader possesses an understanding of how they are going to achieve the goal, i.e., what exactly needs to be done and when.

Both axes are labelled CAN BE ARTICULATED BY THE LEADER or CAN NOT YET BE ARTICULATED BY THE LEADER.

If WHAT SUCCESS LOOKS LIKE and WHAT NEEDS TO BE DONE can both be articulated by the leader, then the leadership style required is much like prescribing what an orchestra must play - each player is given a music score that tells them when, how long and what emphasis to play the notes. It doesn't mean that is necessarily easy, but it does imply adopting a more "command and control" type of leadership.

If WHAT SUCCESS LOOKS LIKE can be articulated by the leader, but WHAT EXACTLY NEEDS TO BE DONE can NOT yet be articulated by the leader, then it is much more like leading a quest for something - like trying to find the Holy Grail. In this instance, the leader might know from the outset that they need to find the Holy Grail, but where it might be is pretty hard to know at the beginning.

As the quest goes on, there are lots of unpredictabilities. Unsurprisingly perhaps, people need constant confirmation and reinforcement that achieving success is worth it. It requires a different style of leadership to the "prescribing-type" project where exactly what needs to be done, and when, has been clearly communicated.

What is key with leading a quest, is that the leadership style must result in *everyone* knowing what the goal is. Unless there is a shared understanding of what the goal is, then people end up going off on their own - and the team falls apart. As such, it's worth being patient, not rushing things and waiting until everyone is on board before setting off.

If WHAT SUCCESS LOOKS LIKE can NOT yet be articulated by the leader, but WHAT EXACTLY NEEDS TO BE DONE can be articulated by the leader, then the project is much more like being a film or TV director. This is when a leadership style is needed that employs sensitive people management skills that helps individuals perfectly coordinate input – making sure people turn up at the right place, at the right time, and follow the plan.

But it is very difficult to predict exactly what the show is actually going to be like until it is over and "in the can". As such, there are usually a lot of nervous people around who need a good deal of reassuring.

This style of leadership requires making sure that all the different parts of the team know what they are meant to be doing, helping them do the right thing at the right time - and then help them check their progress as they go along.

A TV, film or theatre director relies on a well-oiled rehearsal process to assist the team to see how the project is evolving and improving, and allow the team to learn how to best coordinate their individual performances.

Finally, if WHAT SUCCESS LOOKS LIKE <u>can NOT</u> yet be articulated by the leader, and, WHAT EXACTLY NEEDS TO BE DONE <u>can NOT</u> yet be articulated by the leader, the team is genuinely in a space of unknowing – it's called exploration.

Things are, by definition, ambiguous. By analogy, this is much like exploring an uncharted and unknown world.

Here, the explorer might spend some considerable time listening to others, trying things out, making suggestions, etc. The leadership style needed is to be supportive, without imposing too many timetables, or quick judgements being made.

With these types of projects it is important to have a leadership style that allows time for people to make discoveries in their own time, and that critically - just like with any good exploration project - that people commit to coming back together according to an agreed timetable to share progress before any big decisions are made.

If you are running an "exploring-type" project, it is appropriate to initially do some work to try to turn it into a "questing-type" or "coordinating-type" leadership project. This is achieved by successfully answering either the question WHAT ACTIONS NEED TO BE DONE, or, WHAT SUCCESS LOOKS LIKE.

Eventually it may be possible, when both WHAT ACTIONS NEED TO BE DONE, and, WHAT SUCCESS LOOKS LIKE are clearly understood, to turn it into a "prescribing-type" leadership project.

When a leader approaches a project using the wrong type of leadership style, the team gets confused, they get frustrated, and all hell breaks out. They mutiny!

Be like Eddie! Be aware about what you are saying and doing all the time.

TOWEL STORY

"A small change at the beginning of the design process defines an entirely different product experience at the end."
Jonathan Ive
(Chief Design Officer at Apple, Inc)

Pretty much any product, service or experience designer these days will tell you that they are customer centred. But what does that actually mean?

Does it mean that you asked your mum/dad/spouse/kids whether they like your idea — knowing full well that they weren't going to hurt your feelings?

Or perhaps you are the design director that asks your team to go out and test a design - and when they come back, says, "Yes, that's what I wanted to hear".

Or maybe you are the VP of innovation who just likes a bit of confirmation bias — asking some of the most obvious and predictable parts of the target demographic which of three "loaded" options that you've created is the one they liked the best; the one you knew was insane, the one you knew was incredibly boring, and the one you REALLY liked all along.

To be honest — we've probably all done at least one of these at one time or another.

Shortly after graduating, and setting up myself as a freelancing human factors guy for hire, I got my baptism of fire when I was brought in really late into a program to perform some usability testing on a paper towel dispenser.

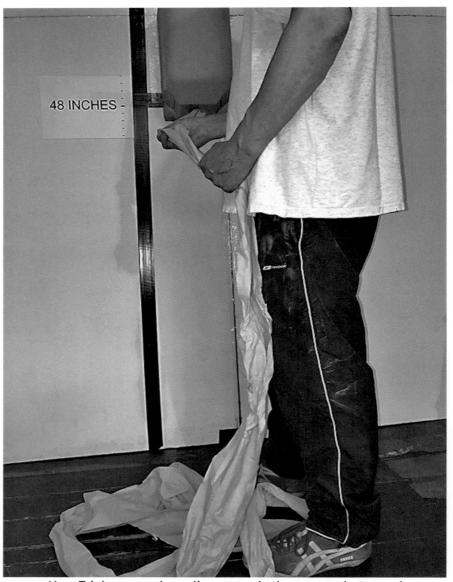

User Trials on mock up dispenser. Authors own photograph

Matt Marsh

I was working for what was a then world leading design agency. They were renowned for inventing corporate identities of 'big' oil companies, designing the look and feel of (then) revolutionary desktop computing companies, and were the go-to agency for all sorts of new product development. They epitomised the cutting edge of design in the 1980's.

I was brought in to help with the "usability" assessment trials of a paper towel dispenser. To be fair - and they were honest with me - bringing me in was an afterthought. I was there primarily because their client had demanded that the usability trials had to be done as part of their sign-off procedure to prove the design was in fact fit for purpose.

The design company wasn't expecting any usability issues. As the design director said to me; "It's only a paper towel dispenser. It's not exactly a revolutionary concept. Pull. Tear. Dry. Dispose".

What they asked me to do is assess if they had got the usability right. Could people successfully get a paper towel out?

Honestly, I thought it couldn't be simpler. Do a usability trial and count how often a user could successfully remove a whole paper towel from said dispenser.

So I went ahead. I selected a range of test participants based on height and strength. I included people who were in wheelchairs, and people who were vision impaired too. Proper inclusivity! Even then.

But the answer was clear before we had even tested 20 people. The design was a failure. It was fundamentally flawed. It didn't work. In fact it was useless.

When you pulled on the paper towel, attempting to tear off a neat napkin, it just pulled more towel down off the roll. Reams and reams, followed by then more reams would roll off onto the floor.

So, I picked up the pieces of paper towel, and I thought about it. I did some analysis. I looked at anthropometric data to tell me where people's hands would be, what direction they would be pulling in relative to the cutting blade, and deduced that the position and angle of the cutting blade was wrong. It wasn't angled correctly relative to where people's hands were to provide a suitable cutting edge.

Ah ha, I thought! All we need to do is change the shape and angle of the blade, tilt it upwards maybe a few degrees so that it would be aligned with the various cutting directions of how people were pulling. Sorted!

I grinned, pleased that I had made a discovery! But alas, this wasn't the happy end of the story.

I was told in no uncertain terms that they couldn't adjust the angle of the blade. The dispenser had already been designed, engineered, and the injection-moulding tool was complete. They couldn't make any changes - the design was going to be as it was.

What a joke! This paper towel dispenser had gone through the hands of designers – it was attractive. It had gone through the hands of an engineer – it was strong and robust. And it had gone through the hands of the marketing department - it had a signature and recognisable look.

But it was useless! Along the way no one had bothered to think what would actually work for people. They hadn't thought about the different types of people who would use the product, they hadn't thought about where the product would be installed, that hadn't included end users at any point to test out or refine ideas, they hadn't made any prototypes to check out what worked.

I was shocked. This was a baptism of fire into the world of design as it so frequently was in the 1980's! Almost always a bunch of young men, sitting in their offices, designing for themselves, leaving it till the end of the process to think about whom they were designing for – and being reluctant or unable to take constructive critique.

Matt Marsh

This experience would shape my attitudes to design and innovation evermore. In short, "How can making new things possibly be this stupid?"

It sowed the seeds of my passion to change the ways that people choose to "make" - and was also why some years later I launched the "people-shaped" campaign.

It is also partly why I decided to write this book. Avoiding mistakes like this isn't rocket science. You just need to move the human centred bit upstream in the process and not think of it as something you tag on the end.

A TRICK . . .
To persuade a team to listen to end users early on in the process – if you want to avoid discovering you've screwed up too late to do anything about it.

WHY YOU NEED TO INCLUDE END USERS EARLY IN THE PROCESS

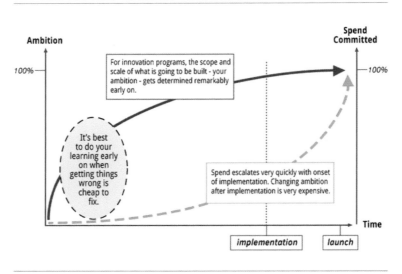

This framework is best used when someone says "let's just leave consulting the end users 'till later, and get right on with the design work now". It provides you with an argument to show your colleagues that it is cheaper and better to understand what end users need and want, before engaging in implementation work.

Fixing things late in the process is often very expensive compared to doing it early in the process. It is no exaggeration to say that it can cost 10 times more to fix something once it has been built and launched, than if the issue had been addressed earlier on before implementation starts.

Matt Marsh

Here's how it works. The X-axis - horizontal - represents time elapsed. At some point implementation activities must begin - for example initiating coding, engineering, tooling, building digital or physical environments or initiating staff training programs. It is at this point that costs tend to rise dramatically.

The right hand Y-axis represents the money you have available to invest in bringing the next new thing to life i.e. your overall budget. At the top of the axis equals 100% of the budget you have available.

The yellow curve represents how you spend your budgets. In the beginning before implementation, costs are relatively low. But as soon as you hit implementation and head towards launch they rise very, very quickly.

The left hand Y-axis represents the clarity of ambition for the project. The top represents certainty, whereas the bottom of the axis represents a state of ambiguity. It is quite hard to explain exactly what the ambition for a project is right at the beginning – but as you can see the ambition actually gets set quite early on and rapidly.

For example, you know quite early on whether you are planning to make a simple App compared to making a new version of Microsoft Word with millions of lines of code! So, the red curve represents the rate at which the ambition for the project is set.

If you get to the end of the budget, and at that point discover that your ambition for the project does not match what end users want, then you need to go back and re-design. Which, if you've already spent your budget is very difficult to do – it's always hard to go back and ask for more money!

It is much better to do your learning early on when it is cheap to discover if the ambition for the project is out of kilter to what your future customers want and need.

Simply, all you are doing is demonstrating that it is highly risky financially - and to the reputation of the company - to leave user input until the late stages of design and development.

Matt Marsh

MELTDOWN

"In my opinion, no single design solution is apt to be optimal for everyone."
Donald Norman
(Author of The Design of Everyday Things)

Doesn't matter if it's a museum, a music festival, a nightclub or a retail park. Compelling visitor experience projects are notoriously difficult to create. There are so many different people and opinions to be considered that it can just turn into an endless debate about who is right, who is wrong, what matters and what doesn't.

Back in late 2008, the issue of climate change was hitting the mainstream media like never before. I was approached by a world famous museum that wanted to say something about it, create a permanent exhibition, and help visitors to the museum explore the concept on their own terms.

But progress was blocked! The museum team had already gathered a great deal of content and had many ideas for what they could *say*, but they were in "analysis paralysis" mode about being able to choose what to actually *do*.

Given the controversies associated with the topic, it was unsurprising that there were many points of view on their board, and that making a decision about how to move forward without alienating some of the most vocal experts was proving challenging.

Contradiction was in the air – it was hard to see how to confidently navigate a way forward.

John Englart, aka Takver. "Think critically, ask for evidence" - Melbourne MarchforScience on Earthday. April 2017. This image is licensed under the Creative Commons Attribution Share Alike 2.0 Generic license.

So, I took up the challenge to try and facilitate collaboration between the various stakeholders, hopefully unblocking the logjam by using a human centred design approach. We suggested that we do four things.

Talk to people about climate change through discussion groups; perform some benchmarking of other exhibitions on the same subject; do some longitudinal analysis about who their visitors actually were, and finally do some design research exploration into what worked and what didn't in terms of museum visitor experience design.

The discussion groups, benchmarking and market analysis of their audience helped us to discover what kinds of exhibition experiences were successful. We agreed as a team that successful should mean challenging perceptions, provoking conversation, informing and educating.

Matt Marsh

And there were LOTS of other climate change exhibitions out there at this time. One organisation had installed huge blocks of ice melting to demonstrate what "global warming" (as it was then called) looked like in real time.

There were also experiential spaces that let people experience the doomsday scenario of a post-climatic change world using visual simulations and movies.

And there were rather dry (forgive the pun) exhibits that offered science-faction descriptions of what the planet might look like in a post 4 degrees Centigrade increase world (essentially, a very soggy world!).

After doing the benchmarking of the other visitor experiences, we followed up by performing some longitudinal analysis of who actually came to this museum in the first place; why they came, how often they came, and what was it they hoped to experience when they were there.

This was very revealing - because it didn't reveal very much. Analysis of visitor feedback forms showed that essentially people came three times in a lifetime; once as a child as part of a school trip; once as a young parent with toddlers; and once as grandparent bringing grandchildren.

To be fair, the data revealed one other visitor type. Tourists who were visiting this city for a long weekend break. It's not to say all this information wasn't interesting. But it didn't tell us how to make this important exhibition a "go to" destination, rather than a "plan b" if the weather was awful!

We needed to discover exactly who the target audience for this new experience was, what their unmet needs were, and how we could stimulate their interest in a climate change exhibition.

By knowing this, we could determine a curation approach would make it novel and exciting, and deliver something that would make visitors talk about it to their friends and family when they got home (seeding the idea of others wanting to come and visit it too!).

We brought together climate change experts, museum-goers, curators from the museum and designers in an intense two-day interdisciplinary workshop format to help flesh out who the intended audience might be.

We explored what experiences we could deliver. And discussed how we could orchestrate those experiences in a way that would enable them to experience it on their own terms and at their own pace.

We performed user research, design research, and contextual design research. This provided the materials necessary to co-create examples of hypothetical visitors, and then apply these hypothetical personas to possible visitor scenarios.

By writing visitor experience storyboards based on these personas, we were able to craft fundamental step-by-step learning moments, and then to collectively plot out and plan how this delicate and nuanced content curation team could work collaboratively.

By going through this human centred proving and testing process, we discovered that there were actually three types of visitor experience we needed to focus on delivering.

The first type was for the climate-change sceptic who would simply pop in and out. The second type of visitor experience needed to accommodate a climate change curious type of person who wanted to know what had changed in terms of climate science since they had last engaged with the issue.

Lastly, there was the third type of experience that needed to be supported. This type of experience was optimised for climate change activist people who wanted to participate in the climate change movement, and continue contributing to the conversation beyond their physical visit to the museum.

As a note. There really was little rationale for an experience aimed at tourists who were in town for a few days. They had MUCH better things to do with their time than get lectured on climate change – things like visit Buckingham Palace, go to the theatre, rave at nightclubs and eat in great restaurants.

After all, most of them had just got an aeroplane to get here. So who wants a reminder of how complicit they are in contributing to impending disaster when you have just spent a small fortune on a mode of travel that is a key factor in climate change?

So a visitor experience designed especially for these types of people was omitted. Obvious really. But only just obvious!

And you can see how this permanent exhibition played out as a design. I've given you a few clues as to where it is. The museum still does an excellent job accommodating the school parties and trans-generational visitors. But this permanent exhibition must work differently because it has to address very some very specific needs of the audience to be effective.

But basically it is laid out so that if you are an in-and out person, you can simply slip though and get the headlines. If you are more interested, then there are zones where you can immerse yourself more deeply. And if you are the right on, balaclava-wearing activist, you can do all the above and also sign up to be part of the museum's climate change community.

A TRICK . . .
To help a team choose research techniques that provide appropriate user perspective – and avoid spending lots of money reinventing the wheel.

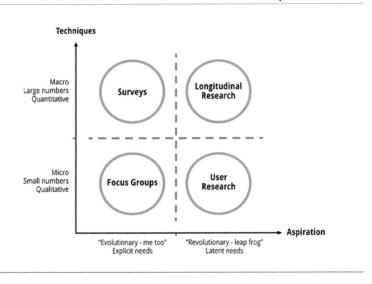

When the human centred designer needs to explain to their marketing colleagues what the difference between marketing and user research are, this framework shows how these two practices can work together and compliment each other.

The Y-axis – vertical - is labelled TECHNIQUE. At the top of the axis are the more quantitative, macro perspective gathering techniques that depend on having a large sample size. Conversely, at the base of the Y-axis are the qualitative, more micro perspective gathering techniques that typically utilise much smaller sample sizes.

Matt Marsh

The X-axis – horizontal - is labelled ASPIRATION. The left hand side describes a project that is "more evolutionary" in nature – something that the world has already seen before, and understands.

If you are dealing with something that is more evolutionary, then people are already familiar with it. Because you are dealing with something that people are familiar with, you are asking them about what are termed "explicit needs". Explicit 's needs are the ones that users are aware of, and can articulate.

Because they are aware of them, they can articulate what they want. You can ask them what their opinion is. Therefore you can use more traditional market research techniques like focus groups or surveys. You can do them online, by phone or perhaps in places like shopping malls where there are lots of people about.

Conversely, the right hand side of the ASPIRATION X-axis describes a challenge that is "more revolutionary" in nature – something that the world is yet to see and experience. If you are doing something more revolutionary, you will be dealing with what are called "latent needs". Latent needs are the ones that users are currently unaware of, or unable to articulate.

As end users are unaware or unable to articulate what it is they need or want next, it is impossible to simply ask them. What you need to do instead is one or both of the following.

Perform some design research to explore and understand their underlying behaviours. Or perhaps you may need to do longitudinal research by carrying out some contextual or trend research work (either digitally, possibly using artificial intelligence). This will reveal their unmet or poorly met needs, and unearth new compelling alternatives.

If the nature of the project is indeed more evolutionary, then it is fine to use traditional focus group or survey type of techniques. However, if the project is more revolutionary in nature, then it is important to perform some user research and longitudinal work.

Two words of caution! The more micro techniques, using small numbers of people, are great for gaining insight and inspiration. But be careful! Remember, that if you just use the more qualitative techniques, with small sample sizes, you are in danger of following the whims of what might be an unrepresentative user population.

You might need to use some more macro techniques, using large numbers of people too. These are great when you need validation. And it is important to validate before your team spends large amounts of money on implementation.

But again, beware. If you are just using the more quantitative techniques you can be pretty sure that other competitors are doing – and learning - exactly the same thing as you. So that leaves no room for coming up with something revolutionary!

So my recommendation is this. First, understand where the project actually lies on the ASPIRATION dimension. But you need to use some caution here too.

A client will often tell you at the beginning that they want to do something revolutionary or "innovative". But do they really? You must question them about it, and make sure that they know what they are getting into - because doing something revolutionary can mess up the status quo.

And messing up the status quo can mean big changes to how they go about their day-to-day business activities. Do they really want this? Best that you find out!

Matt Marsh

If they do still want to do something at the revolutionary end of the ASPIRATIONAL spectrum, then do the following. First, learn from the work done by more traditional market research methods – for example from the focus group or surveys they have performed.

This gives you clues about who to include in your user needs research or your longitudinal research and how you should go about it. Then you should do your user needs research or your longitudinal research informed by these learnings.

Once you have got some insight and inspiration by doing your user needs research or your longitudinal research, you must prototype some of the design responses, and then test those responses using more traditional quantitative techniques to validate your insights and inspiration.

By doing this you mitigate the risk of just following a whim, while at the same time doing sufficient work in order to reveal potential new product features or experiences that will differentiate your proposition in the future marketplace that you are creating.

Matt Marsh

BLIND SIDED

"Any product that needs a manual to work is broken."
Elon Musk
(Founder of Tesla Motors . . . and Spaceman)

To follow through on being an effective human centred designer, it is critical that you take responsibility for shaping the system design, the interaction design, and the brand design too.

By taking this mantle on, you are far more likely to be successful at bringing something to life that the world will genuinely need, understand, and love using.

But sometimes it is easy to lose focus – even getting distracted enough to forget the most basic and obvious things (like usability) that shape the overall user experience.

I learnt this lesson while I was involved in designing a radically new drug delivery device. This device would not only more accurately deliver the right dose, but it was smart enough to ensure that it was delivering the right dose to the right patient too.

Which is a good thing! Bear in mind that (according to my client at the time), in late 1990's within the USA alone, about 450 people died everyday because of some combination of the wrong drug, was given in the wrong dose, through the wrong route, to the wrong patient. Once again . . . . 450 people died unnecessarily every DAY!

That was the equivalent of a jumbo jet going down one day, after another, after another, after another. So this is serious – and an issue that good design should be doing something about!

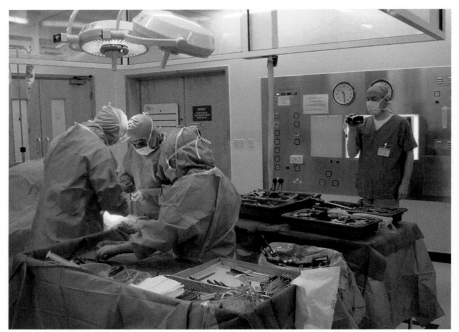

Authors own image. Ethnographic research in clinical environment

Rather than following the usual route to market of charging a high one-off entry price for each piece of kit, it was designed to smooth out the cost of the device over time by charging the healthcare provider on a cost-per-use basis.

Cleverly, this cost-per-use model would be further subsidised by collecting clinical data that could then be sold back to pharmaceutical companies and healthcare providers, thereby further reducing the initial cost of adoption and purchase.

This revolutionary device aimed to democratise access to the device beyond the (very) wealthy that could enjoy the benefits of a "first world" healthcare system. So, all good!

Matt Marsh

My role was not only to design the usability, interaction design and user experience, but to assess how realistic the business model was, and whether the brand promise and healthcare vision associated with this new generation of device was indeed compelling.

To be successful, all aspects of this radical new healthcare proposition had to be perfectly aligned to the needs of all the stakeholders involved - patients, healthcare providers and business managers alike.

It was a challenging project. We ran co-development sessions with nurses, hospital administrators, pharmaceutical companies, and healthcare purchasing representatives. We worked with patients, insurance companies, health providers of all types, and of course with clinicians. And through this consultative process we refined the design to meet all their diverse needs.

We developed separate versions that could reflect the different requirements of unique healthcare markets, tuned the software to create versions that ensured proper integration into alternative healthcare systems, and created bespoke user interfaces that allowed health workers with different levels of skill to use the device properly.

The process was all very rigorous and robust. Feedback was gathered, validation was ensured, and optimisation approaches were proven. And after extensive work, the way that the device would pay for itself, the way it would support improved clinical care and ways it would dovetail into existing work practice were resolved.
We were pleased. The evidence we had gathered suggested that this device could well be a real "game changer". In what we thought were the final throws of development, we built an experience prototype to check some of the fundamental aspects of the design. This meant building something that looked like, worked like and behaved like the final design intention.

And this wasn't an easy deal. We had to prototype something that, had prior to this point, been a technical proof of concept. This prototype had to prove that the data-sets that the device generated could be correctly interpreted by gigantic back-end medical data systems.

And at the same time show that the device was *usable* by staff and patients alike.

Much to my embarrassment, it was on the last qualifier - *being usable* - that I spectacularly failed. Because the device was "smart", it needed to be constantly powered up so that it could transmit data, even when, it wasn't "technically" working to deliver medication.

And because it always needed to be "powered up", the team had made a decision to position the "ON/OFF" switch to the back of the device, hidden away from view. Much like you would "hide" the power switch on a TV that needs to remain on standby mode. We thought it was a good decision and had explored the idea with all the other stakeholders.

But it was a mistake. As part of doing the user trials necessary to obtain FDA (Federal Drug Administration) approval, we invited a series of nurses and clinicians to help us evaluate the device.

First user. First question. "Where's the ON switch?". Second user; first question. "Where's the ON switch? Third user; first question. "Where's the ON switch? Etc. Etc. I needed to understand what I had done wrong – and quickly.

It turned out that the users understood what we were trying to do by putting the ON/OFF switch out of the way – because the device needed to be in a permanent standby mode to work properly. But was there a reason to actually hide the ON/OFF switch?

Did we think that they wouldn't understand the need for a standby mode? Had we been patronising them? Yes we probably had!

Matt Marsh

And by doing so, all we had done was confuse them. And because we had confused them, they didn't know exactly what was going on. And because they didn't know what was going on, they didn't trust the rest of what we had done either. So, by trying to do something to simplify things, we had instead totally undermined everything that this new device stood for.

Simple solution - we moved the switch from the reverse side to the front, changed the LED to offer a gentle flashing amber mode to indicate "sleep" mode and allowed a gentle touch of the user interface to change it from being in "sleep mode" into active mode with a corresponding change in LED behaviour.

Lesson. Make sure you check all your assumptions and preconceptions – including keeping a close eye on the basics - even if it does make you work a bit harder from time-to-time. Hey ho!

A TRICK . . .
To integrate a team's thinking and perspective in an interdisciplinary way – without alienating anybody along the way.

FACILITATING INTERDISCIPLINARY USER EXPERIENCE CONVERSATIONS

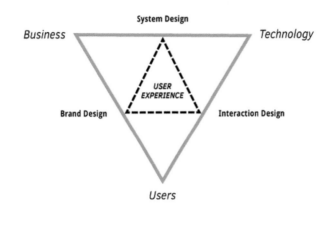

This framework further elaborates on the dynamic between business, technology and user factors described in Dirty Laundry, a story from earlier in this book. And is the second in this book invented by the brilliant Nick Durrant of Plot.

What Nick recognised was that having meaningful conversations about user experience design was often a problem because "different" disciplines often use "different" language to describe what they do and what ultimate success looks like.

Matt Marsh

This powerful tool helps interdisciplinary teams to mediate these difficult conversations by correctly identifying the critical design functions that need to be resolved and coordinated.

Facilitating having these conversations early on in the process helps ensure that a business innovation team will in fact pull together and work collaboratively to deliver an integrated and compelling end user experience.

It works like this. The relationship between business and technology is SYSTEM DESIGN. The relationship between technology and the user is INTERACTION DESIGN. And the relationship between the business and the user is BRAND DESIGN.

As such, including the three previously described conversations (in Dirty Laundry) associated with an innovative business proposition – i.e., what is the business story (viability), what is the user story (desirability) and the technology story (feasibility) – and then adding in the System, Interaction and Brand conversations - there are in fact a total six conversations that the human centred design must keep their eye on in order to deliver a truly compelling user experience.

All of them must be carefully monitored and properly determined during development to deliver a successful product, service or visitor experience. You use this framework much like an aide memoir and deploy it during review meetings when the whole team gets together.

As the custodian of human centred design, you need to make it your job to coordinate the perspective of the various team members responsible for these six conversations, and then work to resolve them through design research, prototyping and testing activities.

By using this framework you can ensure that critical aspects of the overall experience design are not ignored or forgotten.

Please make special note - it is usually the system design conversation that is ignored or forgotten.

This is partly because the team that is responsible for the system design are too often excluded from the design process, and also because the system design is often one of the most hidden and invisible aspects of design. Yet it is one of the most critical to get right when it comes to delivering a consistent and reliable user experience.

Too often, it is when the system design is overlooked, that things don't work properly – and end users become frustrated. This results in complaints to customer support, on social media, or to those who are responsible for running the training programs.

This simple, yet powerful framework ensures that all the parts that contribute to the user experience are addressed early on in development.

Matt Marsh

THE KIDS ARE ALL RIGHT

"Very often the opinion of the clients must be
disregarded in their own interest."
John M Johansen
(US Architect - 1916 to 2012)

In the early noughties, the TV sector was going through a period of
serious soul-searching. How should the old broadcaster model based on
beautifully crafted time-based viewing moments cope with the highly
seductive "my time, my place, my preference" promise of the Internet?

The arguments for this soul-searching were quite compelling – how do
you continue to serve and connect with your audiences in this brave
new Internet enabled world? One instance that exemplified this
revolution involved a TV broadcaster that was tasked with creating
educational programming for younger people as part of their broadcast
licencing obligations.

Here was the rub. These educational TV slots were scheduled for the
afternoon – when all the kids were at school. So no one was watching
them. Then there were the viewing preference statistics that showed
that teenagers were watching less and less live TV – they were on-line
instead.

So, in short, they were making TV shows for people when they weren't
able to watch them - and transmitting them on a platform where they
weren't hanging out. In response, the commissioners decided to do
something new – make fewer educationally based broadcast TV shows,
and start making on-line viewing experiences instead.

And it was this change that led them to think that they wanted to include
a human centred approach to designing – or in their vernacular,
commissioning - these new types of educational experiences.

The project we were asked to come and contribute on was about how kids might best be inspired, and shown how to be successfully entrepreneurial. To start, we spoke to entrepreneurial kids to learn from them about what worked and what didn't.

We ran workshops and interviewed young people. These were kids who were busy printing T-shirts, running market stalls, putting on pop-up nightclubs and selling copies of Banksy artwork (they had got wise to the fact that Banksy didn't copyright his work – gosh, you just have to love South London kids!)

Having completed some fundamental end user research, what became clear very quickly was how different making content for these two different worlds – traditional TV and digital services - was.

Traditional TV commissioners were very used to following their instincts and were comfortable telling people what to do based on those instincts, using their past experience and successes to convince others to act. They were intuitively risk takers!

The digital designers were almost the polar opposite. They wanted evidence, rigour, inclusion, and experimentation. They wanted to mitigate as much risk as possible before committing to building.

And both parties had their points. Commissioning TV and movies is arguably a bit of a dark art. Commissioners excel at bringing things to an audience that the viewer has no idea that they are going to like. Without bold commissioners, "Blackadder", "The Office" or even "Star Trek" would never have gone on to be the blockbuster shows they eventually became. All three were apparently nearly cancelled after the first series!

On the other hand, some commissioning approaches could be viewed as being downright lazy. This is the world of the "re-boot" based purely on past success. Erm, five Bourne Identity films (so far). Eight (at current counting) Star Wars films. Endless re-makes of 1970's TV shows currently proliferate the broadcasting schedules 40 years later.

Matt Marsh

And designers – especially user centred designers – can be an infuriating lot too. Just how much consultation do you need? Does everyone on the team really have to have an equal opinion about what the right thing to do is? How many versions do you need to make before you know which one to go for? How long can a development process practically go on for? Big sigh!

So, this was an interesting clash of creative cultures. Neither was 100% right, but nor was one 100% wrong.

This clash of creative cultures emerged early on with the commissioners wanting to know what the digital programming experience was going to be like before work had even started.

Was it going to be like World of Warcraft with game mechanics? Or would it be like "Etsy" and a community of practice? Or would it be like Facebook with updates, notifications and sharing of content? Or was it going to be like Wikipedia with a repository of constantly updated knowledge?

All were reasonable guesses. And each of the commissioners had a point of view, an idea of what their own favourite was, and were more than willing to confidently tell each other what they thought would be the right thing to do.

But, all this debate just resulted in logjam – because no one had done anything quite like this before! So we stepped up, built some early prototypes to bring a range of ideas to life, and then showed them to some young people to find out what they thought.

We created a tool where the intended end users could explore options. They could experiment what they thought the branding should be, what the information architecture should be, what activities could be performed, what interactions could take place and try out ways that learning experiences could be undertaken – videos, tutorials, text, time logs, real-time posting of events, etc.

And we showed mock ups of the different ideas that the commissions were considering too – a game mechanic, a community mechanic, etc.

And a funny and unexpected thing happened. The kids (actually, younger teenagers) wanted more than anything for the service to be their service - run by kids for kids.

They didn't want adults – like TV execs or designers – telling them what to say, think and do. They wanted to hear from people like themselves – who understood what it was like to be a teenager that wanted to try out being "entrepreneurial".

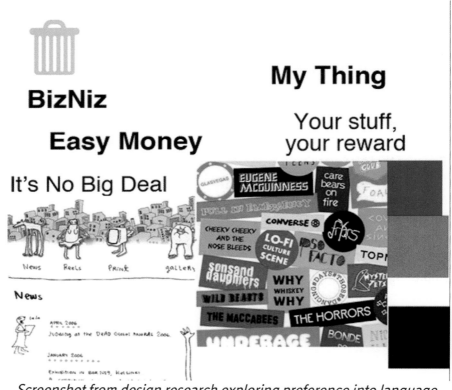

Screenshot from design research exploring preference into language, look, and feel. Authors image.

Matt Marsh

They said that everything we had showed them looked like it had been created by adults, for kids.

They could (metaphorically) smell the lack of authenticity! For example, most of the concepts made it easy to search for content by offering a variety of means to quickly access what was available – as long as you knew beforehand what it was that you were looking for

"No No No", they said.

They would happily trade off speed of interaction for creating a level playing field that helped people like them to *discover* what to do, or to *find* recommendations that came from trusted peers.

What they told us was that adults *always* tried to pigeonhole you by pre-defining what the end goal was. And kids didn't like it when that was done to them.

Interestingly, they didn't like the use of super-slick graphics – even though they appreciated how cool they looked. But again, what this told them was that this wasn't a "kid made and curated" site.

There were countless other mistakes and assumptions we had made. And when you added up all these mistakes together, what it told the teenagers was that this site didn't represent them. It was just another service, purporting to be authentically representing the voice of young people.

What had happened was what the site "was saying", and what it "was doing", was out of kilter. The site was saying it was "for teenagers by teenagers", but what it was doing was "for teenagers by adults"!

It wasn't a genuine peer-to-peer service, it wasn't about authentic sharing of life experience, and it wasn't about enabling each person to find his or her own path.

What we were proposing came across as being a sophisticated, yet ultimately patronising offer that could easily be from any other government agency, cynical TV company or arrogant digital start up company.

Phew. Good catch kids!

So we took this back to the team, ate a large chunk of humble pie, re-evaluated what we were doing, and how we should do it. Then we started all over again. This time, doing it with some informed sensitivity and empathy.

Matt Marsh

A TRICK . . .
To help a team gain foresight about what needs to be built and how to fulfil promises

BUILDING A USER EXPERIENCE IN A HOLISTIC AND STABLE WAY

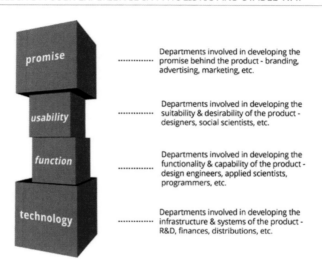

promise .... Departments involved in developing the promise behind the product - branding, advertising, marketing, etc.

usability .... Departments involved in developing the suitability & desirability of the product - designers, social scientists, etc.

function .... Departments involved in developing the functionality & capability of the product - design engineers, applied scientists, programmers, etc.

technology .... Departments involved in developing the infrastructure & systems of the product - R&D, finances, distributions, etc.

You can use this framework to ensure that a new business proposition perfectly aligns the technology experience with the brand promise experience. Essentially that the "walk" – what you do - is consistent with the "talk" – what you say.

It was invented by the amazing Kathleen Holman, a pioneer of User Experience Design that I was lucky enough to work with when we were both working at IDEO London at the turn of the Century.

As such, I like to call it "Holman's Blocks". Imagine the four cubes as children's building blocks; each one stacked on top of the other. The team can work together to assess, and then manipulate the sizes of the blocks to construct a stable structure reflecting the amount of development funding available and the ambition of the project.

If the PROMISE block is very large, and is sitting on top of a very small TECHNOLOGY block, then the overall structure is very unstable. On the other hand if the TECHNOLOGY block is very large and the PROMISE block is small, then the proposition is unlikely to meet it's potential.

This is because too much resource and investment has been put into the technology, and yet the promise is too small to build a sustainable business. Then all you do is lose money, brand reputation and the respect of your workforce.

After all, if a business proposition mis-aligns the technology experience and the brand promise, than people tend to get confused. And if they get confused, they tend to go somewhere else instead. In short, it becomes much harder to build-in loyalty and the creation of customer advocates.

Conceptually, sitting above the TECHNOLOGY lie the FEATURES and FUNCTIONS. These are the things that translate the enabling technologies into doing something useful for people – the benefits of the business proposition.

Between FEATURES and FUNCTIONS and the PROMISE blocks lies USABILITY. This is what makes the features and functions delightful to the end user. It's what makes a new business proposition intuitive to learn, easy to use and simple to explain to someone else.

So the idea is to try to build the size of the blocks up in concert – with each one of approximately the same size. As such, it is better to launch a service with equivalently sized blocks, and then build up from there.

Matt Marsh

This means that you don't disappoint customers by over-promising using an impoverished technology platform. Conversely, you don't disappoint investors by piling money into a technology that doesn't deliver a sufficiently large audience.

So you can use this framework as a way to mediate conversations between the different parts of an interdisciplinary team to ensure that the investment in enabling technologies, selection of the functions, the manner in which you make them usable, and the way the business proposition is crafted, are all perfectly aligned with the external marketing and brand messaging activities.

However even if the blocks are conceptually of the same size and magnitude, they could be poorly aligned with respect to each other and be offset. And in this case, even though the business proposition is well proportioned, it is still unstable.

By involving the end user, you can ensure that the various building blocks are optimally aligned – it is almost as though there are "user experience" and "brand expression" cables passing through the blocks.

As you focus on the nuances of the user need and wants, this shared perspective pulls the blocks into alignment, thereby creating a stable and perfectly balanced proposition.

The best way to "make the blocks" is, first, for the team to work together to list out the attributes and enablers for each of the blocks – promise, usability, functionality and technology.

The second step, is for each of the lists to be broken down into two new lists – what is the "minimum viable" required, and what is the "ultimate it could be". Then you can visualise those lists as the blocks. If there isn't much difference between the "minimum" and the "ultimate" variants, then the blocks should be about the same size. And vice versa.

By sketching out the lists and representing them as these physical forms, the team can quickly and easily begin to see if mis-matches and mis-alignments exist, and then work to address any of these by modifying their development strategy accordingly.

Matt Marsh

I QUIT !

"Design is a funny word. Some people think design means how it looks. But of course, if you dig deeper, it's really how it works."
Steve Jobs
(Founder of Apple, Inc, Grid and Pixar - 1955 to 2011)

One of the most challenging service design projects I've worked on was creating an effective smoking cessation experience. This was in 2004 (mea culpa, I was still a user of the evil weed) and the products available to help you quit were in many ways still in their infancy.

There were the nicotine replacement approaches that addressed the physiological aspects of smoking - nicotine gum, nicotine mints and nicotine patches. The gum and mints tasted pretty awful and the patches tended to make your skin itchy or give you a burning sensation. I know - I tried them all.

Then there were therapy-based approaches that attempted to address the psychological aspects of smoking - like hypnotherapy, cognitive behavioural therapy or counselling. And of course there was the willpower approach – just stop smoking. And yes, I tried all of them too.

When I was given the opportunity to re-invent the smoking cessation experience, it was of great interest to me. Curious anecdote – I was the only person on the team who was a smoker, or at least would admit to being a smoker (the others all worked for a pharmaceutical company where smoking was strictly frowned upon!).

We performed user research in different parts of Europe where different laws regarding smoking in public places existed. In Poland and Germany, for example, it was still permissible to smoke inside pubs and restaurants. In Italy, smoking in pubs and restaurants had just been made illegal. In the UK, smoking indoors in public places had been prohibited for some time.

In Japan and Korea, it was still common for people to be smoking in their bedrooms and nicotine replacement therapy products of any kind were extremely hard to find. Whereas in California, hardly anyone smoked anywhere indoors - the habit had been expelled to the back garden many years previously.

We interviewed stop-smoking therapists and counsellors of all types and approaches. And we spoke to people who had gone "cold-turkey" and decided to stop completely, and we also talked to people who had adopted the cutting down slowly approach.

What we discovered was that most people improvised in order to try and discover an approach that worked for them. There were dozens and dozens of individual workarounds in play – and different strategies appeared to work depending on what sort of smoker the person wanted to be.

For example, a common strategy was to cut nicotine patches in half or quarter to try and slowly reduce the nicotine dose they received. Another strategy was to cut down their cigarette consumption by limiting when they allowed themselves to smoke - perhaps after work, or after the children went to bed.

Some people were straightforward nicotine addicts who enjoyed the "hit" – but hated all the smell, smoke and financial (or health) cost associated with it. So they often choose to switch to higher nicotine cigarettes with the intention of smoking fewer of them (kind of counter intuitive).

Matt Marsh

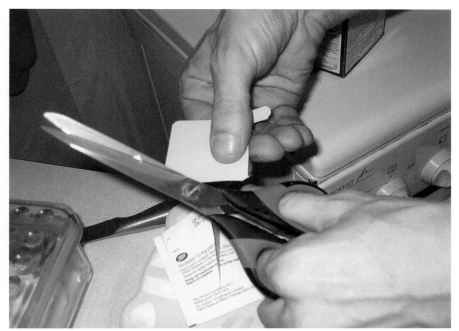
Authors own image. In home ethnographic research

Others genuinely loved the ritualised parts of smoking, such as the artisanal rolling of a cigarette, blowing smoke rings, or, the social parts of smoking - yet claiming they didn't crave the nicotine at all!

It was, to say the least, a complicated picture. Yet a number of insights did eventually emerge.

First, that a "one size fits all" cessation approach rarely matched the majority of needs of the user population. People needed to try things out and learn what worked for *them* – and at that time there was no smoking cessation service that supported this.

Second, that cessation meant different things to different people. For some, the goal was for a total stop. But for others, stopping smoking meant just having the odd one at the weekend or at a party. For others still, it meant stop smoking tobacco in joints.

Third, that some people found quitting smoking much, much harder than others. It appeared that if you started when you were young - perhaps in your formative years as a teenager - smoking was frequently tied to powerful ideas surrounding identity and social standing. For example, enjoying the signalling to others of being "rebellious", "cool", "sexy" or "glamorous".

Fourth, that people wanted feedback to give encouragement as they progressed along the cessation journey. It was important for them to discover that cravings were slowly reducing, that lung capacity was improving, that clothes (and bodies) didn't smell of tobacco anymore, or that money was being saved, etc.

And finally, that people needed to be "relapse ready". One of the key discoveries was how stopping smoking was frequently a long and unpredictable journey. We heard many stories about how a year or more after their last cigarette, people experienced incredibly powerful urges to "just have one", and by just having one, thereby prove that they were not a smoker anymore. And bang! Within days they were puffing away, and back to the cessation starting point.

This told us that smoking cessation needed a special kind of approach; one that started with knowing what kind of smoker you were, and assisted in finding a cessation strategy that would indeed get you to where you wanted to be at the end.

It needed to offer a variety of interventions that dealt with both the psychological and physiological aspects of the addiction, as well as one that would equip you to be ready and prepared for a relapse moment at some point in the distant future. All had to be built into the system.

It was about designing a nuanced path to participation – or rather in this case - a path to cessation. It was hopeless to simply contemplate repackaging up nicotine gum in a different flavour. Especially, if that gum, mint or patch wasn't going to be available during a relapse moment (like in a nightclub!).

Matt Marsh

You also needed a range of trusted people to turn to for advice - even if it was at the weekend. You needed to be able to try different products and approaches, so that you didn't get bored and so you could fine-tune your approach to your own social circumstances. And you needed accessories and peripherals as part of the service to provide you with the encouragement and feedback, when and if, you needed it.

It is pleasurable to see that, over ten years on, a lot of these parts of the cessation service now exist. You can get sample packs of different products. You can use your smart phone to log your progress and receive motivational messages. You can get help and advice from many different places – from your gym to your doctor.

Most critically, there are now products available to help with those relapse moments - such as nicotine sprays, drinks and items that are designed to sit dormant in your wallet or purse until the moment you really need them.

A TRICK . . .
To help a team to design for participation – and avoid losing the future customer along the way.

CREATING A COHERENT PATH TO PARTICIPATION

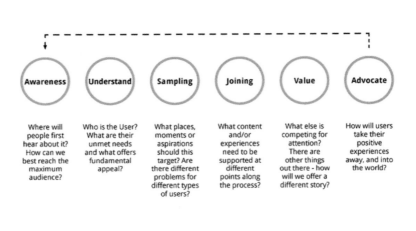

Awareness	Understand	Sampling	Joining	Value	Advocate
Where will people first hear about it? How can we best reach the maximum audience?	Who is the User? What are their unmet needs and what offers fundamental appeal?	What places, moments or aspirations should this target? Are there different problems for different types of users?	What content and/or experiences need to be supported at different points along the process?	What else is competing for attention? There are other things out there - how will we offer a different story?	How will users take their positive experiences away, and into the world?

During early planning and strategy phases, this framework is invaluable for crafting those intangible business propositions like digital products, services and visitor experiences. I like to call it "Heron's Steps" after a colleague and friend upon whose work it is derived (Steve Heron of Nodding Dog consulting).

For these sorts of propositions, it is critical to design the overall path to participation; thinking holistically from when someone first hears about the new offer, to the point when they start telling other people that they should try it out too!

It is important to understand how intangible propositions (like services or visitor experiences) differ from standard physical products. When you buy a physical product – something tangible - there is typically a singular transaction point. Once you have bought the product, there is no going back. They have your money and you have the product.

But with intangible business propositions, there is usually a subscription or joining up model. And as such, you as the customer can cancel, and then choose another option at anytime. So with intangible propositions you need to design the whole customer journey - from what happens when the user sees the advertising and promotion of it, to when they start using it, and eventually to how you support them talking about it to others in a positive way.

This is a simple framework. It begins by thinking about designing the AWARENESS experience – making sure that information about the new service appears in places where it is most relevant to the prospective new customer.

That is then followed by designing the UNDERSTAND experience – explaining what is it and why is it relevant to their needs. Then there is the SAMPLING experience – defining what happens when you first start using the service and showing how to become familiar with the service's features and benefits.

After this point comes the JOINING IN experience - which is about helping people to gain confidence by providing a number of ways to try the service out and, critically, provide positive feedback to reward their efforts.

The penultimate point in the path to participation is designing the VALUING experience – when an end user begins to enjoy and take delight in the choices that they have made and helping them recognise how the service is enhancing their life.

Finally there is designing the ADVOCATE experience, which is about supporting them to express the pleasure they have experienced, and assisting them in promoting that pleasure or delight on to the outside world.

This creates a virtuous cycle where the advocate begins to add to the initial AWARENESS experience and therefore stimulate others to join in and try it out.

At each point along the path to participation, the design team can populate the customer journey with different ideas and design interventions. It is then possible to weave together a customer journey from those alternative ideas and interventions to suit customer personas of different types.

Thus, you can create a service experience that maps directly onto the varied needs of different kinds of user. It provides an effective mechanism for the many disciplines working on a service design project to collaborate as an effective team and correctly coordinate the whole customer journey.

Matt Marsh

CHAPTER THREE – THE PEOPLE-SHAPED MANIFESTO FOR CHANGE

Matt Marsh

The people-shaped manifesto

First Published 23-02-09 by **firsthand** Experience (with special thanks to Ian Willingham)

The top line

We want to see an end to the wasteful manner in which products, services and brands have been designed, developed and manufactured over the last 50 years.

Do it now.

Stop, think and press the ***reset*** button on the old way of doing things.

Embrace a better, more effective way of making; fit for a more thoughtful, responsible and challenging 21st Century.

You will need to reinvent your *process* – from the very beginning of how strategy is formed right the way through to implementation.

In this complex era of high expectation and change, process needs to put ***people*** at the heart of its thinking and doing in order to be effective.

Make it ***people-shaped***.

The waste story

Far too many companies are still developing new products and services destined to become market failures. Whether they start off on the wrong foot or get binned soon after launch, all are an entirely *avoidable* waste of time, money, energy and, worst of all, perfectly good opportunity.

We understand how difficult making new 'stuff' is. But it shouldn't (and doesn't have to) cost the earth! A **people-shaped approach** creates significant improvements to business profitability in terms of both the financial savings and the brand's reputation.

The traditional, high-risk approach to business is increasingly ineffective in the face of the complexity of 21st Century customer demand. Its 'throw spaghetti against the wall' approach is now failing to respond or adapt to the idiosyncratic and rapidly shifting markets that business was once able to predict and affect. It is not that companies don't want to change, they just don't know how too.

By placing the needs, motivations and behaviour of people at the centre of the business thinking, at the very beginning of a project, you can figure out exactly what the right proposition to develop is – when it's cheap to find out rather than much later on, when you really can't afford to discover that you've backed the wrong horse.

Customers are only capricious because companies give them a license to be fickle. Meet, or exceed, their expectations and they will not only be delighted and come back for more, but tell their friends about you too.

Matt Marsh

The era of disconnect

There is clear evidence that most organisations are so out of touch with the daily reality of people's lives that the disconnect is beginning to turn on them, biting back in the form of a more-in-control and discerning consumer, fed up with a poor customer experience and continually disappointed by a lack of follow-though on promise.

Business has no choice but to respond accordingly by making end users part of the whole story – or it will simply fail. And this means going way beyond the tired old cliché of 'getting to know the consumer', or the rather exploitative approach of "co-creative" development.

*A **people-shaped** approach creates meaningful, practical dialogues between companies and end-users for the sole purpose that everybody will benefit from the end result.*

Many organisations are not set up with the ability to implement new projects with the kind of agility demanded by today's world. This is as much down to the way in which individuals behave on a day-to-day basis as the internal cultures and working practices of a company. We can see how easy it is to drift off-course, away from end-users' needs, when developing a new product or service, and here are the four most common examples why...

i) The 'Siren Effect'

Makers tend to grow very close to whichever new concepts and technologies they are currently using. So much so, that they often want to add a personal touch to their work, as their involvement increases and the potential of their 'legacy' grows. This hypnotic 'Siren Effect', draws them in even closer and they become further removed from focusing on the needs of their end-user. What happens is that they end up designing more for themselves, their peers, or worse, their investor, and less for the very people who will be using it in the context of their daily lives. This happens more than you'd care to imagine!

People-shaped thinking keeps strategists, designers, marketers and manufactures on track. By starting with people at the centre of the thinking, projects can be clearly shaped around the end user needs throughout development and thus maximising the opportunity for success.

ii) 'Miscommunication'

As a project is passed from one department to another, just like a relay baton in a race, a game starts to take place. What started as a clearly articulated concept starts to get muddled, diffused and confused as it moves from research to development, to design, to manufacture, to marketing and beyond. This is worsened by the fact that the very people involved in these sequential stages are not only in different departments, but also often in a different building – or even company – from each other.

Matt Marsh

***People-shaped** thinking breaks these 'silos' by installing new cultures of practice and carrying the central concept throughout different teams in an integrated and user-centred way. It prevents the proposition from getting lost, confused or diffused by the time it is launched.*

iii) 'Spec Creep'

Failing to connect your central thinking to the end user can also create a phenomenon called 'Spec creep'. Similar to the 'Siren Effect', but usually when a project is nearing completion, the impulse to change the design by adding on features and functionalities proves all too strong for some, resulting in a mediocre and muddled proposition that nobody wants or needs. This sudden urge to bolt things on is usually a panic reaction to sudden market changes just before launch.

***People-shaped** thinking maintains a mantra of 'simple is beautiful', keeping projects focused on their end user needs and not diluting or damaging a great opportunity.*

iv) 'The cult of design'

We see so many design teams who are culturally and physically removed from the people they are designing for. In consequence they often design to either satisfy themselves, their bosses, or for a mythic "everyone", resulting in ineffective, inappropriate, insufficient or, at worst, insulting end results.

Within academia, it is even more important that a user-centred perspective is taught and this should be ingrained within the process. By learning to tackle any given brief within a broader, user-friendly context, their future work will truly be richer, whether eventually within the world of design or any type of industry.

*A **people-shaped** approach complements and enrichens a person's existing skills with the ability to observe, understand, empathise with and then respond effectively to your end users' real needs.*

The last word

The last word is truly **people-shaped**.

It goes to you, the user.

It's your time.

If things aren't good enough, show them!

Vote with your feet and with your pockets!

Eventually, they will listen.

They might even thank you...

[END]

Matt Marsh

BIBLIOGRAPHY, NOTES AND CONTACTS

FORWARD

Derived from Bain & Company. Closing the delivery gap: How to achieve true customer-led growth. October 2005, 2005; James Allen, Frederick F. Reichheld, Barney Hamilton and Rob Markey.

BOOK REFERENCES

The Lean Start Up – Eric Ries. ISBN 978-0-670-92160-7. The Audacity of Zero, Page 52.
"Zero invites the imagination, but small numbers invite questions about whether large numbers will ever materialize."

QUOTES

brainyquote.com
99 Designs.com
Design Synopsis.com

IMAGES

Never Give Up, Art Installation. The Boom Boom Club. PunchDrunk at The Old Vic Tunnels 2011. Authors photograph.

Women workers with shells in Chilwell filling factory 1917. Nicholls Horace. Q 30040. Imperial War Museum.

In December 2013, the German Deutsche Post AG tested a microdrones md4-1000 for delivery. 6 January 2014 by Frankhöffner This image is licensed under the Creative Commons Attribution-Share Alike 3.0 Unported license.

FONT
BODY TEXT: Officina Display ITCTT. COVER: A Day Without The Sun

CONTACTS

Eddie Obeng	eddie.obeng (at) pentaclethevbs.com
Steve Heron	steve (at) noddingdogcompany.com
Kathleen Holman	kathleenholman (at) gmail.com
Nick Durrant	nick (at) plotlondon.net
Gill Wildman	gill (at) plotlondon.net
Dodger Phillips	dodgerphillips (at) me.com
Ian Willingham	ianwltd (at) gmail.com

ABOUT MATT MARSH

It's true; he is bit passionate, a bit provocative, and yes can be a bit "punchy" too. But you wouldn't expect anything less from a design radical like him.

Matt started his first human centred design firm shortly after graduating from Loughborough University in 1986. He went on to work in San Francisco during the 1990's, returning to London at the turn of the Century to set up his own consulting firm.

Matt started his career in the mid eighties when the world was entering a phase of massive cultural change – end of the cold war, a "big bang" going on in the financial sector, a time when consumerism was on the rise - and of course the beginning of the leap into everything digital.

And at that time, the design world was suddenly being thrust into this new world, and had to adapt fast. Along with the many other people, he learnt by being curious, deferring judgement, trying new things out - and by making mistakes that all of us were all too willing to share with each other.

Today people are almost trained to live in fear of failure, and too often only ask the questions they think they already know the answers too. But what Matt and his contemporaries know is that through inquisitiveness, you can learn how to be comfortable with the unknown.

And more, if you are prepared to listen to people, most times you'll succeed sooner and better.

Printed in Great Britain
by Amazon